Frommer's®

PORTABLE

Bahamas

6th Edition

by Darwin Porter & Danforth Prince

Y0-CBF-562

Here's what critics say about Frommer's:

"Amazingly easy to use. Very portable, very complete."

—*Booklist*

"Detailed, accurate, and easy-to-read information for all price ranges."

—*Glamour Magazine*

Wiley Publishing, Inc.

Published by:

WILEY PUBLISHING, INC.
111 River St.
Hoboken, NJ 07030-5774

Copyright © 2007 Wiley Publishing, Inc., Hoboken, New Jersey. All rights
reserved. No part of this publication may be reproduced, stored in a
retrieval system or transmitted in any form or by any means, electronic,
mechanical, photocopying, recording, scanning or otherwise, except as per-
mitted under Sections 107 or 108 of the 1976 United States Copyright
Act, without either the prior written permission of the Publisher, or
authorization through payment of the appropriate per-copy fee to the
Copyright Clearance Center, 222 Rosewood Drive, Danvers, MA 01923,
978/750-8400, fax 978/646-8600. Requests to the Publisher for permission should be addressed to the Legal Department, Wiley Publishing, Inc.,
10475 Crosspoint Blvd., Indianapolis, IN 46256, 317/572-3447, fax 317/
572-4355, or online at http://www.wiley.com/go/permissions.

Wiley and the Wiley Publishing logo are trademarks or registered trademarks
of John Wiley & Sons, Inc. and/or its affiliates. Frommer's is a trademark or
registered trademark of Arthur Frommer. Used under license. All other trademarks are the property of their respective owners. Wiley Publishing, Inc. is
not associated with any product or vendor mentioned in this book.

ISBN: 978-0-470-16546-1

Editor: Jamie Ehrlich
Production Editor: M. Faunette Johnston
Cartographer: Andrew Murphy
Photo Editor: Richard Fox
Anniversary Logo Design: Richard Pacifico
Production by Wiley Indianapolis Composition Services

For information on our other products and services or to obtain technical
support, please contact our Customer Care Department within the U.S. at
800/762-2974, outside the U.S. at 317/572-3993 or fax 317/572-4002.

Wiley also publishes its books in a variety of electronic formats. Some con-
tent that appears in print may not be available in electronic formats.

Manufactured in the United States of America

5 4 3 2 1

Contents

Index

List of Maps

ABOUT THE AUTHORS

As a team of veteran travel writers, **Darwin Porter** and **Danforth Prince** have produced numerous titles for Frommer's, including best-selling guides to Italy, France, the Caribbean, England, and Germany. Porter, a former bureau chief of *The Miami Herald,* is also a Hollywood biographer, and his most recent release is *Howard Hughes: Hell's Angel.* Prince was formerly employed by the Paris bureau of the *New York Times,* and is today the president of Blood Moon Productions and other media-related firms.

AN INVITATION TO THE READER

In researching this book, we discovered many wonderful places—hotels, restaurants, shops, and more. We're sure you'll find others. Please tell us about them, so we can share the information with your fellow travelers in upcoming editions. If you were disappointed with a recommendation, we'd love to know that, too. Please write to:

Frommer's Portable Bahamas, 6th Edition
Wiley Publishing, Inc. • 111 River St. • Hoboken, NJ 07030-5774

AN ADDITIONAL NOTE

Please be advised that travel information is subject to change at any time—and this is especially true of prices. We therefore suggest that you write or call ahead for confirmation when making your travel plans. The authors, editors, and publisher cannot be held responsible for the experiences of readers while traveling. Your safety is important to us, however, so we encourage you to stay alert and be aware of your surroundings. Keep a close eye on cameras, purses, and wallets, all favorite targets of thieves and pickpockets.

FROMMER'S STAR RATINGS, ICONS & ABBREVIATIONS

Every hotel, restaurant, and attraction listing in this guide has been ranked for quality, value, service, amenities, and special features using a **star-rating system.** In country, state, and regional guides, we also rate towns and regions to help you narrow down your choices and budget your time accordingly. Hotels and restaurants are rated on a scale of zero (recommended) to three stars (exceptional). Attractions, shopping, nightlife, towns, and regions are rated according to the following scale: zero stars (recommended), one star (highly recommended), two stars (very highly recommended), and three stars (must-see).

In addition to the star-rating system, we also use **seven feature icons** that point you to the great deals, in-the-know advice, and unique experiences that separate travelers from tourists. Throughout the book, look for:

Finds	Special finds—those places only insiders know about
Fun Fact	Fun facts—details that make travelers more informed and their trips more fun
Kids	Best bets for kids—advice for the whole family
Moments	Special moments—those experiences that memories are made of
Overrated	Places or experiences not worth your time or money
Tips	Insider tips—some great ways to save time and money
Value	Great values—where to get the best deals

The following **abbreviations** are used for credit cards:

AE	American Express	DISC	Discover	V	Visa
DC	Diners Club	MC	MasterCard		

FROMMERS.COM

Now that you have this guidebook to help you plan a great trip, visit our website at **www.frommers.com** for additional travel information on more than 3,600 destinations. We update features regularly to give you instant access to the most current trip-planning information available. At Frommers. com, you'll find scoops on the best airfares, lodging rates, and car rental bargains. You can even book your travel online through our reliable travel booking partners. Other popular features include:

- Online updates of our most popular guidebooks
- Vacation sweepstakes and contest giveaways
- Newsletters highlighting the hottest travel trends
- Online travel message boards with featured travel discussions

The Best of
The Bahamas

The Bahamas is one of the most geographically complicated nations of the Atlantic. A coral-based archipelago, it is composed of more than 700 islands, 2,000 cays (pronounced "keys," from the Spanish word for small islands), and hundreds of rocky outcroppings that have damaged the hulls of countless ships since colonial days.

But don't worry: We're here to help you plan the perfect getaway. In this chapter, you'll find clear and concise lists of The Bahamas' best beaches, honeymoon resorts, family vacations, and restaurants.

For more information on choosing the island that best suits your taste and budget, refer to "The Islands in Brief" in chapter 2. There, we'll explain the pros and cons of each island in detail.

1 The Best Beaches

- **Cable Beach** (New Providence Island): The glittering shore-line of Cable Beach has easy access to shops, casinos, restaurants, watersports, and bars. It's a sandy 6.5km-long (4-mile) strip, with a great array of facilities and activities. See p. 78.
- **Cabbage Beach** (Paradise Island): Think Vegas in the tropics. It seems as if most of the sunbathers dozing on the sands here are recovering from the previous evening's partying, and it's likely to be crowded near the megahotels. But you can find a bit more solitude on the beach's isolated northwestern extension (Paradise Beach), which is accessible only by boat or on foot. Lined with palms, sea grapes, and casuarinas, the sands are broad and stretch for at least 3km (2 miles). See p. 121.
- **Xanadu Beach** (Grand Bahama Island): Grand Bahama has 97km (60 miles) of sandy shoreline, but Xanadu Beach is most convenient to Freeport's resort hotels, several of which offer shuttle service to Xanadu. There's more than a kilometer of white sand and (usually) gentle surf. Don't expect to have

Xanadu to yourself, but if you want more quiet and privacy, try any of the beaches that stretch from Xanadu for many miles in either direction. See p. 160.

2 The Best Honeymoon Resorts

- **Sandals Royal Bahamian Hotel & Spa** (Cable Beach, New Providence Island; ℂ **800/SANDALS** or 242/327-6400; www.sandals.com): This Jamaican chain of couples-only, all-inclusive hotels is a honeymooners' favorite. The Bahamas' branch of the chain is more upscale than many of its Jamaican counterparts, and it offers 27 secluded honeymoon suites with semiprivate plunge pools. Staff members lend their experience and talent to on-site wedding celebrations; Sandals will provide everything from a preacher to flowers, as well as champagne and a cake. It's more expensive than most Sandals resorts, but you can usually get better prices than the official "rack rates" through a travel agent or a package deal. See p. 60.
- **One&Only Ocean Club** (Paradise Island; ℂ **800/321-3000** in the U.S. only, or 242/363-2501; www.oneandonlyresorts.com): It's elegant, low-key, and low-rise, and it feels exclusive. The guests include many older honeymoon couples. With waterfalls, fountains, reflecting pools, and a stone gazebo, the Ocean Club's formal terraced gardens were inspired by the club's founder (an heir to the A&P fortune) and are the most impressive in The Bahamas. At the center is a French cloister, with carvings from the 12th century. See p. 106.
- **Old Bahama Bay** (Grand Bahama Island; ℂ **800/444-9469** in the U.S., or 242/350-3500; www.oldbahamabay.com): Perfect for honeymooners seeking a quiet hideaway in a boutique-style hotel with cottages adjacent to a marina. The casinos, entertainment, shopping, and dining of Freeport/Lucaya are 40km (25 miles) away, but here you can sneak away for luxury, solitude, and romance. See p. 146.

3 The Best Family Vacations

- **Sheraton Cable Beach Hotel** (Cable Beach, New Providence Island; ℂ **800/325-3535** or 242/327-6000; www.sheraton.com/cablebeach): A family could spend their entire vacation on the grounds of this vast resort. There's a pool area that features the most lavish artificial waterfall this side of Tahiti; a health club at

The Best Beaches

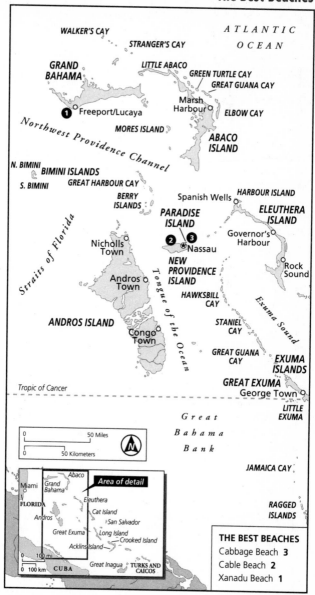

WALKER'S CAY

STRANGER'S CAY

ATLANTIC OCEAN

GRAND BAHAMA

LITTLE ABACO

GREEN TURTLE CAY

GREAT GUANA CAY

Marsh Harbour

ELBOW CAY

❶ Freeport/Lucaya

Northwest Providence Channel

MORES ISLAND

ABACO ISLAND

N. BIMINI

BIMINI ISLANDS

S. BIMINI

GREAT HARBOUR CAY

BERRY ISLANDS

HARBOUR ISLAND

Spanish Wells

ELEUTHERA ISLAND

PARADISE ISLAND

❷ ❸ Nassau

Governor's Harbour

Straits of Florida

Nicholls Town

NEW PROVIDENCE ISLAND

Rock Sound

Andros Town

HAWKSBILL CAY

Exuma Sound

ANDROS ISLAND

Congo Town

Tongue of the Ocean

STANIEL CAY

GREAT GUANA CAY

EXUMA ISLANDS

Tropic of Cancer

GREAT EXUMA

George Town

LITTLE EXUMA

Great Bahama Bank

| 0 | 50 Miles |
| 0 | 50 Kilometers |

JAMAICA CAY

Area of detail

Miami

Abaco

Grand Bahama

FLORIDA

Eleuthera

Cat Island

Andros

San Salvador

Great Exuma

Long Island

Crooked Island

Acklins Island

0   100 mi

0   100 km

CUBA

Great Inagua

TURKS AND CAICOS

RAGGED ISLANDS

THE BEST BEACHES
Cabbage Beach **3**
Cable Beach **2**
Xanadu Beach **1**

the nearby Crystal Palace that welcomes both guests and their children; Camp Junkanoo, with supervised play for children 3 through 12; and a long list of in-house activities that includes dancing lessons. Major changes and redevelopment are planned for this resort. See p. 62.

- **Atlantis Paradise Island Resort & Casino** (Paradise Island; © **800/ATLANTIS** in the U.S., or 242/363-3000; www. atlantis.com): This is one of the largest hotel complexes in the world, with endless rows of shops and watersports galore. Both children and adults will enjoy the 5.6-hectare (14-acre) sea world with waterslides, a lagoon for watersports, white sandy beaches, and underground grottoes plus an underwater viewing tunnel and 240m (787 ft.) of cascading waterfalls. Its children's menus and innovative, creative children's programs are the best in The Bahamas and perhaps even in the Caribbean. See p. 100.

- **Best Western Castaways Resort & Suites** (Grand Bahama Island; © **800/780-7234** in the U.S., or 242/352-6682; www.bestwestern.com): Here's a good choice for families on a budget. The pagoda-capped lobby is set a very short walk from the ice-cream stands, souvenir shops, and fountains of the International Bazaar. Children under 12 stay free in their parents' room, and the in-house lounge presents limbo and fire-eating shows several evenings a month. The hotel offers a babysitting service and a free shuttle to Williams Town Beach. See p. 138.

4 The Best Restaurants

- **Sun and . . .** (Nassau, New Providence Island; © **242/393-1205**) has made a comeback after being closed for many years. Once again, it is the leading independent choice on New Providence Island, serving a finely honed international cuisine. It's a throwback to Nassau in its grand heyday. Originally built in the 1930s as a private residence, it lies in an upscale residential neighborhood east of the center of Nassau. See p. 68.

- **Moso** (in the Wyndham Nassau Resort, Cable Beach, New Providence Island; © **242/327-6200**) is the best Asian restaurant on island. A well-trained staff here has learned the secrets of the cuisines of the Far East, and they dispense an array of some of the best known and tastiest dishes including teriyaki specialties. See p. 75.

- **Nobu** (the Atlantis Paradise Island Resort's Royal Towers; Paradise Island; ℂ **242/363-3000**) brings a member of this celebrated chain to The Bahamas. It's the most talked-about and arguably the best restaurant on island, attracting a string of celebrities. The setting is glamorous and the cuisine is top-rated, prepared either with market-fresh ingredients or exotic products shipped in. See p. 116.
- **Dune** (in the One&Only Ocean Club, Paradise Island; ℂ **242/363-2501,** ext. 64739): The most cutting-edge restaurant in either Paradise Island or Nassau, Dune is the creation of French-born restaurant guru Jean-Georges Vongerichten, the moving force behind several of New York City's top dining spots. Every dish served here is something special—from shrimp dusted with orange powder to chicken and coconut milk soup with shiitake cakes. See p. 114.
- **Bahamian Club** (Paradise Island; ℂ **242/363-3000**): A notch down from the superb Dune, this establishment is nevertheless one of the leading restaurants in The Bahamas and our favorite at the sprawling megaresort of Atlantis. Strictly upscale, it presents superb French and international cuisine against a backdrop that evokes the British Colonial era. The restaurant serves the island's finest cuts of meats. See p. 112.

2

Planning Your Trip to The Bahamas

You can be in The Bahamas after a quick 35-minute jet hop from Miami. And it's never been easier to take advantage of great package deals that can make these islands a terrific value.

1 The Islands in Brief

The Bahamian chain of islands, cays, and reefs stretches from Grand Bahama Island, 121km (75 miles) almost due east of Palm Beach, Florida, to Great Inagua, the southernmost island, which lies 97km (60 miles) northeast of Cuba and fewer than 161km (100 miles) north of Haiti.

The most developed islands for tourism in The Bahamas are **New Providence Island,** site of Nassau (the capital) and Cable Beach; **Paradise Island;** and **Grand Bahama,** home of Freeport and Lucaya. If you're after glitz, gambling, bustling restaurants, nightclubs, and a beach-party scene, these big three islands are where you'll want to be. Package deals are easily found here.

Set sail (or hop on a short commuter flight) for one of the **Out Islands,** such as Andros, the Exumas, or the Abacos, and you'll find fewer crowds—and often lower prices, too. Though some of the Out Islands are accessible mainly (or only) by boat, it's still worth your while to make the trip if you like the idea of having an entire beach to yourself. Space doesn't permit us to cover all these islands in this small guide, so if you're interested, please pick up a copy of *Frommer's Bahamas* for complete coverage.

NEW PROVIDENCE ISLAND (NASSAU/CABLE BEACH)
New Providence isn't the largest of the Bahamian Islands, but it's the historic heart of the nation, with a strong maritime tradition and the largest population in the country. Home to more than 125,000 residents, it offers groves of palms and casuarinas; sandy, flat soil; the closest thing in The Bahamas to urban sprawl; and superb anchorages sheltered from rough seas by the presence of nearby Paradise

Island. New Providence has the country's busiest airport and is dotted with hundreds of villas owned by foreign investors. Its two major resort areas are Cable Beach and Nassau.

The resort area of **Cable Beach** is a glittering beachfront strip of hotels, restaurants, and casinos; only Paradise Island has been more developed. Its center is the Marriott Resort & Crystal Palace Casino. Often, deciding between Cable Beach and Paradise Island isn't so much a choice of which island you prefer as a choice of which hotel you prefer. But it's easy to sample both, since it takes only about 30 minutes to drive between the two.

Nassau, the Bahamian capital, isn't on a great stretch of shoreline and doesn't have as many first-rate hotels as either Paradise Island or Cable Beach—with the exception of the British Colonial Hilton, which has a small private beach. The main advantages of Nassau are colonial charm and price. Its hotels may not be ideally located, but they are relatively inexpensive; some offer very low prices even during the winter high season. You can base yourself here and commute easily to the beaches at Paradise Island or Cable Beach. Some travelers even prefer Nassau because it's the seat of Bahamian culture and history—not to mention the shopping mecca of The Bahamas.

PARADISE ISLAND   If high-rise hotels and glittering casinos are what you want, along with some of the best beaches in The Bahamas, there is no better choice than Paradise Island, directly off the coast of Nassau. It has the best food, the best entertainment, terrific beaches, casinos, and the best hotels. Its major drawbacks are that it's expensive and often overcrowded. Boasting a colorful history, yet some unremarkable architecture, Paradise Island remains one of the most intensely marketed pieces of real estate in the world. The sands and shoals of the elongated and narrow island protect the wharves and piers of Nassau, which rise across a narrow channel only 180m (590 ft.) away.

Owners of the 277-hectare (684-acre) island have included brokerage mogul Joseph Lynch (of Merrill Lynch) and Huntington Hartford (heir to the A&P supermarket fortune). More recent investors have included Merv Griffin. The island today is a carefully landscaped residential and commercial complex with good beaches, lots of glitter (some of it tasteful, some of it way too over-the-top), and many diversions.

GRAND BAHAMA ISLAND (FREEPORT/LUCAYA)   The island's name derives from the Spanish term *gran bajamar* (great shallows), which refers to the shallow reefs and sandbars that, over the centuries, have destroyed everything from Spanish galleons to English clipper ships on Grand Bahama's shores. Thanks to the tourist development schemes of U.S. financiers such as Howard Hughes, Grand Bahama boasts a well-developed tourist infrastructure. Casinos, beaches, and restaurants are now plentiful here.

Grand Bahama's **Freeport/Lucaya** resort area is another popular destination for American tourists, though it has a lot more tacky development than Paradise Island or Cable Beach. The compensation for that is a lower price tag on just about everything. Freeport/Lucaya offers plenty of opportunities for fine dining, entertainment, and gambling. Grand Bahama also offers the best hiking in The Bahamas and has some of the finest sandy beaches. Its golf courses attract players from all over the globe, and the island hosts major tournaments several times a year. You'll find some of the world's best diving here, as well as UNEXSO, the internationally famous diving school. Grand Bahama Island is especially popular with families.

2 Visitor Information

The two best sources to try before you leave home are your travel agent and **The Bahamas Tourist Office** nearest you. Visit the nation's official tourism office at www.bahamas.com, or call ℭ **800/ BAHAMAS** or 242/302-2000. You can also walk in at these branch offices:

Chicago: 8600 W. Bryn Mawr Ave., Suite 820, North Chicago, IL 60631 (ℭ **312/693-1500**)

Miami: 1 Turnberry Pl., 19495 Biscayne Blvd., Suite 80, Aventura, FL 33180 (ℭ **305/932-0051**)

Fort Lauderdale: 1100 Lee Wagener Blvd., Suite 204, Ft. Lauderdale, FL 33315 (ℭ **954/359-8099**)

Los Angeles: 3450 Wilshire Blvd., Suite 208, Los Angeles, CA 90010 (ℭ **213/385-0033**)

New York: 150 E. 52nd St., New York, NY 10022 (ℭ **212/ 758-2777**)

Texas: 3102 Oak Lawn Ave., Suite 700, Dallas, TX 75219 (ℭ **214/560-2280**)

Toronto: 121 Bloor St. E., Suite 1101, Toronto, ON M4W 3M5 (ℭ **416/968-2999**)

United Kingdom: 10 Chesterfield St., London W1J 5JL (ℭ **020/7355-0800**)

You may also want to contact the U.S. State Department for background bulletins, which supply up-to-date information on crime, health concerns, import restrictions, and other travel matters. Call © **888/407-4747** or visit www.travel.state.gov.

A travel agent can be a great source of information. Make sure your agent is a member of the American Society of Travel Agents (ASTA). If you get poor service from an ASTA agent, you can write to the ASTA Consumer Affairs Department, 1101 King St., Alexandria, VA 22314 (© **800/440-ASTA** or 703/739-2782; www.astanet.com).

SEARCHING THE WEB
Bahamas websites include:

The Bahamas Ministry of Tourism (www.bahamas.com or www.tourismbahamas.org): Official tourism site.

The Bahamas Out Islands Promotion Board (www.myout islands.com): Focuses on remote isles.

Bahamas Tourist Guide (www.interknowledge.com/bahamas): Travelers' opinions.

Bahamas Vacation Guide (www.bahamasvg.com): Service listings.

Nassau/Paradise Island Promotion Board (www.nassau paradiseisland.com): Service listings.

3 Entry Requirements

ENTRY REQUIREMENTS
PASSPORTS

To enter The Bahamas, **citizens of Britain** and **Canada** coming in as visitors *must* bring a passport to demonstrate proof of citizenship. Under new Homeland Security regulations that started December 31, 2005, **U.S. travelers** must have a valid passport to re-enter the United States by January 1, 2008. During the life of this edition (2007), Americans can—perhaps—get by with a voter registration card or an original birth certificate *plus* a government-issued photo ID. But since rules are in a state of flux, there could be delays upon re-entering the U.S. Therefore we recommend that all Frommer's readers carry a passport for travel in 2007.

Onward or return tickets must be shown to immigration officials in The Bahamas. Citizens of other countries, including Australia, Ireland, and New Zealand, should carry a valid passport.

For information on how to get a passport, go to "Passports" in the "Fast Facts: The Bahamas" section of this chapter—the websites listed provide downloadable passport applications as well as the current fees for processing passport applications. For an up-to-date, country-by-country listing of passport requirements around the world, go to the "Foreign Entry Requirement" Web page of the U.S. State Department at **http://travel.state.gov**.

VISAS

The Commonwealth of The Bahamas does not require visas. On entry to The Bahamas, you'll be given an Immigration Card to complete and sign. The card has a carbon copy that you must keep until departure, at which time it must be turned in. You'll also have to pay a departure tax before you can exit the country (see "Taxes," under "Fast Facts: The Bahamas," later in this chapter).

MEDICAL REQUIREMENTS

For information on medical requirements and recommendations, see "Health & Safety," p. 18.

CUSTOMS
WHAT YOU CAN BRING INTO THE BAHAMAS

Bahamian Customs allow you to bring in 200 cigarettes, or 50 cigars, or 1 pound of tobacco, plus 1 quart of spirits (hard liquor). You can also bring in items classified as "personal effects," and all the money you wish.

WHAT YOU CAN TAKE HOME FROM THE BAHAMAS

Visitors leaving Nassau or Freeport/Lucaya for most U.S. destinations clear U.S. Customs & Border Protection before departing The Bahamas. Charter companies can make special arrangements with the Nassau or Freeport flight services and U.S. Customs & Border Protection for pre-clearance. No further formalities are required upon arrival in the United States once the pre-clearance has taken place in Nassau or Freeport.

Collect receipts for all purchases you make in The Bahamas. *Note:* If a merchant suggests giving you a false receipt, misstating the value of the goods, beware—the merchant might be an informer to U.S. Customs. You must also declare all gifts received while abroad.

If you purchased an item during an earlier trip abroad, carry proof that you have already paid customs duty on the item at the time of your previous reentry. To be extra careful, compile a list of expensive carry-on items and ask a U.S. Customs agent to stamp your list at the airport before your departure.

U.S. Citizens

For specifics on what you can bring back and the corresponding fees, download the invaluable free pamphlet *Know Before You Go* online at **www.cbp.gov**. (Click on "Travel," and then click on "Know Before You Go") Or contact the **U.S. Customs & Border Protection (CBP),** 1300 Pennsylvania Ave., NW, Washington, DC 20229 (© **877/287-8667**), and request the pamphlet.

Canadian Citizens

For a clear summary of Canadian rules, write for the booklet *I Declare,* issued by the **Canada Border Services Agency** (© **800/ 461-9999** in Canada, or 204/983-3500; **www.cbsa-asfc.gc.ca**).

U.K. Citizens

For information, contact **HM Revenue & Customs** at © **0845/ 010-9000** (from outside the U.K., 02920/501-261), or consult their website at **www.hmrc.gov.uk**.

Australian Citizens

A helpful brochure available from Australian consulates or Customs offices is *Know Before You Go.* For more information, call the **Australian Customs Service** at © **1300/363-263,** or log on to **www. customs.gov.au**.

New Zealand Citizens

Most questions are answered in a free pamphlet available at New Zealand consulates and Customs offices: *New Zealand Customs Guide for Travellers, Notice no. 4.* For more information, contact **New Zealand Customs Service,** The Customhouse, 17–21 Whitmore St., Box 2218, Wellington (© **04/473-6099** or 0800/428-786; **www.customs.govt.nz**).

4 When to Go

THE WEATHER

The temperature in The Bahamas averages between 75°F and 85°F (24°C–29°C) in both winter and summer, although it can get chilly in the early morning and at night. The Bahamian winter is usually like a perpetual late spring—naturally the high season for North Americans rushing to escape snow and ice. Summer brings broiling hot sun and humidity. There's a much greater chance of rain during the summer and fall.

THE HURRICANE SEASON

The curse of Bahamian weather, the hurricane season, lasts (officially) from June 1 to November 30. But there is no cause for panic.

More tropical cyclones pound the U.S. mainland than The Bahamas. Hurricanes are actually fairly infrequent here, and when one does come, satellite forecasts generally give adequate advance warning so that precautions can be taken.

If you're heading for The Bahamas during the hurricane season, you might want to visit the National Weather Service at www.nws.noaa.gov.

For an online 5-day forecast anytime, check the Weather Channel at www.weather.com (for free!).

Average Temperatures & Rainfall (in.) in The Bahamas

Note that these numbers are daily averages, so expect temperatures to climb significantly higher in the noonday sun and to cool off a good deal in the evening.

	Jan	Feb	Mar	Apr	May	June	July	Aug	Sept	Oct	Nov	Dec
Temp. °F	70	70	72	75	77	80	81	82	81	78	74	71
Temp. °C	21	21	22	24	25	27	27	28	27	26	23	22
Rainfall (in.)	1.9	1.6	1.4	1.9	4.8	9.2	6.1	6.3	7.5	8.3	2.3	1.5

THE "SEASON"

In The Bahamas, hotels charge their highest prices during the peak winter period from mid-December to mid-April, when visitors fleeing from cold north winds flock to the islands. Winter is the driest season.

If you plan to visit during the winter, try to make reservations at least 2 to 3 months in advance. At some hotels, it's impossible to book accommodations for Christmas and the month of February without even more lead time.

5 Getting There

Lying off the east coast of Florida, the archipelago of The Bahamas is the easiest and most convenient foreign destination you can fly to unless you live close to the Canadian or Mexican borders.

Nassau is the busiest and most popular point of entry (this is where you'll fly if you're staying on Paradise Island). Freeport, on Grand Bahama, also has its own airport, which is served by flights from the U.S. mainland, too.

Flight time to Nassau from Miami is about 35 minutes; from New York, 2½ hours; from Atlanta, 2 hours and 5 minutes; from Philadelphia, 2 hours and 45 minutes; from Charlotte, 2 hours and 10 minutes; from central Florida, 1 hour and 10 minutes; and, from Toronto, 3 hours.

> ⸤Tips⸥ **Getting Through the Airport**
>
> - Arrive at the airport at least 1 hour before a domestic flight and 2 hours before an international flight. You can check the average wait times at your airport by going to the TSA **Security Checkpoint Wait Times** site (waittime.tsa.dhs.gov).
> - Know what you can carry on and what you can't. For the latest updates on items you are prohibited to bring in carryon luggage, go to **www.tsa.gov/travelers/airtravel.**
> - Help speed up security before you're screened. Remove jackets, shoes, belt buckles, heavy jewelry, and watches and place them either in your carryon luggage or the security bins provided. Place keys, coins, cellphones, and pagers in a security bin. If you have metallic body parts, carry a note from your doctor. When possible, keep packing liquids in checked baggage.

THE MAJOR AIRLINES

From the U.S. mainland, about a half-dozen carriers fly nonstop to the country's major point of entry and busiest airline hub, Nassau's **Lynden Pindling International Airport** (② 242/377-1759). Some also fly to the archipelago's second-most-populous city of Freeport.

American Airlines (② 800/433-7300; www.aa.com) has several flights per day from Miami to Nassau as well as four daily flights from Fort Lauderdale to Nassau. In addition, the carrier flies three times daily from Miami to Freeport.

Delta (② 800/221-1212; www.delta.com) has several connections to The Bahamas, with service from Atlanta, Orlando, and New York's LaGuardia.

The national airline of The Bahamas, **Bahamasair** (② 800/222-4262 or 242/377-8451; www.bahamasair.com), flies to The Bahamas from Miami and Fort Lauderdale, landing at either Nassau (with seven nonstop flights daily) or Freeport (with two nonstop flights daily).

US Airways (② 800/428-4322; www.usairways.com) offers daily direct flights to Nassau from Philadelphia and Charlotte, North Carolina.

JetBlue (② 800/JET-BLUE; www.jetblue.com) has one direct flight daily to Nassau, from JFK in New York.

Other carriers include **Continental Airlines** (© 800/231-0856; www.continental.com), which has greatly expanded its link to The Bahamas through South Florida through its regional affiliate, Gulfstream International. In addition, it maintains frequent links between Fort Lauderdale, Freeport, and destinations in the Out Islands.

Air Canada (© 888/247-2262; www.aircanada.com) is the only carrier offering scheduled service to Nassau from Canada. Direct flights from Toronto and Montreal leave daily; other flights from Toronto and Montreal, as well as other Canadian cities, make connections in the U.S.

British travelers opt for transatlantic passage aboard **British Airways** (© 800/AIR-WAYS in the U.S. or 0870/850-9850 in the U.K.; www.britishairways.com), which offers four weekly direct flights from London to Nassau. The airline also has at least one flight daily to Miami. From here, many connections are available to Nassau and many other points within the archipelago on several carriers.

6 Money & Costs

It's always advisable to bring money in a variety of forms on a vacation: a mix of cash, credit cards, and traveler's checks. You should also exchange enough petty cash to cover airport incidentals, tipping, and transportation to your hotel before you leave home, or withdraw money upon arrival at an airport ATM.

In many international destinations, ATMs offer the best exchange rates. Avoid exchanging money at commercial exchange bureaus and hotels, which often have the highest transaction fees.

CURRENCY

The currency is the **Bahamian dollar (B$1),** pegged to the U.S. dollar so that they're always equivalent. (In fact, U.S. dollars are accepted widely throughout The Bahamas.) There is no restriction on bringing foreign currency into The Bahamas. Most large hotels and stores accept traveler's checks, but you may have trouble using a personal check. It's a good idea to exchange enough money to cover airport incidentals and transportation to your hotel before you leave home.

You can change currencies at a local American Express (© 800/807-6233; www.americanexpress.com) or Thomas Cook (© 800/223-7373; www.thomascook.com) or at your bank.

Be sure to carry some small bills or loose change when traveling. Petty cash will come in handy for tipping and public transportation. Consider keeping the change separate from your larger bills, so that it's readily accessible and you'll be less of a target for theft. In general prices are about the same as in urban America, but they are less expensive than costs in the U.K. Food is often more expensive, however, since so much of it has to be imported.

ATMs

The easiest way to get cash away from home is from an ATM (automated teller machine). The **Cirrus** (© **800/424-7787;** www.mastercard.com) and **PLUS** (© **800/843-7587;** www.visa.com) networks span the globe; look at the back of your bank card to see which network you're on, then call or check online for ATM locations at your destination. Know your personal identification number (PIN) and your daily withdrawal limit. Ask your card carrier if your current PIN works in The Bahamas. Every card is different, but some need a four-digit, rather than a six-digit, PIN to withdraw cash abroad.

Many banks impose a fee every time a card is used at a different bank's ATM, and that fee can be higher for international transactions (up to $5/£2.60 or more) than for domestic ones (rarely more than $1.50/80p). On top of this, the bank from which you withdraw cash may charge its own fee. To compare banks' ATM fees within the U.S., use **www.bankrate.com**. For international withdrawal fees, ask your bank.

You can also get cash advances on your credit card at an ATM. Credit card companies do try to protect themselves from theft by limiting the funds someone can withdraw outside their home country, so notify your credit card company before you leave home. And keep in mind that you'll pay interest from the moment of your withdrawal, even if you pay your monthly bills on time.

On New Providence Island and Paradise Island, there are plenty of ATMs, including one at the Nassau International Airport. There are far fewer ATMs on Grand Bahama Island (Freeport/Lucaya), but those that are here are strategically located—including ones at the airport and the casino (of course).

CREDIT CARDS

Credit cards are another safe way to carry money. They also provide a convenient record of all your expenses, and they generally offer relatively good exchange rates. You can withdraw cash advances from your credit cards at banks or ATMs but high fees make credit-card cash advances a pricey way to get cash. Keep in mind that you'll pay interest from the moment of your withdrawal, even if you pay your monthly bills on time. Also, note that many banks now assess a

1–3% "transaction fee" on **all** charges you incur abroad (whether you're using the local currency or your native currency).

TRAVELER'S CHECKS

You can buy traveler's checks at most banks. They are offered in denominations of $20, $50, $100, $500, and sometimes $1000. Generally, you'll pay a service charge ranging from 1% to 4%.

The most popular traveler's checks are offered by **American Express** (© **800/807-6233** or © **800/221-7282** for card holders—this number accepts collect calls, offers service in several foreign languages, and exempts Amex gold and platinum cardholders from the 1% fee.); **Visa** (© **800/732-1322**)—AAA members can obtain Visa checks for a $9.95 fee (for checks up to $1,500) at most AAA offices or by calling © **866/339-3378;** and **MasterCard** (© **800/223-9920**).

Be sure to keep a record of the traveler's checks serial numbers separate from your checks in the event that they are stolen or lost. You'll get a refund faster if you know the numbers.

American Express, Thomas Cook, Visa, and **MasterCard** offer **foreign currency traveler's checks**, useful if you're traveling to one country or to the Euro zone; they're accepted at locations where dollar checks may not be.

Another option is the new prepaid traveler's check cards, reloadable cards that work much like debit cards but aren't linked to your checking account. The **American Express Travelers Cheque Card,** for example, requires a minimum deposit, sets a maximum balance, and has a one-time issuance fee of $14.95. You can withdraw money from an ATM (for a fee of $2.50 per transaction, not including bank fees), and the funds can be purchased in dollars, euros, or pounds. If you lose the card, your available funds will be refunded within 24 hours.

7 Travel Insurance

Buying insurance might make sense because The Bahamas is not necessarily a "safe" destination. Although crimes against individual tourists are rare, your property, if left unprotected, could be stolen. Tour operators, airlines, and cruise ships can all go out of business suddenly, making default insurance a wise move on some Bahamian trips. Trip delay insurance might cover expenses that rise suddenly, as in the event of a hurricane.

Check your existing insurance policies and credit card coverage before you buy travel insurance. You may already be covered for lost luggage, canceled tickets, or medical expenses.

The cost of travel insurance varies widely, depending on the cost and length of your trip, your age and health, and the type of trip you're taking, but expect to pay between 5% and 8% of the vacation itself. You can get estimates from various providers through **Insure-MyTrip.com**. Enter your trip cost and dates, your age, and other information, for prices from more than a dozen companies.

TRIP-CANCELLATION INSURANCE

Trip-cancellation insurance will help retrieve your money if you have to back out of a trip or depart early, or if your travel supplier goes bankrupt. Permissible reasons for trip cancellation can range from sickness to natural disasters to the State Department declaring a destination unsafe for travel.

For more information, contact one of the following recommended insurers: **Access America** (✆ 800/729-6021; www.access america.com); **Travel Guard International** (✆ 800/826-4919; www.travelguard.com); **Travel Insured International** (✆ 800/ 243-3174; www.travelinsured.com); and **Travelex Insurance Services** (✆ 800/228-9792; www.travelex-insurance.com).

MEDICAL INSURANCE

For travel overseas, most U.S. health plans (including Medicare and Medicaid) do not provide coverage, and the ones that do often require you to pay for services upfront and reimburse you only after you return home. As a safety net, you may want to buy travel medical insurance, particularly if you're traveling to a remote or high-risk area where emergency evacuation might be necessary. If you require additional medical insurance, try **MEDEX Assistance** (✆ 800/732-5309; www.medexassist.com) or **Travel Assistance International** (✆ **800/821-2828;** www.travelassistance.com; for general information on services, call the company's Worldwide Assistance Services, Inc., at ✆ **800/777-8710**).

LOST-LUGGAGE INSURANCE

On flights within the U.S., checked baggage is covered up to $2,500 per ticketed passenger. On international flights (including U.S. portions of international trips), baggage coverage is limited to approximately $9.07 per pound, up to approximately $635 per checked bag. If you plan to check items more valuable than what's covered by the standard liability, see if your homeowner's policy covers your valuables. As an added discretion, you might also ask for baggage insurance as part of your comprehensive travel-insurance package.

If your luggage is lost, immediately file a lost-luggage claim at the airport, detailing the luggage contents. Most airlines require that you report delayed, damaged, or lost baggage within 4 hours of arrival. The airlines are required to deliver luggage, once found, directly to your house or destination free of charge.

8 Health & Safety

STAYING HEALTHY

We list **hospital** and **emergency numbers** under "Fast Facts," in each chapter. Even on the remotest island, you'll find, if not a hospital, a local medicine man (or woman, in many cases). Many Bahamians are fond of herbal remedies. But you don't need to rely on these primitive treatments, as most resorts have either hospitals or clinics on-site.

The major health risk here is not tropical disease, as it is in some Caribbean islands, but rather the bad luck of ingesting a bad piece of shellfish, exotic fruit, or too many rum punches. If your body is not accustomed to some of these foods, or they haven't been cleaned properly, you may suffer diarrhea. If you tend to have digestive problems, then drink bottled water and avoid ice, unpasteurized milk, and uncooked food such as fresh salads. However, fresh food served in hotels is usually safe to eat.

The Bahamas has excellent medical facilities. Physicians and surgeons in private practice are readily available in Nassau, Cable Beach, and Freeport/Lucaya. (We've listed the names and telephone numbers of specific clinics in the individual island coverage that follows throughout this book.) If intensive or urgent care is required, patients are brought by the Emergency Flight Service to **Princess Margaret Hospital** (© 242/322-2861) on Shirley St., Nassau. Some of the big resort hotels have in-house physicians or can quickly secure one for you.

There are also a government-operated hospital, **Rand Memorial** (© 242/352-6735), on E. Atlantic Dr., Freeport, and several government-operated clinics on Grand Bahama Island. Nassau and Freeport/Lucaya also have private hospitals.

Dentists are plentiful in Nassau, somewhat less so on Grand Bahama.

Contact the **International Association for Medical Assistance to Travelers (IAMAT;** © 716/754-4883 or, in Canada, 416/652-0137; **www.iamat.org**) for tips on travel and health concerns in the countries you're visiting, and for lists of local, English-speaking doctors. The United States **Centers for Disease Control and Prevention**

Healthy Travels to You

The following government websites offer health-related travel advice:

- **Australia:** www.dfat.gov.au/travel/
- **Canada:** www.hc-sc.gc.ca/index_e.html
- **U.K.:** www.dh.gov.uk/PolicyAndGuidance/HealthAdvice ForTravellers/fs/en
- **U.S.:** www.cdc.gov/travel/

(© **800/394-1945;** www.cdc.gov) provides up-to-date information on health hazards by region or country and offers tips on food safety. The website **www.tripprep.com**, sponsored by a consortium of travel medicine practitioners, may also offer helpful advice on traveling abroad. You can find listings of reliable clinics overseas at the **International Society of Travel Medicine** (www.istm.org).

COMMON AILMENTS

EXPOSURE TO THE SUN   Getting too much sun can be a real issue in The Bahamas. You must, of course, take the usual precautions you would anywhere against sunburn and sunstroke. Your time in the sun should be wisely limited for the first few days until you become accustomed to the more intense rays of the Bahamian sun. Also bring and use strong UVA/UVB sunblock products.

WHAT TO DO IF YOU GET SICK AWAY FROM HOME

In most cases, your existing health plan will provide the coverage you need. But double-check; you may want to buy **travel medical insurance** instead (see the section on insurance above). Bring your insurance ID card with you wherever you travel.

We list **hospitals** and **emergency numbers** under "Fast Facts," in each chapter.

If you suffer from a chronic illness, consult your doctor before your departure. Pack **prescription medications** in your carry-on luggage, and carry them in their original containers, with pharmacy labels—otherwise they won't make it through airport security. Carry the generic name of prescription medicines, in case a local pharmacist doesn't know the brand name.

For travel abroad, you may have to pay medical costs upfront and be reimbursed later. See "Medical Insurance," under "Travel Insurance," above.

STAYING SAFE

When going to Nassau (New Providence), Cable Beach, Paradise Island, or Freeport/Lucaya, exercise the same caution you would if visiting Miami. Whatever you do, if people peddling drugs approach you, steer clear of them.

Crime is increasing, and visitors should use caution and good judgment when visiting The Bahamas. While most criminal incidents take place in a part of Nassau not usually frequented by tourists (the "Over-the-Hill" area south of downtown), crime and violence have moved into more upscale tourist and residential areas.

Women, especially, should take caution if walking alone on the streets of Nassau after dark, particularly if those streets appear to be deserted.

In the last year the U.S. Embassy has received several reports of sexual assaults, including against teenage girls. Most assaults have been perpetrated against intoxicated young women, some of whom were reportedly drugged. To minimize the potential for sexual assault, the embassy recommends that young women stay in groups, consume alcohol in moderation, and not accept rides or drinks from strangers.

Pickpockets (often foreigners) work the crowded casino floors of both Paradise Beach and Cable Beach. See that your wallet, money, and valuables are well secured.

Travelers should avoid walking alone after dark or in isolated areas, and avoid placing themselves in situations where they are alone with strangers. Be cautious on deserted areas of beaches at all hours. Don't leave valuables such as cameras and purses lying unattended on the beach while you go for a swim.

If you're driving a rental car, always make sure your car door is locked, and never leave possessions in view.

Hotel guests should always lock their doors and should never leave valuables unattended, especially on beaches. Visitors should store passport/identity documents, airline tickets, credit cards, and extra cash in hotel safes. Avoid wearing expensive jewelry, particularly Rolex watches, which criminals have specifically targeted. Use only clearly marked taxis and make a note of the license plate number for your records.

The loss or theft of a passport overseas should be reported to the local police and the nearest embassy or consulate. A lost or stolen birth certificate and/or driver's license generally cannot be replaced outside the United States. U.S. citizens may refer to the Department of State's pamphlets, *A Safe Trip Abroad* and *Tips for Travelers to the Caribbean,* for ways to promote a trouble-free journey. The pamphlets are available by mail from the Superintendent of Documents, U.S. Government Printing Office, Washington, DC 20402, via the Internet at www.gpoaccess.gov/index.html, or via the Bureau of Consular Affairs home page at www.travel.state.gov.

9 Specialized Travel Resources

TRAVELERS WITH DISABILITIES

A disability should not stop anyone from traveling to the Bahamian islands. Because these islands are relatively flat, it is fairly easy to get around, even for persons with disabilities.

Many travel agencies offer customized tours and itineraries for travelers with disabilities. Among them are **Flying Wheels Travel** (© 507/451-5005; www.flyingwheelstravel.com); **Access-Able Travel Source** (© 303/232-2979; www.access-able.com); and **Accessible Journeys** (© 800/846-4537 or 610/521-0339; www. disabilitytravel.com).

Organizations that offer assistance to disabled travelers include **MossRehab** (© 800/225-5667; www.mossresourcenet.org), the **American Foundation for the Blind** (AFB; © 800/232-5463 or 212/502-7600; www.afb.org), and **SATH (Society for Accessible Travel & Hospitality;** © 212/447-7284; www.sath.org). **AirAmbulanceCard.com** is partnered with SATH and allows you to pre-select top hospitals in case of an emergency.

Also check out the quarterly magazine *Emerging Horizons* (www.emerginghorizons.com), and *Open World* magazine, published by SATH.

TIPS FOR BRITISH TRAVELERS WITH DISABILITIES

Contact the Royal Association for Disability and Rehabilitation (RADAR), Unit 12, City Forum, 250 City Rd., London, EC1V 8AF (© 020/7250-3222; www.radar.org.uk).

Tips Finding an Accessible Hotel

You can call the **Bahamas Association for the Physically Disabled** (BAPD) (© 242/322-2393) for information about accessible hotels in The Bahamas. This agency will also send a van to the airport to transport you to your hotel for a fee, and can provide ramps.

GAY & LESBIAN TRAVELERS

Generally speaking, The Bahamas isn't a gay-friendly destination. Think twice before choosing to vacation here. Although many gay people visit or live here, the country has very strict antihomosexual laws. Relations between homosexuals, even when between consenting adults, are subject to criminal sanctions carrying prison terms. If you would like to make visiting gay beaches, bars, or clubs part of your vacation, consider South Miami Beach, Key West, or Puerto Rico instead.

Of course, the big resorts welcome one and all, even if forced to do so. For many years, the all-inclusive Sandals Royal Bahamian on Cable Beach refused to accept same-sex couples and booked only heterosexual guests. However, rights groups in Canada and Great Britain lobbied successfully, and the Sandals people found they could no longer advertise their resorts, and their discriminatory policies, in those countries. As a result, Sandals capitulated and ended its previous ban. However, gay and lesbian couples looking for a carefree holiday should seriously consider whether they want to spend their hard-earned dollars in a resort like Sandals that did not voluntarily end its ban against homosexuals until forced to do so by more liberal and far-sighted governments.

Single gays or gay couples should travel here with great discretion. If you're intent on visiting, **The International Gay and Lesbian Travel Association (IGLTA; ✆ 800/448-8550** or 954/776-2626; www.iglta.org) is the trade association for the gay and lesbian travel industry, and offers an online directory of gay- and lesbian-friendly travel businesses; go to their website and click on "Members."

Many agencies offer tours and travel itineraries specifically for gay and lesbian travelers. Among them are **Above and Beyond Tours** (✆ 800/397-2681; www.abovebeyondtours.com), **Now, Voyager** (✆ 800/255-6951; www.nowvoyager.com), and **Olivia Cruises & Resorts** (✆ 800/631-6277; www.olivia.com).

Gay.com Travel (✆ 415/644-8044; www.gay.com/travel or www. outandabout.com), is an excellent online successor to the popular *Out & About* print magazine. It provides regularly updated information about gay-owned, gay-oriented, and gay-friendly lodging, dining, sightseeing, nightlife, and shopping establishments in every important destination worldwide.

The following travel guides are available at many bookstores, or you can order them from any online bookseller: *Spartacus International Gay Guide* (Bruno Gmünder Verlag; www.spartacusworld. com/gayguide) and *Odysseus: The International Gay Travel*

Planner (Odysseus Enterprises Ltd.); and the *Damron* guides (www.damron.com), with separate, annual books for gay men and lesbians.

SENIOR TRAVEL

In The Bahamas, the standard adult rate usually applies to all ages more than 21 years of age. The careful, frugal travel shopper, however, might find some deals if arrangements are made before you go.

Members of **AARP** (formerly known as the American Association of Retired Persons), 601 E St. NW, Washington, DC 20049 (© 888/687-2277; www.aarp.org), get discounts on hotels, airfares, and car rentals. AARP offers members a range of benefits, including *AARP: The Magazine* and a monthly newsletter. Anyone over 50 can join.

Many reliable agencies and organizations target the 50-plus market. **Elderhostel** (© 800/454-5768; www.elderhostel.org) arranges study programs for those aged 55 and over. **ElderTreks** (© 800/741-7956; www.eldertreks.com) offers small-group tours to off-the-beaten-path or adventure-travel locations, restricted to travelers 50 and older. **INTRAV** (© 800/456-8100; www.intrav.com) is a high-end tour operator that caters to the mature, discerning traveler (not specifically seniors), with trips around the world that include guided safaris, polar expeditions, private-jet adventures, and small-boat cruises down jungle rivers.

Recommended publications offering travel resources and discounts for seniors include: the quarterly magazine *Travel 50 & Beyond* (www.travel50andbeyond.com); *Travel Unlimited: Uncommon Adventures for the Mature Traveler* (Avalon); *101 Tips for Mature Travelers,* available from Grand Circle Travel (© 800/959-0405 or 617/350-7500; www.gct.com); and *Unbelievably Good Deals and Great Adventures That You Absolutely Can't Get Unless You're Over 50* (McGraw-Hill), by Joann Rattner Heilman.

FAMILY TRAVEL

The Bahamas is one of the top family-vacation destinations in North America. The smallest toddlers can spend blissful hours on sandy beaches and in the shallow seawater or in swimming pools constructed with them in mind. There's no end to the fascinating pursuits offered for older children, ranging from boat rides to shell collecting to horseback riding, hiking, or even dancing. Some children are old enough to learn to snorkel and to explore an underwater wonderland. Some resorts will even teach kids to swim or windsurf.

Most families with kids head for New Providence (Nassau), Paradise Island, or Grand Bahama Island (Freeport). Look for our "Kids" icon, indicating attractions, restaurants, or hotels and resorts that are especially family friendly. See also "The Best Family Vacations," in chapter 1, for additional recommendations.

Every country's regulations differ, but in general children traveling abroad should have plenty of documentation on hand, particularly if they're traveling with someone other than their own parents (in which case a notarized form letter from a parent is often required).

For details on entry requirements for children traveling abroad, go to the U.S. State Department website (http://travel.state.gov).

Recommended family travel websites include **Family Travel Forum** (www.familytravelforum.com), **Family Travel Network** (www.familytravelnetwork.com), **Traveling Internationally with Your Kids** (www.travelwithyourkids.com), and **Family Travel Files** (www.thefamilytravelfiles.com).

WOMEN TRAVELERS

Should a woman travel alone to The Bahamas? Opinions and reports vary. A woman traveling alone in such countries as Jamaica face certain dangers, and safety is often an issue. Women traveling alone in The Bahamas rarely encounter aggressive, potentially dangerous behavior from males, and are usually treated with respect. However, some Bahamian men may assume that a woman traveling alone is doing so in order to find a male partner. To avoid such unwanted attention, dress a bit conservatively and don't go wandering the streets of Nassau unescorted at night. It's always advisable to wear a cover-up to your swimsuit when leaving the beach and heading into town. For additional details, see "Staying Safe" above.

Women Welcome Women World Wide (5W); (© 01494/ 465441; www.womenwelcomewomen.org.uk) works to foster international friendships by enabling women of different countries to visit one another (men can come along on the trips; they just can't join the club). It's a big, active organization, with more than 3,500 members from all walks of life in some 70 countries.

Also check out the award-winning website **Journeywoman** (www.journeywoman.com), a "real life" women's travel-information network where you can sign up for a free e-mail newsletter and get advice on everything from etiquette to safety; or the travel guide *Safety and Security for Women Who Travel* by Sheila Swan and Peter Laufer (Travelers' Tales, Inc.), offering common-sense tips on safe travel.

Frommers.com: The Complete Travel Resource

For an excellent travel-planning resource, we highly recommend **Frommers.com** (www.frommers.com), voted Best Travel Site by *PC Magazine*. We're a little biased, of course, but we guarantee that you'll find the travel tips, reviews, monthly vacation giveaways, bookstore, and online-booking capabilities thoroughly indispensable.

AFRICAN-AMERICAN TRAVELERS

Black Travel Online (www.blacktravelonline.com) posts news on upcoming events and includes links to articles and travel-booking sites. **Soul of America** (www.soulofamerica.com) is a comprehensive website, with travel tips, event and family-reunion postings, and sections on historically black beach resorts and active vacations.

Agencies and organizations that provide resources for black travelers include **Rodgers Travel** (© **800/825-1775;** www.rodgers travel.com) and the **African American Association of Innkeepers International** (© **877/422-5777;** www.africanamericaninns.com). For more information, check out the following collections and guides: *Go Girl: The Black Woman's Guide to Travel & Adventure* (Eighth Mountain Press), a compilation of travel essays by writers including Jill Nelson and Audre Lorde; *The African American Travel Guide* by Wayne Robinson (Hunter Publishing; www. hunterpublishing.com); *Steppin' Out* by Carla Labat (Avalon); *Travel and Enjoy Magazine* (© **866/266-6211;** www.travel andenjoy.com); and *Pathfinders Magazine* (© **215/438-2140;** www.pathfinderstravel.com), which includes articles on everything from Rio de Janeiro to Ghana as well as information on upcoming ski, diving, golf, and tennis trips.

SINGLE TRAVELERS

Single tourists often find the dating scene better in The Bahamas during the winter when there are more visitors, especially unattached ones.

On package vacations, single travelers are often hit with a "single supplement" to the base price. To avoid it, you can agree to room with other single travelers or find a compatible roommate before you go, from one of the many roommate-locator agencies.

TravelChums (© 212/787-2621; www.travelchums.com) is an Internet-only travel-companion matching service with elements of an online personals-type site, hosted by the respected New York–based Shaw Guides travel service. Many reputable tour companies offer singles-only trips.

For more information, check out Eleanor Berman's guide *Traveling Solo: Advice and Ideas for More Than 250 Great Vacations* (Globe Pequot), with advice on traveling alone, either solo or as part of a group tour.

10 Sustainable Tourism/Ecotourism

Each time you take a flight or drive a car, CO_2 is released into the atmosphere. You can help neutralize this danger to our planet through "carbon offsetting"—paying someone to reduce your CO_2 emissions by the same amount you've added. Carbon offsets can be purchased in the U.S. from companies such as **Carbonfund.org** (www.carbonfund.org) and **TerraPass** (www.terrapass.org), and from **Climate Care** (www.climatecare.org) in the U.K.

Although one could argue that any vacation that includes an airplane flight can't be truly "green," you can go on holiday and still contribute positively to the environment. You can offset carbon emissions from your flight in other ways. Choose forward-looking companies that embrace responsible development practices, helping preserve destinations for the future by working alongside local people. An increasing number of sustainable tourism initiatives can help you plan a family trip and leave as small a "footprint" as possible on the places you visit.

Responsible Travel (www.responsibletravel.com) contains a great source of sustainable travel ideas run by a spokesperson for responsible tourism in the travel industry. **Sustainable Travel International** (www.sustainabletravelinternational.org) promotes responsible tourism practices and issues an annual Green Gear & Gift Guide.

You can find eco-friendly travel tips, statistics, and touring companies and associations—listed by destination under "Travel Choice"—at the TIES website, www.ecotourism.org. Also check out **Conservation International** (www.conservation.org)—which, with *National Geographic Traveler,* annually presents **World Legacy Awards** (www.wlaward.org) to those travel tour operators, businesses, organizations, and places that have made a significant contribution to sustainable tourism. **Ecotravel.com** is part online magazine and part ecodirectory that lets you search for touring companies in several categories (water-based, land-based, spiritually oriented, and so on).

For information about the ethics of swimming with dolphins and other outdoor activities, visit the **Whale and Dolphin Conservation Society** (www.wdcs.org) and **Tread Lightly** (www.treadlightly.org).

11 Staying Connected

INTERNET ACCESS AWAY FROM HOME
WITHOUT YOUR OWN COMPUTER

In lieu of the cybercafe that exists in most cities today, in The Bahamas you may have to rely on the good graces of your hotel to get your e-mail.

To see whether there are any cybercafes in your destination, check **www.cybercaptive.com** and **www.cybercafe.com**. Aside from formal cybercafes, most **youth hostels** and **public libraries** have Internet access. Avoid **hotel business centers** unless you're willing to pay exorbitant rates.

Most major airports now have **Internet kiosks** scattered throughout their gates. These give you basic Web access for a per-minute fee that's usually higher than cybercafe prices.

WITH YOUR OWN COMPUTER

More and more hotels, cafes, and retailers are signing on as Wi-Fi (wireless fidelity) "hot spots." Mac owners have their own networking technology: Apple AirPort. **T-Mobile Hotspot** (www.t-mobile.com/hotspot) serves up wireless connections at more than 1,000 Starbucks coffee shops nationwide. **Boingo** (www.boingo.com) and **Wayport** (www.wayport.com) have set up networks in airports and high-class hotel lobbies. IPass providers (see below) also give you access to a few hundred wireless hotel lobby setups. To locate other hotspots that provide **free wireless networks** in cities around the world, go to **www.personaltelco.net.**

For dial-up access, most business-class hotels throughout the world offer dataports for laptop modems, and a few thousand hotels in The Bahamas now offer free high-speed Internet access. In addition, major Internet Service Providers (ISPs) have **local access numbers** around the world, allowing you to go online by placing a local call. The **iPass** network also has dial-up numbers around the world. You'll have to sign up with an iPass provider, who will then tell you how to set up your computer for your destination(s). For a list of iPass providers, go to www.ipass.com and click on "Individuals Buy Now." One solid provider is **i2roam** (www.i2roam.com; ℂ **866/ 811-6209** or 920/233-5863).

Wherever you go, bring a **connection kit** of the right power and phone adapters, a spare phone cord, and a spare Ethernet network cable—or find out whether your hotel supplies them to guests. See "Electricity" in the "Fast Facts: The Bahamas" section later in this chapter.

CELLPHONE USE

The three letters that define much of the world's wireless capabilities are GSM (Global System for Mobiles), a big, seamless network that makes for easy cross-border cellphone use throughout Europe and dozens of other countries worldwide. In the U.S., T-Mobile, AT&T Wireless, and Cingular use this quasi-universal system; in Canada, Microcell and some Rogers customers are GSM, and all Europeans and most Australians use GSM. If your cellphone is on a GSM system, and you have a world-capable multiband phone such as many Sony Ericsson, Motorola, or Samsung models, you can make and receive calls across civilized areas around much of the globe. Just call your wireless operator and ask for "international roaming" to be activated on your account. Unfortunately, per-minute charges can be high—usually $1 to $1.50 (50p-80p) in Western Europe and up to $5 (£2.60) in places like Russia and Indonesia.

For many, **renting** a phone is a good idea. (Even worldphone owners will have to rent new phones if they're traveling to non-GSM regions, such as Japan or Korea.) While you can rent a phone from any number of overseas sites, including kiosks at airports and at car-rental agencies, we suggest renting the phone before you leave home. North Americans can rent one before leaving home from **InTouch USA** (ℂ 800/872-7626; www.intouchglobal.com) or **RoadPost** (ℂ 888/290-1616 or 905/272-5665; www.roadpost.com). InTouch will also, for free, advise you on whether your existing phone will work overseas.

Buying a phone can be economically attractive, as many nations have cheap prepaid phone systems. Once you arrive at your destination, stop by a local cellphone shop and get the cheapest package; you'll probably pay less than $100 (£52) for a phone and a starter calling card. Local calls may be as low as 10¢ (5p) per minute, and in many countries incoming calls are free.

Wilderness adventurers, or those heading to less-developed countries, might consider renting a **satellite phone ("satphone").** It's different from a cellphone in that it connects to satellites and works where there's no cellular signal or ground-based tower. You can rent satellite phones from RoadPost (see above). InTouch USA (see above) offers a wider range of satphones but at higher rates. Per-minute call charges can be even cheaper than roaming charges with a regular cellphone, but the phone itself is more expensive. As of this writing, satphones were outrageously expensive to buy, so don't even think about it.

12 Packages for the Independent Traveler

Before you search for the lowest airfare on your own (see earlier in this chapter), you may want to consider booking your flight as part of a package deal—a way to travel independently but pay group rates.

A package tour is not an escorted tour, in which you're led around by a guide. Except by cruise ships visiting certain islands, the option of being escorted around six or so Bahamian islands on an escorted tour does not exist.

Package tours are simply a way to buy the airfare, accommodations, and other elements of your trip (such as car rentals, airport transfers, and sometimes even activities) at the same time and often at discounted prices.

One good source of package deals is the airlines themselves. Most major airlines offer air/land packages, including **American Airlines Vacations** (© 800/321-2121; www.aavacations.com), **Delta Vacations** (© 800/654-6559; www.deltavacations.com), **Continental Airlines Vacations** (© 800/301-3800; www.covacations.com), and **United Vacations** (© 888/854-3899; www.unitedvacations.com). Several big **online travel agencies**—Expedia, Travelocity, Orbitz, Site59, and Lastminute.com—also do a brisk business in packages.

Liberty Travel (© **888/271-1584;** www.libertytravel.com) is one of the biggest packagers in the U.S. Northeast, and it usually boasts a full-page ad in Sunday papers. There's also **TourScan, Inc.,** 1051 Boston Post Rd., Darien, CT 06820 (© **800/962-2080** in the U.S.; www.tourscan.com), which researches the best value vacation at each hotel and condo.

For British travelers, package tours to The Bahamas can be booked through **Kuoni Travel,** Kuoni House, Dorking, Surrey RH5 4AZ (© **01306/744-442;** www.kuoni.co.uk), which offers both land and air packages to destinations such as Nassau and

Freeport, and to some places in the Out Islands. They also offer packages for self-catering villas on Paradise Island.

For an all-inclusive package, **Just-A-Vacation, Inc.,** 15501 Ebbynside Ct., Bowie, MD 20716 (© **301/559-0510;** www.justa vacation.com), specializes in all-inclusive resorts on the islands of The Bahamas, plus other destinations in the Caribbean including Barbados, Jamaica, Aruba, St. Lucia, and Antigua. **Club Med** (© **888/WEB-CLUB;** www.clubmed.com) has various all-inclusive options throughout the Caribbean and The Bahamas.

Travel packages are also listed in the travel section of your local Sunday newspaper. Or check ads in the national travel magazines such as *Arthur Frommer's Budget Travel Magazine, Travel & Leisure, National Geographic Traveler,* and *Condé Nast Traveler.*

13 Getting Around The Bahamas

If your final destination is Paradise Island, Freeport, or Nassau (Cable Beach) and you plan to fly, you'll have little trouble in reaching your destination.

BY PLANE

The national airline of The Bahamas, **Bahamasair** (© **800/222-4262;** www.bahamasair.com), serves 19 airports on 12 Bahamian islands.

BY RENTAL CAR

Many travelers don't really need to rent a car in The Bahamas, especially those who are coming for a few days of soaking in the sun at their resort's own beach. In Nassau and Freeport, you can easily rely on public transportation or taxis.

Most visitors need transportation only from the airport to their hotel; perhaps you can arrange an island tour later, and an expensive private car won't be necessary. Your hotel can always arrange a taxi for you if you want to venture out.

You may decide that you want a car to explore beyond the tourist areas of New Providence Island, and you're very likely to want one on Grand Bahama Island.

Just remember: Road rules are much the same as those in the U.S., but you *drive on the left.*

The major U.S. car-rental companies operate in The Bahamas, but not on all the remote islands. We always prefer to do business with one of the major firms if they're present because you can call ahead and reserve from home via a toll-free number, they tend to offer better-maintained vehicles, and it's easier to resolve any disputes after the fact. Call **Budget** (© **800/472-3325;** www.budget.com), **Hertz** (© **800/654-3001;** www.hertz.com), **Dollar** (© **800/800-3665;** www.dollarcar.com), or **Avis** (© **800/331-1084;** www.avis.com). Budget rents in Nassau and Paradise Island. Liability insurance is compulsory.

"Petrol" is easily available in Nassau and Freeport, though quite expensive. The major towns of the islands have service stations. You should have no problems on New Providence or Grand Bahama Island unless you start out with a nearly empty tank.

Visitors may drive with their home driver's license for up to 3 months. For longer stays, you'll need to secure a Bahamian driver's license.

As you emerge at one of the major airports, including those of Nassau (New Providence) and Freeport (Grand Bahama Island), you can pick up island maps that good for routine touring around those islands. However, if you plan to do extensive touring, you should go first to a bookstore in either Nassau or Freeport and ask for a copy of *Atlas of The Bahamas.* It provides touring routes (outlined in red) through all the major islands.

BY TAXI

Once you've reached your destination, you'll find that taxis are plentiful in the Nassau–Cable Beach–Paradise Island area and in the Freeport/Lucaya area on Grand Bahama Island. These cabs, for the most part, are metered—but they take cash only, no credit cards. See "Getting Around," in the chapters on each island that follow for further details.

BY CHARTERED BOAT

For those who can afford it, this is the most luxurious way to see The Bahamas. On your private boat, you can island-hop at your convenience. Well-equipped marinas are on every major island and many cays. There are designated ports of entry at Great Abaco (Marsh Harbor), Andros, the Berry Islands, Bimini, Cat Cay, Eleuthera, Great Exuma, Grand Bahama Island (Freeport/Lucaya), Great Inagua, New Providence (Nassau), Ragged Island, and San Salvador.

Vessels must check with Customs at the first port of entry and receive a cruising clearance permit to The Bahamas. Carry it with you and return it at the official port of departure.

The Yachtsman's Guide to The Bahamas (Tropical Island Publishers) covers the entire Bahamas. Copies are available at major marine outlets and bookstores, and by mail direct from the publisher for $40, U.S., plus postage: Tropical Island Publishers, P.O. Box 12, Adelphia, NJ 07710 (© **877/923-9653;** www.yachtsmans guide.com).

Experienced sailors with a sea-wise crew can charter **"bareboat"** (a fully equipped boat with no crew). You're on your own, and you'll have to prove you can handle it before you're allowed to take out such a craft. You may want to take along an experienced yachter familiar with local waters, which may be tricky in some places.

Most yachts are rented on a weekly basis. Contact **Abaco Bahamas Charters** (© **800/626-5690** or 242/366-0151; www. abacocharters.com), or the **Moorings** (© **888/952-8420** or 727/535-1446; www.moorings.com).

14 Tips on Accommodations

The Bahamas offers a wide selection of accommodations, ranging from small private guesthouses to large luxury resorts. Hotels vary in size and facilities, from deluxe (offering room service, sports, swimming pools, entertainment, and so on) to fairly simple inns.

There are package deals galore, and they are always cheaper than "rack rates." (A rack rate is what an individual pays if he or she literally walks in from the street. These are the rates we've listed in the chapters that follow, though you can almost always do better—especially at the big resorts.) It's sometimes good to go to a reliable travel agent to find out what, if anything, is available in the way of a land-and-air package before booking a particular accommodation. See section 12, "Packages for the Independent Traveler," above, for details on a number of companies that usually offer good-value packages to The Bahamas.

There is no rigid classification of hotel properties in the islands. The word "deluxe" is often used (or misused) when "first class" might have been a more appropriate term. "First class" itself often isn't. For that and other reasons, we've presented fairly detailed descriptions of the properties so that you'll get an idea of what to expect. However, even in the deluxe and first-class resorts and hotels, don't expect top-rate service and efficiency. When you go to turn on the shower, sometimes you get water and sometimes you don't. You may even experience power failures.

What the Hotel Symbols Mean

As you're shopping around for your hotel, you may see the following terms used:

- **AP (American Plan):** Includes three meals a day (sometimes called full board or full pension).
- **EP (European Plan):** Includes only the room—no meals.
- **CP (Continental Plan):** Includes continental breakfast of juice, coffee, bread, and jam.
- **MAP (Modified American Plan):** Sometimes called half board or half pension, this room rate includes breakfast and dinner (or lunch instead of dinner if you prefer).

The winter season in The Bahamas runs roughly from the middle of December to the middle of April, and hotels charge their highest prices during this peak period. Winter is generally the dry season in the islands, but there can be heavy rainfall regardless of the time of year. During the winter months, make reservations 2 months in advance if you can. You can't book early enough if you want to travel over Christmas or in February.

The off season in The Bahamas—roughly from mid-April to mid-December (although this varies from hotel to hotel)—amounts to a sale. In most cases, hotel rates are slashed a startling 20% to 60%. It's a bonanza for cost-conscious travelers, especially for families who can travel in the summer. Be prepared for very strong sun, though, plus a higher chance of rain. Also note that hurricane season runs through summer and fall.

MAP VS. AP, OR DO YOU WANT TO GO EP?

All Bahamian resorts offer a **European Plan (EP)** rate, which means that you pay for the price of a room. That leaves you free to dine around at night at various other resorts or restaurants without restriction. Another plan preferred by many is the **Continental Plan (CP),** which means you get a continental breakfast of juice, coffee, bread, and jam included in a set price. This plan is preferred by those who don't like to look around for a place to eat breakfast.

Another major option is the **Modified American Plan (MAP),** which includes breakfast and one main meal of the day, either lunch or dinner. The final choice is the **American Plan (AP),** which includes breakfast, lunch, and dinner. At certain resorts you will save money by booking in on either MAP or AP, because discounts are granted. If you dine a la carte often for lunch and dinner, your dining costs will be much higher than if you stay on the MAP or AP.

Dining at your hotel at night cuts down on transportation costs. Taxis especially are expensive. Nonetheless, if dining out and having many different culinary experiences is your idea of a vacation, and you're willing to pay the higher price, avoid AP plans or at least make sure the hotel where you're staying has more than one dining room.

One option is to ask if your hotel has a dine-around plan. You might still keep costs in check, but you can avoid a culinary rut by taking your meals in some other restaurants if your hotel has such a plan. Such plans are rare in The Bahamas, which does not specialize in all-inclusive resorts the way that Jamaica or some other islands do.

Before booking a room, check with a good travel agent or investigate on your own what you are likely to save by booking on a dining plan. Under certain circumstances in winter you might not have a choice if MAP is dictated as a requirement for staying there. It pays to investigate, of course.

THE RIGHT ROOM AT THE RIGHT PRICE

Ask detailed questions when booking a room. Specify your likes and dislikes. There are several logistics of getting the right room in a hotel. In general, back rooms cost less than oceanfront rooms, and lower rooms cost less than upper-floor units. If budget is a major consideration with you, opt for the cheaper rooms. You won't have a great view, but you'll save your money for something else. Just make sure that it isn't next to the all-night drummers.

Of course, all first-class or deluxe resorts feature air-conditioning, but many Bahamian inns do not, especially in the Out Islands. Cooling might be by ceiling fans or, in more modest places, the breeze from an open window, which also brings the mosquitoes. If sleeping in a climate-controlled environment is important to your vacation, check this out in advance.

If you're being your own travel agent, it pays to shop around by calling the local number given for a hotel and its toll-free number if it has one. You can check online and call a travel agent to see where you can obtain the best price.

Another tip: Ask if you can get an upgrade or a free night's stay if you stay an extra few days. If you're traveling during the "shoulder" periods (between low and high season), you can sometimes get a substantial reduction by delaying your travel plans by a week or 10 days. For example, a $300 (£156) room booked on April 12 might have been lowered to $180 (£93.60) by April 17, as mid-April marks the beginning of the low season in The Bahamas.

Transfers from the airports or the cruise dock are included in some hotel bookings, most often in a package plan but usually not in ordinary bookings. This is true of first-class and deluxe resorts but rarely of medium-priced or budget accommodations. Always ascertain whether transfers (which can be expensive) are included.

When using the facilities at a resort, make sure that you know exactly what is free and what costs money. For example, swimming in the pool is nearly always free, but you might be charged for use of a tennis court. Nearly all watersports cost extra, unless you're booked on some special plan such as scuba package. Some resorts seem to charge every time you breathe and might end up costing more than a deluxe hotel that includes most everything in the price.

Some hotels are right on the beach. Others involve transfers to the beach by taxi or bus, so factor in transportation costs, which can mount quickly if you stay 5 days to a week.

THE ALL-INCLUSIVES

A hugely popular option in Jamaica, the all-inclusive resort hotel concept finally has a foothold in The Bahamas. At these resorts, everything is included—sometimes even drinks. You get your room and all meals, plus entertainment and many watersports (although some cost extra). Some people find the cost of this all-inclusive holiday cheaper than if they'd paid individually for each item, and some simply appreciate knowing in advance what their final bill will be.

The first all-inclusive resort hotel in The Bahamas was **Club Med** (© **888/WEB-CLUB;** www.clubmed.com) on Paradise Island. This is not a swinging-singles kind of place; it's popular with everybody, from honeymooners to families with kids along. Families with kids like it a lot here, and the resort also attracts scuba divers.

The biggest all-inclusive of them all, **Sandals** (© **888/SAN-DALS;** www.sandals.com), came to The Bahamas in 1995 on Cable Beach. This Jamaican company is now walking its sandals across the Caribbean, having established firm beachheads in Ocho Rios, Montego Bay, and Negril. The most famous of the all-inclusives (but not necessarily the best), ended its ban against same-sex couples. See chapter 3 for details.

RENTAL VILLAS & VACATION HOMES

You might rent a big villa, a good-size apartment in someone's condo, or even a small beach cottage (more accurately called a cabana).

Private apartments come with or without maid service (ask upfront exactly what to expect). This is more of a no-frills option than the villas and condos. The apartments may not be in buildings with swimming pools, and they may not have a front desk to help you.

Many cottages or cabanas ideally open onto a beach, although others may be clustered around a communal swimming pool. Most of them are fairly simple, containing only a plain bedroom plus a small kitchen and bathroom. In the peak winter season, reservations should be made at least 5 or 6 months in advance.

Hideaways Aficionado (℘ 877/843-4433 in the U.S. or 603/430-4433; www.hideaways.com) publishes *Hideaways Life,* a 24-page pictorial directory of home rentals throughout the world, with full descriptions so you know what you're renting. Rentals range from cottages to staffed villas to whole islands! On most rentals you deal directly with owners. At condos and small resorts, Hideaways offers member discounts. Other services include specialty cruises, yacht charters, airline ticketing, car rentals, and hotel reservations. Annual membership costs $185 (£96.20).

Sometimes local tourist offices will also advise you on vacation-home rentals if you write or call them directly.

THE BAHAMIAN GUESTHOUSE

Many Bahamians stay at a guesthouse when traveling in their own islands. In The Bahamas, however, the term "guesthouse" can mean anything. Sometimes so-called guesthouses are really like simple motels built around swimming pools. Others are small individual cottages, with their own kitchenettes, constructed around a main building in which you'll often find a bar and restaurant serving local food.

FAST FACTS: The Bahamas

American Express Representing American Express in The Bahamas is **Destinatinos**, 303 Shirley St. (between Charlotte and Parliament sts.), Nassau (℘ **242/322-2931**). Hours are 9am to 5pm Monday through Friday. The travel department is also open Saturday 9am to 1pm. If you present a personal check and an Amex card, you can buy traveler's checks here.

Area Code The area code for The Bahamas is **242**.

ATM Networks See "Money & Costs," p. 14.

Business Hours   In Nassau, Cable Beach, and Freeport/ Lucaya, commercial banking hours are 9:30am to 3pm Monday through Thursday, 9:30am to 5pm on Friday. Most government offices are open Monday through Friday from 9am to 5pm, and most shops are open Monday through Saturday from 9am to 5pm.

Camera & Film   Purchasing film in Nassau/Paradise Island or Freeport/Lucaya is relatively easy, if a little expensive.

Car Rentals   See "Getting Around The Bahamas," p. 30.

Cashpoints   See "Money & Costs," p. 14.

Currency   See "Money & Costs," p. 14.

Driving Rules   See "Getting Around The Bahamas," p. 30.

Drug Laws   Importing, possessing, or dealing unlawful drugs, including marijuana, is a serious offense in The Bahamas, with heavy penalties. Customs officers may at their discretion conduct body searches for drugs or other contraband goods.

Drugstores   Nassau and Freeport are amply supplied with pharmacies (see individual listings).

Electricity   Electricity is normally 120 volts, 60 cycles, AC. American appliances are fully compatible; British or European appliances will need both converters and adapters.

Embassies & Consulates   The U.S. Embassy is on 42 Queen St., P.O. Box N-8197, Nassau (✆ 242/322-1181), and the Canadian consulate is on Shirley Street Shopping Plaza, Nassau (✆ 242/ 393-2123). The British High Commission is located in Kingston, Jamaica at 28 Trafalgar Rd. (✆ 876/510-0700).

Emergencies   Throughout most of The Bahamas, the number to call for a medical, dental, or hospital emergency is ✆ 911. In the Out Islands, the number is ✆ 919. To report a fire, however, call ✆ 411.

Holidays   Public holidays observed in The Bahamas are New Year's Day, Good Friday, Easter Sunday, Easter Monday, Whitmonday (7 weeks after Easter), Labour Day (the first Fri in June), Independence Day (July 10), Emancipation Day (the first Mon in Aug), Discovery Day (Oct 12), Christmas, and Boxing Day (the day after Christmas). When a holiday falls on Saturday or Sunday, stores and offices are usually closed on the following Monday.

Hospitals In Nassau, **Princess Margaret Hospital** (② 242/322-2861) and in Freeport, **Rand Memorial** (② 242/352-6735).

Internet Access Access is limited on the islands, but it can be obtained at **Cybercafe,** in the Mall at Marathon in Nassau (② 242/394-6254), or in Freeport at **CyberClub** at Seventeen Center (② 242/351-4560). Web access is increasingly common at hotels in The Bahamas. But if this issue is especially important to you, check with specific accommodations before booking. Also see *"Staying Connected,"* earlier.

Language In The Bahamas, locals speak English, but sometimes with a marked accent that provides the clue to their ancestry—African, Irish, or Scottish, for example.

Liquor Laws Liquor is sold in liquor stores and various convenience stores; it's readily available at all hours though not sold on Sundays. The legal drinking age is 18.

Lost & Found Be sure to tell all of your credit card companies the minute you discover your wallet has been lost or stolen and file a report at the nearest police precinct. Your credit card company or insurer may require a police report number or record of the loss. Most credit card companies have an emergency toll-free number to call if your card is lost or stolen; they may be able to wire you a cash advance immediately or deliver an emergency credit card in a day or two. **Visa's** U.S. emergency number is ② **800/847-2911. American Express** cardholders and traveler's check holders should call ② **800/221-7282. MasterCard** holders should call ② **800/307-7309.** For other credit cards, call the toll-free number directory at ② **800/555-1212.**

If you need emergency cash over the weekend when all banks and American Express offices are closed, you can have money wired to you via **Western Union** (② **800/325-6000;** www.westernunion.com).

Mail You'll need Bahamian (not U.S.) postage stamps to send postcards and letters. Most of the kiosks selling postcards also sell the stamps you'll need to mail them, so you probably won't need to visit the post office. Sending a postcard or an airmail letter (up to ½-oz. in weight) from The Bahamas to anywhere outside its borders (including the U.S., Canada, and the U.K.) costs 65¢ (34p), with another charge for each additional half ounce of weight.

Mail to and from the Out Islands is sometimes slow. Airmail may go by air to Nassau and by boat to its final destination. If a resort has a U.S. or Nassau address, it is preferable to use it.

Measurements   See the chart on the inside front cover of this book for details on converting metric measurements to non-metric equivalents.

Newspapers & Magazines   Three newspapers are circulated in Nassau and Freeport: the *Nassau Guardian* (www.thenassau guardian.com), the *Tribune,* and the *Freeport News.* You can find such papers as the *New York Times, Wall Street Journal, USA Today, The Miami Herald, Times of London,* and *Daily Telegraph* at newsstands in your hotel and elsewhere in Nassau.

Passports   Allow plenty of time before your trip to apply for a passport; processing normally takes 3 weeks but can take longer during busy periods (especially spring). And keep in mind that if you need a passport in a hurry, you'll pay a higher processing fee.

For Residents of Australia: You can pick up an application from your local post office or any branch of Passports Australia, but you must schedule an interview at the passport office to present your application materials. Call the **Australian Passport Information Service** at © **131-232,** or visit the government website at www.smartraveller.gov.au.

For Residents of Canada: Passport applications are available at travel agencies throughout Canada or from the central **Passport Office,** Department of Foreign Affairs and International Trade, Ottawa, ON K1A 0G3 (© **800/567-6868;** www.ppt.gc.ca).

For Residents of Ireland: You can apply for a 10-year passport at the **Passport Office,** Setanta Centre, Molesworth Street, Dublin 2 (© **01/671-1633;** www.irlgov.ie/iveagh). Those under age 18 and over 65 must apply for a €12 3-year passport. You can also apply at 1A South Mall, Cork (© **021/494-4700**) or at most main post offices.

For Residents of New Zealand: You can pick up a passport application at any New Zealand Passports Office or download it from their website. Contact the **Passports Office** at © **0800/ 225-050** in New Zealand or 04/474-8100, or log on to www.passports.govt.nz.

For Residents of the United Kingdom: To pick up an application for a standard 10-year passport (5-year passport for children under 16), visit your nearest passport office, major post office, or travel agency or contact the **United Kingdom Passport Service** at ℂ **0870/521-0410** or search its website at www.ukpa.gov.uk.

For Residents of the United States: Whether you're applying in person or by mail, you can download passport applications from the U.S. State Department website at **http://travel.state.gov**. To find your regional passport office, either check the U.S. State Department website or call the **National Passport Information Center** toll-free number (ℂ **877/487-2778**) for automated information.

Pets   You'll have to get a valid import permit to bring any animal into The Bahamas. Application for such a permit must be made in writing, accompanied by a $10 (£5.20) processing fee and a $5 (£2.60) fax fee, to the **Director of Agriculture,** Department of Agriculture, P.O. Box N-3028, Nassau, The Bahamas (ℂ **242/325-7502**), at least 4 weeks in advance.

Police   Dial ℂ **911.**

Safety   See "Health & Safety," earlier in this chapter.

Taxes   Departure tax is $15 ($18 from Grand Bahama Island) for visitors ages 7 and up. An 8% tax is imposed on hotel bills; otherwise there is no sales tax in The Bahamas.

Telephones   Direct long-distance dialing is available between North America and Nassau or Grand Bahama.

 To call The Bahamas:
 1. Dial the international access code: 011 from the U.S.; 00 from the U.K., Ireland, or New Zealand; or 0011 from Australia
 2. Dial the country code **242**
 3. Dial the seven-digit local number.

 To make international calls: To make international calls from The Bahamas, first dial 00 and then the country code (U.S. or Canada 1, U.K. 44, Ireland 353, Australia 61, New Zealand 64). Next you dial the area code and number. For example, if you wanted to call the British Embassy in Washington, D.C., you would dial 00-1-202-588-7800.

 For local calls within The Bahamas: Simply dial the seven-digit number. To call from one island to another within The Bahamas, dial 1-242 and then the seven-digit local number.

 For directory assistance: Dial ℂ **916** if you're looking for a number inside The Bahamas, and dial "0" for numbers to all other countries.

For operator assistance: To reach an international or a domestic operator within The Bahamas, dial **0**. There is no distinction made in The Bahamas between the two types of operators.

Toll-free numbers: Numbers beginning with **881** within The Bahamas are toll-free. However, calling a normally toll-free number within the United States (that is, one beginning with 800, 887, or 888) usually involves a charge within The Bahamas. In fact, it usually costs the same as an overseas call unless the merchant has made arrangements with the local telephone authorities. *Note:* Major airlines generally maintain toll-free 800, 887, or 888 provisions for calls made to them within The Bahamas. If you dial what you think is a toll-free phone number and it ends up costing the long-distance rate, an automated recording will inform you of this fact. In some cases, the recording will suggest a local toll-free alternative—usually one beginning with 881.

To reach the major international services of **AT&T,** dial *C* **800/CALL-ATT,** or head for any phone with AT&T or USA Direct marked on the side of the booth. Picking up the handset will connect you with an AT&T operator. These phones are often positioned beside cruise-ship docks to help passengers disembarking on shore leave for the day. **MCI** can be reached at *C* **800/888-8000.**

Note that the old coin-operated phones are still prevalent in The Bahamas and still swallow coins. Each local call costs 25¢ (13p); you can use either Bahamian or U.S. quarters. Those old phones, however, are gradually being replaced by phones that use calling cards (debit cards), similar in appearance to a credit card, that come in denominations of $5, $10, $20, and $50. They can be bought from any office of **BATELCO** (Bahamas Telephone Co.). BATELCO's main branch is on Kennedy Drive, Nassau (*C* **242/302-7008**), although a popular local branch lies in the heart of Nassau, on East Street off Bay Street.

Time Zone   Eastern Standard Time is used throughout The Bahamas, and daylight saving time is observed in the summer.

Tipping   Many establishments add a service charge, but it's customary to leave something extra if service has been exceptional. If you're not sure whether service has been included in your bill, don't be shy—ask.

Bellboys and porters, at least in the expensive hotels, expect a tip of $1 (52p) per bag. It's also customary to tip your maid at least $2 (£1.05) per day—more if she or he has performed special services such as getting a shirt or blouse laundered. Most service personnel, including taxi drivers, waiters, and the like, expect 15% (20% in deluxe restaurants).

Useful Phone Numbers   Sources of information include:

U.S. Dept. of State Travel Advisory ⓒ 202/647-5225 (manned 24 hrs.)

U.S. Passport Agency ⓒ 202/647-0518

U.S. Centers for Disease Control International Traveler's Hotline: ⓒ 404/332-4559

Water   Technically, tap water is drinkable throughout The Bahamas. But we almost always opt for bottled. Resorts tend to filter and chlorinate tap water more aggressively than other establishments; elsewhere, bottled water is available at stores and supermarkets, and tastes better than that from a tap.

Weddings   The bride and groom must both be in The Bahamas at the moment they apply for the $100 (£52) wedding license here. If both are single and U.S. citizens, a declaration certifying this fact must be sworn before a consul at the American Embassy in Nassau. The fee is $55 (£28.60) per person; you'll need to appear in person with ID such as a passport (and, if applicable, proof of divorce). If all of these requirements are met, you can then get married after staying for 24 hours in The Bahamas. No blood test is necessary. Contact the **Registrar General** at P.O. Box N-532, Nassau, The Bahamas (ⓒ 242/322-3316), for more details.

3

New Providence (Nassau/Cable Beach)

One million visitors a year have cast their vote: They want to visit New Providence Island, setting for Nassau, adjoining Cable Beach, and Paradise Island (which is covered separately in chapter 4). This is the center of all the action: the best shopping, the best entertainment, the most historic attractions—plus some of the best beaches in The Bahamas.

The capital of The Bahamas, the historic city of Nassau is a 35-minute flight from Miami. Despite the development and the modern hotels, a laid-back tropical atmosphere still pervades the city, and it still offers a good dose of colonial charm. The commercial and banking hub of The Bahamas, as well as a mecca for shoppers, Nassau lies on the north side of New Providence, which is 34km (21 miles) long and 11km (6¾ miles) wide at its greatest point.

Cable Beach, a stretch of sand just west of the city, is lined with luxury resorts—in fact, the Nassau/Cable Beach area has the largest tourist infrastructure in The Bahamas, though there's another concentration of luxury hotels on Paradise Island. If you want to stay right on the sands, don't choose a hotel in downtown Nassau itself. Head for Cable Beach or Paradise Island. You can easily reach the beach from a base in Nassau, but it won't be right outside your window.

When you're based in Nassau/Cable Beach, you have an array of watersports, golf, tennis, and plenty of duty-free shopping nearby—not to mention those fine powdery beaches. In addition, the resorts, restaurants, and beaches of Paradise Island, discussed in the next chapter, are just a short distance away. Paradise Island, which lies just opposite Nassau, is connected to New Providence Island by a toll bridge. For northbound traffic (that is, from New Providence Island to Paradise Island), the bridge costs $1 (55p) for cars, $2 (£1.05) for taxis, and is free for pedestrians. Southbound traffic for all vehicles is free. There's also frequent ferry and water-taxi service between Nassau and Paradise Island.

As the sun goes down, Cable Beach and Paradise Island heat up, offering fine dining, glitzy casinos, cabaret shows, moonlight cruises, dance clubs, and romantic evening strolls. (We'd confine the evening stroll to Cable Beach or Paradise Island, and not the streets of downtown Nassau, which can be dangerous at night.)

The shops might draw a lot more business than the museums, but no city in The Bahamas is as rich in history as Nassau. You can take a "royal climb" up the Queen's Staircase to Fort Fincastle. These 66 steps are said to have been cut in the sandstone cliffs by slaves in the 1790s. Other Nassau attractions include Ardastra Gardens, which feature 2 hectares (5 acres) of landscaping and more than 300 exotic birds, mammals, and reptiles. Most popular are the trained pink flamingos that march for audiences daily to their trainer's commands.

It's surprising that Nassau has retained its overlay of British colonial charm despite its proximity to Florida and the massive influx of North American business. It hasn't become completely Americanized, at least not yet; despite new development, traffic, and cruise-ship crowds, Nassau's still a long way from becoming another Miami. Stately old homes and public buildings still stand proudly among the modern high-rises and bland government buildings. Tropical foliage lines streets where horse-drawn surreys still trot by, carrying visitors on leisurely tours. Police officers in white starched jackets and dome-shaped pith helmets still direct traffic on the main streets, as they have long done. It could almost be England—but for the weather, that is, and for the staunch and sometimes defiant presence of a deeply entrenched sense of Bahamian nationalism.

1 Orientation

ARRIVING

BY PLANE   Planes land at Nassau's **Lynden Pindling International Airport** (© 242/377-1759), which lies 13km (8 miles) west of Nassau, in the pine forests beside Lake Killarney.

No bus service goes from the airport to Cable Beach, Nassau, or Paradise Island. Your hotel may provide airport transfers if you've made arrangements in advance; these are often included in package deals. There are also any number of car-rental offices here if you plan to have a car while on New Providence Island (see "Getting Around," below), though we don't really think you need one.

If you don't have a lift arranged, take a taxi to your hotel. From the airport to the center of Nassau, expect to pay around $22 (£12);

New Providence Island

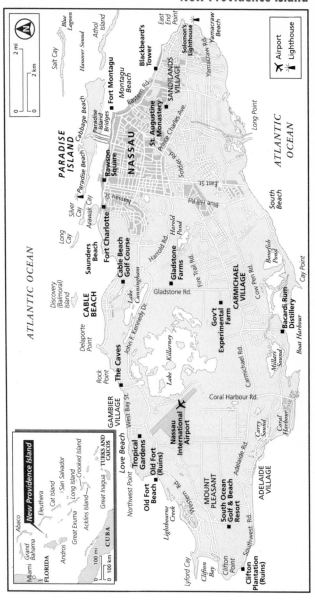

from the airport to Cable Beach, $15 (£7.95); from the airport to
Paradise Island, $28 (£15), a rate which includes the $10 (£5.30)
bridge toll for passage between New Providence Island and Paradise
Island. Drivers expect to be tipped 15%, and some will remind you
should you "forget." You don't need to stop at a currency exchange
office before departing the airport: U.S. currency is fine for these
(and any other) transactions.

BY CRUISE SHIP   Nassau has spent millions of dollars expanding its port so that a number of cruise ships can come into port at
once. Sounds great in theory. Practically speaking, however, facilities
in Nassau, Cable Beach, and Paradise Island become extremely over-
crowded as soon as the big boats dock. You'll have to stake out your
space on the beach, and you will find downtown streets, shops, and
attractions overrun with visitors every day you're in port.

Cruise ships dock near Rawson Square, the heart of the city and
the shopping area—and the best place to begin a tour of Nassau.
Unless you want to go to one of the beach strips along Cable Beach
or Paradise Island, you won't need a taxi. You can go on a shopping
expedition near where you dock: The Straw Market is nearby, at
Market Plaza; Bay Street—the main shopping artery—is also close;
and the Nassau International Bazaar is at the intersection of Woodes
Rogers Walk and Charlotte Street.

The government has added **"Festival Place"** (© 242/322-7680)
to the Prince George dock (where the cruise ships arrive). Designed
as a welcome point and service center for cruise ship visitors, Festival Place is a multicolored structure with about 45 shops selling sun-
dries, gift items, duty-free luxury goods, and Bahamian-themed
arts, crafts, and souvenirs. It also contains a tourist information
booth (© **242/323-3182** or 242/323-3183) and various snack bars
and cafes. This mall-like facility is open daily 8am to 8pm, but if
cruise ships are in port that day, closing is extended to as late as
10pm. You can lounge and have a daiquiri while you listen to the
live calypso entertainment, or even get your hair braided. From a
point nearby, you can catch a ride by horse and surrey, or take a
water taxi across the channel to Paradise Island. (For more on that,
see chapter 4.)

VISITOR INFORMATION
The Bahamas Ministry of Tourism maintains a **tourist information
booth** at the Nassau International Airport in the arrivals terminal
(© **242/377-6806;** www.bahamas.com). Hours are from 9am to
10pm daily.

Information can also be obtained from the Information Desk at the **Ministry of Tourism's Office,** Bolam House, George Street (℗ **242/302-2000**), which is open Monday to Friday 9am to 5pm. It's also available from the tourist information booth at Festival Place (℗ **242/323-3182** or 242/323-3183), where the cruise ships dock. The Festival Place Tourist information kiosk is usually open daily year-round from 7:45am to 6pm.

THE LAY OF THE LAND

Most of the hotels in Nassau are city hotels and are not on the water. If you want to stay right on the sands, choose a hotel in Cable Beach (later in this chapter) or on Paradise Island (see chapter 4).

Rawson Square is the heart of Nassau, positioned just a short walk from **Prince George Wharf,** where the big cruise ships, many of them originating in Florida, berth. Here you'll see the Churchill Building, which contains the offices of the Bahamian prime minister along with other government ministries.

Busy **Bay Street,** the main shopping artery, begins on the south side of Rawson Square. This was the turf of the infamous "Bay Street Boys," a group of rich white Bahamians who once controlled political and economic activity on New Providence.

On the opposite side of Rawson Square is **Parliament Square,** with a statue of a youthful Queen Victoria. Here are more government houses and the House of Assembly. These are Georgian and neo-Georgian buildings, some dating from the late 1700s.

The courthouse is separated by a little square from the **Nassau Public Library and Museum,** which opens onto Bank Lane. It was the former Nassau Gaol (jail). South of the library, across Shirley Street, are the remains of the **Royal Victoria Hotel,** which opened the same year the American Civil War began (1861) and once hosted blockade runners and Confederate spies.

A walk down Parliament Street leads to the post office. Philatelists may want to stop in, since some Bahamian stamps are collector's items.

Going south, moving farther away from the water, Elizabeth Avenue takes you to the **Queen's Staircase.** One of the major landmarks of Nassau, it leads to Bennet's Hill and Fort Fincastle.

If you return to Bay Street, you'll discover the oversized tent which contains the **Straw Market,** a handicrafts emporium where you can buy all sorts of souvenirs.

In Nassau, and especially in the rest of The Bahamas, you will seldom, if ever, find street numbers on hotels or other businesses. In the more remote places, you sometimes won't even find street names. Get directions before heading somewhere in particular. Of course, you can always ask along the way, as most Bahamians are very helpful.

2 Getting Around

BY TAXI

You can easily rely on taxis and skip renting a car. The rates for New Providence, including Nassau, are set by the government. Although working meters are required in all taxis, some of them don't work. Consequently, the government has established a well-defined roster of rates for passage between the airport and various points around the island. When you get in, the fixed rate is $3 (£1.60), plus 40¢ (20p) for each additional quarter-mile. Each passenger over 2 years old pays an extra $3 (£1.60). For sightseeing purposes, taxis can also be hired at the hourly rate of $45 (£24) for a five-passenger cab. Luggage is carried at a surcharge of $1 (55p) extra per piece, although the first two pieces are transported free. The radio-taxi call number is ⓒ **242/323-5111.** It's easy to get a taxi at the airport or at any of the big hotels.

BY CAR

You really don't need to rent a car. It's a lot easier to rely on taxis when you're ready to leave the beach and do a little exploring.

However, if you choose to drive (perhaps for a day of touring the whole island), some of the biggest U.S. car-rental companies maintain branches at the airport, in downtown Nassau, at Cable Beach, and on Paradise Island. **Avis** (ⓒ **800/331-1212** or 242/326-6380; www.avis.com) operates at the airport and also has branches at the cruise-ship docks at Bay Street and Cumberland Street, across from the British Colonial Hilton (ⓒ 242/326-6380). **Budget Rent-a-Car** (ⓒ **800/527-0700** or 242/377-9000; www.budgetrentacar.com) has a branch at the airport and on Shirley Street in downtown Nassau. **Dollar/Thrifty Rent-a-Car** (ⓒ **800/654-3131** or 242/377-8300; www.dollar.com) rents at the airport and also from within a kiosk at the British Colonial Hilton. **Hertz** (ⓒ **800/654-3131** or 242/ 377-8684; www.hertz.com) has only one location: at the airport.

Remember: Drive on the left!

BY BUS

The least expensive means of transport is by any of the medium-sized buses (some locals refer to them as "jitneys") that make runs from downtown Nassau to outposts on New Providence. The fare is

> ### *Tips* **On Your Own Sturdy Feet**
>
> This is the only way to see Old Nassau, unless you rent a horse and carriage. All the major attractions and the principal stores are within walking distance. You can even walk to Cable Beach or Paradise Island, although it's a hike in the hot sun. Confine your walking to the daytime, and beware of the occasional pickpocket and purse snatcher. In the evening, avoid walking the streets of downtown Nassau, where, from time to time, muggings have been reported.

$1 (55p), and exact change, in coins or with a dollar bill, is required. The jitneys operate daily from 6:30am to 7pm. Buses to the Cable Beach area and points west of that include the much-used #10, the 10A, and the "Western" bus. They depart from the corner of Bay Street and George Street, and stop at various clearly designated spots along Bay Street. Buses headed to the eastern (mostly residential and rarely accessed by short-term visitors) part of New Providence Island depart from the Frederick Street North depot.

BY BOAT

Water taxis operate daily from 9am to 6pm at 20-minute intervals between Paradise Island and Prince George Wharf. An alternative service involves ferryboats, which link the wharves at the end of Casuarina Drive on Paradise Island to Rawson Square, across the channel on New Providence Island. The ferry operates daily from 9:30am to 4:15pm, with departures every half-hour from both sides of the harbor. Both the ferryboats and the water taxis charge the same fixed rate: $3 (£1.60) per person, each way, for passage across the channel.

BY MOPED

Lots of visitors like to rent mopeds to explore the island. Unless you're an experienced moped rider, stay on quiet roads until you feel at ease. (Don't start out in all the congestion on Bay St.) Some hotels maintain rental kiosks on their premises. If yours doesn't, try **Knowles** (*©* **242/356-0741**), at Festival Place, near the cruise ship dock, which rents mopeds for $50 (£27) per day. Included in the rental price are insurance and mandatory helmets for both drivers and passengers. Mopeds are rented daily between 8am and 5pm.

FAST FACTS: **New Providence**

American Express   The local representative is **Destinations,** 303 Shirley St., between Charlotte and Parliament streets, Nassau (© 242/322-2931). Hours are Monday to Friday 9am to 5pm.

ATMs   Major banks with ATMs in Nassau include the **Royal Bank of Canada** (© 242/322-8700), **Bank of Nova Scotia** (© 242/356-1517), and **The First Caribbean Bank** (formerly known as Barclays; © 242/356-8000). However, some accept cards only in the **Cirrus** network (© 800/424-7787), while others take only **PLUS** (© 800/843-7587). ATMs at both the Paradise Island and Cable Beach casinos dispense quick cash. Be alert to the fact that whereas ATM machines within large hotels and casinos tend to dispense U.S. dollars, ATM machines within banks and at the airport dispense Bahamian dollars. Since both U.S. and Bahamian currencies are readily accepted anywhere, it's not a crucial issue, but it's a good idea to read the information on the individual ATM machine before proceeding with your transaction.

Babysitting   Hotel staff can help you hire an experienced sitter. Expect to pay around $10 to $15 (£5.30–£7.95) an hour, plus $3 (£1.60) an hour for each additional child.

Climate   See "When to Go," in chapter 2.

Dentist   Try the dental department of the **Princess Margaret Hospital** on Sands Road (© 242/322-2861).

Doctor   For the best service, use a staff member of the **Princess Margaret Hospital** on Sands Road (© 242/322-2861).

Drugstores   Try **Lowes Pharmacy,** Palm Dale, in downtown Nassau (© 242/322-8594), open Monday to Saturday 8am to 6:30pm. They also maintain three branches in the Harbour Bay Shopping Center (© 242/393-4813), open Monday to Saturday 8am to 8:30pm and Sunday 9am to 5pm; in the **Town Center Mall** (© 242/325-6482), open Monday to Saturday 9:30am to 8pm; and an additional outlet on Soldier Road (© 242/394-6312), which is open Monday to Saturday 8am to 8pm. Nassau has no late-night pharmacies.

Embassies & Consulates   See "Fast Facts: The Bahamas," in chapter 2.

Emergencies   For any major emergency, call © either **911** or **919**.

Eyeglass Repair   The **Optique Shoppe,** 22 Parliament St. at the corner of Shirley Street ((C) **242/322-3910**), is convenient to the center of Nassau. Hours are Monday to Friday 9am to 5pm and on Saturday 9am to noon.

Hospitals   The government-operated **Princess Margaret Hospital** on Sands Road ((C) **242/322-2861**) is one of the major hospitals in The Bahamas. The privately owned **Doctors Hospital,** 1 Collins Ave. ((C) **242/322-8411**), is the most modern private health care facility in the region.

Hot Lines   For information about help or assistance of any kind, call (C) **242/326-HELP.**

Information   See "Visitor Information," earlier.

Internet Access   Check out **Cyberjack** at the **Mall on Marathon Road** ((C) **242/394-6254**). Here you can get online from your own laptop or log on to one of their computers. The cost is 15¢ (8p) per minute. Most of the larger hotels also offer guests Internet access for a fee. Payable by credit card, the fee can in some cases be as high as 50¢ (25p) per minute of use, which can add up quickly if you're an addictive web-surfer.

Laundry & Dry Cleaning   **Superwash** ((C) **242/323-4018**), at the corner of Nassau Street and Boyd Road, offers coin-operated machines; it's open 24 hours a day, 7 days a week. Drop-off service is available for a small additional fee. In the same building is the **New Oriental Dry Cleaner** ((C) **242/323-7249**).

Newspapers & Magazines   *The Tribune Daily* and *The Nassau Guardian,* both published in the morning, are the country's two competing daily newspapers. At your hotel and visitor information stations, you can find various helpful magazines, brochures, and booklets.

Photographic Needs   The largest camera store in Nassau is **John Bull** ((C) **242/302-2800**), on Bay Street 3 blocks west of Rawson Square. They maintain four additional branches scattered at heavily visited tourist sites across New Providence and Paradise Island. Each of these outlets also sells perfume, watches, and jewelry.

Police   Dial (C) **911** or 919.

Post Office   The **Nassau General Post Office,** at the top of Parliament Street on East Hill Street ((C) **242/322-3344**), is open Monday to Friday 9am to 5pm and on Saturday 8:30am to 12:30pm. Note that you can buy stamps from most postcard kiosks. A postcard sent airmail to the U.S. or Canada costs 50¢ (25p); a letter to the same destinations costs 65¢ (35p) per half-ounce.

Safety   Avoid walking along lonely side streets in downtown Nassau at night, where there are sometimes robberies and muggings. (Because the local government is particularly punitive against crimes against tourists, most visitors from outside The Bahamas are never affected, but it's probably better to be safe than sorry.) Cable Beach and Paradise Island tend to be safer than downtown Nassau after dark.

Taxes   There is no sales tax on any purchases made within The Bahamas, though there is a 12% hotel tax. Although it isn't immediately obvious, since the fee is automatically included in the price of any airline or cruise ship ticket, visitors leaving The Bahamas each pay a $20 (£11) departure tax.

3 Where to Stay

In the hotel descriptions that follow, we've listed regular room prices or "rack rates," but these are simply for ease of comparison. They are likely to be accurate for smaller properties, but you can almost always do better at the larger hotels and resorts. *Note:* Read the section "Packages for the Independent Traveler" in chapter 2 before you book a hotel separately from your airfare, and if you do book yourself, always inquire about honeymoon specials, golf packages, summer weeks, and other discounts. In many cases, too, a travel agent can get you a package deal that would be cheaper than these official rates.

Hotels add a 12% "resort levy" tax to your rate. Sometimes this is quoted in advance as part of the net price; at other times, it's added as an unexpected last-minute afterthought to your final bill. When you are quoted a rate, always ask if the tax is included. Many hotels also add a 15% service charge to your bill. Ask about these charges in advance so you won't be shocked when you receive the final tab.

Taxes and service are not included in the rates listed below. We'll lead off with a selection of hotels within the heart of Nassau, followed by accommodations in Cable Beach. Most visitors prefer to stay at Cable Beach since the resorts here are right on the sand. But you can stay in Nassau and commute to the beaches at Cable Beach or Paradise Island; it's cheaper but less convenient. Those who prefer the ambience of Old Nassau's historic district and being near the best shops may decide to stay in town.

NASSAU
EXPENSIVE

British Colonial Hilton ✹✹ In the restored British Colonial Hilton, there's a palpable air of the long-ago days when The Bahamas was firmly within the political and social orbit of Britain. This landmark seven-story hotel has seen its share of ups and downs over the years. Plush and glamorous when it was built in 1900, it burned to the ground in 1920 and was rebuilt 3 years later before deteriorating into a flophouse. Between 1996 and 1999, a Canadian entrepreneur poured $68 million into its restoration.

Don't expect the glitz and glitter of Cable Beach or Paradise Island here—the Hilton is after business travelers rather than the casino crowd. It also lacks the aristocratic credentials of Graycliff (see below). Nonetheless, it's a dignified and friendly, but rather sedate, hotel with a discreetly upscale decor (no Disney-style themes or gimmicks). Bedrooms, each renovated sometime during 2006 or 2007, are a bit on the small side but capped with rich crown moldings and accessorized with tile or stone-sheathed bathrooms with tub/showers. The staff, incidentally, is well trained and motivated; we've found them upbeat and hardworking. There's a small beach a few steps away, but it's not very appealing (it's on the narrow channel separating New Providence from Paradise Island, with no wave action at all).

1 Bay St. (P.O. Box N-7148), Nassau, The Bahamas. ℭ **800/HILTONS** in the U.S. and Canada, or 242/322-3301. Fax 242/302-9009. www.hilton.com. 291 units. Winter $379–$409 (£201–£217) double, $509–$1,400 (£270–£742) suite; off season $299–$369 (£158–£196) double, $429–$1,400 (£227–£742) suite. AE, DC, DISC, MC, V. Bus: 10. **Amenities:** 2 restaurants; 2 bars; outdoor pool; health club; full-service spa; tour desk; business center; secretarial service; room service; babysitting; laundry service; dry cleaning. *In room:* A/C, TV, minibar, coffeemaker, hair dryer, iron, safe, trouser press.

Graycliff ✹ Now in a kind of nostalgic decay, Graycliff remains the grande dame of downtown Nassau hotels even though her tiara is a bit tarnished and her age showing. In spite of its drawbacks, this place still has its devotees, especially older visitors. Originally an 18th-century private home reflecting Georgian colonial architecture, it's now an intimate inn with old-fashioned atmosphere. Even though the inn isn't on the beach, people who can afford to stay anywhere sometimes choose Graycliff because it epitomizes the old-world style and grace that evokes Nassau back in the days when the Duke and Duchess of

Where to Stay & Dine in Nassau

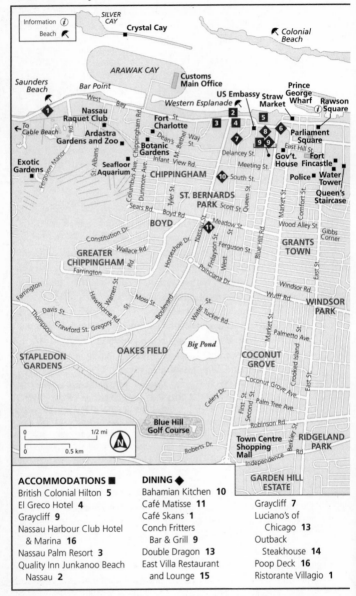

ACCOMMODATIONS ■

British Colonial Hilton **5**
El Greco Hotel **4**
Graycliff **9**
Nassau Harbour Club Hotel
  & Marina **16**
Nassau Palm Resort **3**
Quality Inn Junkanoo Beach
  Nassau **2**

DINING ◆

Bahamian Kitchen **10**
Café Matisse **11**
Café Skans **1**
Conch Fritters
  Bar & Grill **9**
Double Dragon **13**
East Villa Restaurant
  and Lounge **15**

Graycliff **7**
Luciano's of
  Chicago **13**
Outback
  Steakhouse **14**
Poop Deck **16**
Ristorante Villagio **1**

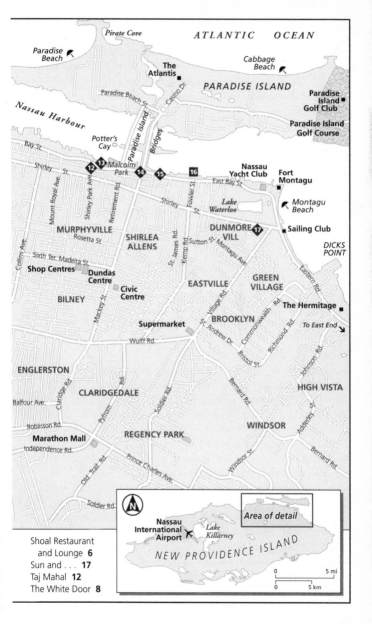

ATLANTIC OCEAN

Pirate Cove

Paradise Beach 🢔

Cabbage Beach 🢔

The Atlantis ∎

PARADISE ISLAND

Paradise Island Golf Club ∎

Paradise Beach St

Nassau Harbour

Paradise Island Bridges

Paradise Island Golf Course

Potter's Cay

Casina Dr.

Bay St.

Shirley St.

Mount Royal Ave.

Shirley Park Ave.

Retirement Rd.

⓬ ⓭ Malcolm Park

⓮ ⓯ ⓰

Nassau Yacht Club

Fort Montagu ∎

East Bay St.

Fowler St.

Shirley St.

Lake Waterloo

Montagu Beach 🢔

Sailing Club ∎

DICKS POINT

MURPHYVILLE

Rosetta St.

SHIRLEA ALLENS

St. James Rd.

Kemp Rd.

Sutton St.

DUNMORE VILL ⓱

Montagu Ave.

Collins Ave.

Sixth Ter. Madeira St.

Shop Centres ∎

Dundas Centre ∎

Mackey St.

Civic Centre ∎

EASTVILLE

GREEN VILLAGE

Eastern Rd.

BILNEY

Supermarket ∎

BROOKLYN

Village Rd.

St. Andrew Dr.

Commonwealth Rd.

Richmond Rd.

The Hermitage ∎

To East End 🢖

Wulff Rd.

Bristol St.

Johnson Rd.

ENGLERSTON

Claridge Rd.

CLARIDGEDALE

Pyfrom Rd.

Soldier Rd.

Bernard Rd.

HIGH VISTA

Balfour Ave.

Robinson Rd.

Marathon Mall ∎

Independence Rd.

REGENCY PARK

WINDSOR

Adderley St.

Prince Charles Ave.

Windsor St.

Bernard Rd.

Old Trail Rd.

Soldier Rd.

Shoal Restaurant and Lounge **6**
Sun and . . . **17**
Taj Mahal **12**
The White Door **8**

🧭 N

Nassau International Airport ✈

Lake Killarney

Area of detail

NEW PROVIDENCE ISLAND

0 ___ 5 mi
0 ___ 5 km

55

Windsor were in residence. Churchill, of course, can no longer be seen paddling around in the swimming pool with a cigar in his mouth, and the Beatles are long gone, but the three-story Graycliff marches onward, without the visiting celebs who today head for Paradise Island. Beach lovers usually go by taxi to either nearby Goodman's Bay or the Western Esplanade Beach, nearly adjacent to Arawak Cay. The bigger British Colonial Hilton is Graycliff's main competitor; they both have a rather staid, deliberately unflashy ambience.

The historic garden rooms in the main house are large and individually decorated with antiques, though the better units are the more modern garden rooms. The Yellow Bird, Hibiscus, and Pool cottages are ideal choices, but the most luxurious accommodation of all is the Mandarino Suite, with Asian decor, a king-size bed, an oversize bathroom, and a private balcony overlooking the swimming pool. Bathrooms are spacious, with tub/showers, deluxe toiletries, and robes.

8–12 W. Hill St. (P.O. Box N-10246), Nassau, The Bahamas. ⓒ **242/302-9150** or 242/326-6188. Fax 242/326-6188. www.graycliff.com. 18 units. Winter $325–$370 (£172–£196) double, $450 (£239) cottage; off season $290 (£154) double, $400 (£212) cottage. AE, MC, V. Bus: 10 or 21A. **Amenities:** 2 restaurants; 2 bars; 2 outdoor pools; spa; Jacuzzi; sauna; room service; massage; babysitting; laundry service; dry cleaning. *In room:* A/C, TV, minibar, hair dryer, iron, safe.

MODERATE
Nassau Palm Resort *(Value)* A short walk west of downtown Nassau, within a cluster of other cost-conscious hotels that include both the (also-recommended) El Greco and The Quality Inn, this hotel lies across the often-busy West Bay Street from the relatively narrow confines of Junkanoo Beach (which is also known as Lighthouse Beach or the Western Esplanade). Although not as fine or dramatic as Cable Beach, a few miles to the west, it's a safe urban beach with tranquil waters and a lot of shells. This place is a good value for those who don't demand particularly attentive service and who don't want to pay the higher prices charged by the more deluxe and better-accessorized hotels along Cable Beach. Bedrooms are outfitted in a standardized motel style, most with a view of Nassau Harbour, and they come with extras you don't always find in a moderately priced choice, such as alarm clocks, two-line phones, and a working desk. All have relatively well-maintained bathrooms containing tub/showers.

There's a bar and two restaurants within a few steps of the hotel itself, and several others within a 5-minute walk.

W. Bay St. (P.O. Box SS-19055), Nassau, The Bahamas. © **242/356-0000.** Fax 242/323-1408. www.nassau-hotels.com. 183 units. Winter $95 (£50) double, $135 (£72) suite; off season $89 (£47) double, $95 (£500) suite. AE, DISC, MC, V. Bus: 10 or 17. **Amenities:** 2 restaurants; 2 bars; 2 outdoor pools; health club; spa; salon; room service; laundry service; dry cleaning; nonsmoking rooms; rooms for those w/limited mobility. *In room:* A/C, TV, fridge, coffeemaker, hair dryer, iron, safe, Wi-Fi.

INEXPENSIVE

El Greco Hotel   This hotel is across the street from Junkanoo Beach/Lighthouse Beach/The Western Esplanade, and a short walk from the sometimes raucous nightlife of Arawak Cay. It's also a quick walk from the shops and restaurants of downtown Nassau. El Greco is a well-managed bargain choice that attracts many European travelers. The Greek owners and staff genuinely seem to care about their guests—in fact, the two-story hotel seems more like a small European B&B than your typical Bahamian hotel.

The midsize rooms aren't that exciting, but they're clean and comfortable, with decent beds and small tile bathrooms, containing tub/showers. Bedrooms have a bright decor—a sort of Mediterranean motif, each with two ceiling fans and carpeted floors. Accommodations are built around a courtyard that contains statues crafted in the Italian baroque style, draped with lots of bougainvillea. A restaurant isn't on-site, but you can walk to many places nearby for meals.

W. Bay St. (P.O. Box N-4187), Nassau, The Bahamas. © **242/325-1121.** Fax 242/325-1124. 27 units. Winter $140 (£74) double, $160–$200 (£85–£106) suite; off season $120 (£64) double, $140–$170 (£74–£90) suite. AE, MC, V. Free parking. Bus: 10. **Amenities:** Bar; pool; babysitting. *In room:* A/C, TV.

Nassau Harbour Club Hotel & Marina   Don't expect lush and sprawling gardens or much peace and privacy here—this battered, much-used hotel is in the heart of a busy commercial neighborhood of downtown Nassau that's devoted to boats, boat repair, and the fishing and warehousing industry, even though the more formal showcase neighborhoods of Nassau lie within a 15-minute walk. A compound of two-story pink buildings from the early 1960s arranged like a horseshoe around a concrete terrace, it occupies a bustling strip of land between busy Bay Street and the edge of the channel that separates New Providence from Paradise Island. Rooms offer views of yachts and boats moored at a nearby marina, and easy access to the shops, bars, and restaurants of downtown Nassau and within the Harbour Bay Shopping Centre. Throughout, it's down-to-earth, aggressively unpretentious, and just a bit funky. Bedrooms are simple and compact but comfortable, and equipped with bathrooms with tub/showers. However, they are just a bit beat-up and worn.

E. Bay St. (P.O. Box SS-5755), Nassau, The Bahamas. 🕾 **242/393-0771**. Fax 242/393-5393. 50 units. Year-round $120 (£64) double; $130 (£69) suite. Extra person $20 (£11) per day. AE, MC, V. Free parking. Bus: 9, 11, or 19. **Amenities:** Restaurant; bar; outdoor pool, babysitting. *In room:* A/C, TV, fridge.

Quality Inn Junkanoo Beach Nassau   This no-nonsense, efficiently designed, green-fronted hotel rises prominently across the sometimes busy traffic of West Bay Street, from the narrow sands known variously as Junkanoo Beach, Lighthouse Beach, Long Wharf, and the Western Esplanade. Partly because of its compact rooms, it's the least desirable, and also the least expensive, of the also-recommended hotels (the Nassau Palm and the El Greco) that lie nearby within this congested neighborhood of downtown Nassau. But during the peak of winter, when other competitors might be more expensive or sold out completely, it offers comfortable, unpretentious lodgings in a six-story venue that might be appealing if you don't expect tons of amenities and superlative service.

W. Bay St. and Nassau St., Nassau, The Bahamas. 🕾 **242/322-1515**. Fax 242/322-1514. www.choicehotels.com. 63 units. Winter $111–$123 (£59–£65) double; off season $89–$112 (£47–£59) double. AE, DC, MC, V. Bus: 10, 16. **Amenities:** Bar; outdoor pool; business center; dry-cleaning service; nonsmoking rooms; rooms for those w/limited mobility. *In room:* A/C, TV, hair dryer, iron, beverage maker.

CABLE BEACH

The glittering shoreline of Cable Beach, located west of Nassau, is topped only by Paradise Island (see chapter 4). It has loyal fans, many of whom find Paradise Island too expensive or artificial. Cable Beach has for years attracted visitors with its broad stretches of beachfront, variety of restaurants and sports facilities, and one of the biggest casinos in The Bahamas. Come here for comfortable lodgings, diversion, distraction, and lots of flash.

WHERE TO STAY IN CABLE BEACH
VERY EXPENSIVE

Breezes Bahamas 🅡   In 1996, SuperClubs, an all-inclusive chain which competes successfully with Sandals (see below), spent $125 million transforming a tired old relic—the Ambassador Beach Hotel—into this all-inclusive resort. Major renovations were completed in 2006, which included an upgrade of most of the plumbing and electrical systems. Today Breezes' biggest competitor is the nearby Sandals Royal Bahamian, which is more imposing, more elegant, more stylish, more expensive, and more upscale. Rowdier and

Where to Stay & Dine in Cable Beach

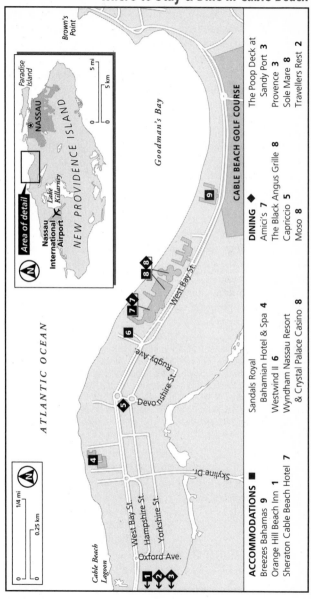

ACCOMMODATIONS ■
Breezes Bahamas **9**
Orange Hill Beach Inn **1**
Sheraton Cable Beach Hotel **7**
Sandals Royal
Bahamian Hotel & Spa **4**
Westwind II **6**
Wyndham Nassau Resort
& Crystal Palace Casino **8**

DINING ◆
Amici's **7**
The Black Angus Grille **8**
Capriccio **5**
Moso **8**
The Poop Deck at
Sandy Port **3**
Provence **3**
Sole Mare **8**
Travellers Rest **2**

more raucous, and located on a prime 450m (1,476-ft.) beachfront along Cable Beach, Breezes attracts a more middle-of-the-road crowd; it's unpretentious and more affordable (though it isn't exactly cheap, and we think it's a bit overpriced for what it is). This U-shaped beachfront resort has two wings of rooms plus a main club-house facing a large, sometimes-overcrowded terrace with a swimming pool that serves as the social centerpiece. Both couples and single travelers are accepted here. Everything is included—the room, meals, snacks, unlimited wine (not the finest) with lunch and dinner, even premium-brand liquor at the bars, plus activities and airport transfers.

The air-conditioned hotel rooms contain pastel-painted furniture with Formica tops. Accommodations are not as luxurious as those at Sandals, but rates are kept deliberately lower. Tiled bathrooms are medium-size, each equipped with a shower and bathtub.

Diners can sample unremarkable international fare at the food court, although the Italian restaurant serves better food. A beachside grill and snacks are available throughout the day. Entertainment includes a high-energy disco, a piano bar, and a nightclub. Karaoke is inevitable, but the professional Junkanoo live shows, which are presented every Saturday night, are more entertaining, and local bands often perform.

P.O. Box CB-13049, Cable Beach, Nassau, The Bahamas. © 800/GO-SUPER or 242/327-5356. Fax 242/327-5155. www.superclubs.com. 391 units. Year-round $144–$219 (£76–£116) per person per night, double occupancy; $234–$269 (£124–£143) per person per night, double occupancy, suite. Rates include all meals, drinks, tips, airport transfers, and most activities. AE, DISC, MC, V. Free parking. Bus: 10. No children under 14 year-round; no one under 18, unless accompanied by an adult 21 or older, Mar–May. **Amenities:** 3 restaurants; 4 bars; 2 outdoor pools; 3 tennis courts; health club; watersports equipment; laundry service; nonsmoking rooms; rooms for those w/limited mobility. *In room:* A/C, TV, coffeemaker, hair dryer, iron, safe.

Sandals Royal Bahamian Hotel & Spa 𝒶𝒶𝒶 This all-inclusive property is the most upscale Sandals resort in the world. It's shockingly expensive, though you can often get special promotional rates that make it more reasonable. The property originated as a very posh hotel, the Balmoral Beach, in the 1940s. In 1996, the Jamaica-based Sandals chain poured $20 million into renovating and expanding the resort, and additional renovations have been ongoing ever since. Everywhere, you'll find some of the trappings of Edwardian England in the tropics: manicured gardens, rich cove moldings, neoclassical/Palladian architectural themes, plus hidden courtyards

Moments   Junkanoo Festivals

No Bahamian celebration is as raucous as the Junkanoo (which is also the name of the music associated with this festival). The special rituals originated during the colonial days of slavery, when African-born newcomers could legally drink and enjoy themselves only on certain strictly predetermined days of the year. In its celebration, Junkanoo closely resembles Carnaval in Rio and Mardi Gras in New Orleans. Its major difference lies in the costumes and the timing (the major Junkanoo celebrations occur the day after Christmas, a legacy of the English celebration of Boxing Day on Dec 26, and New Year's Day). On a more touristy note, a 2-month festival, the **Junkanoo Summer Festival,** takes place in June and July annually.

In the old days, Junkanoo costumes were crafted from crepe paper, often in primary colors, stretched over wire frames. (One sinister offshoot of the celebrations was that Junkanoo costumes and masks were used to conceal the identity of anyone seeking vengeance on a white or on another slave.) Today locals have more money to spend on costumes and Junkanoo festivals than they did in the past. The finest costumes can cost up to $15,000 (£7,950) and are sometimes sponsored by local bazaars, lotteries, church groups, and charity auctions. Everyday folks from all walks of Bahamian life also join in, often with homemade costumes that are sensuous or humorous. The best time and place to observe Junkanoo is New Year's Day in Nassau, when throngs of cavorting, music-making, and costumed figures prance through the streets. Find yourself a good viewing position on Bay Street. Less elaborate celebrations take place in major towns on the other islands, including Freeport on Grand Bahama Island.

tastefully accentuated with sculptures. The resort is located on a beach a short walk west of the more glittery megahotels of Cable Beach.

A favorite for honeymoon getaways, Sandals offers well-furnished and often elegant rooms, all classified as suites and positioned within either the resort's core Manor House or the circa-1998

Windsor Building. Others, including some of the most upscale and expensive, occupy outlying villas known collectively as The Royal Village. The villas are preferred because of their rigorously secluded settings and easy access to nearby semiprivate plunge pools. Bedrooms, regardless of their location, have thick cove moldings, formal English furniture, and tub/shower bathrooms loaded with perfumed soaps and cosmetics. The rooms that face the ocean offer small curved terraces with ornate iron railings and views of an offshore sand spit, Sandals Key.

For a long time, only heterosexual guests were allowed at this resort. But the British and Canadian governments said they wouldn't allow Sandals to advertise its resorts if it continued discriminatory policies against same-sex couples. In 2004, Sandals capitulated and ended the ban. Today self-defined gay couples are accepted as guests, but their numbers since the corporate policy changes haven't been particularly visible.

Bahamian and international fare is offered in generous portions in the property's restaurants. In addition to spectacular buffets, the options include white-glove service and continental dishes in the Baccarat Dining Room. The two latest additions include Kimono's, offering Japanese cuisine, and Casanova, specializing in Italian fare. Other choices include Arizona for Southwestern-style grilled specialties, and Spices for upscale buffets three times a day. The pool here is one of the most appealing on Nassau, with touches of both Vegas and ancient Rome (outdoor murals and replicas of ancient Roman columns jutting skyward above the water). Complimentary shuttle bus service goes to the casino and nightlife options at the nearby Wyndham Crystal Palace complex; concierge service is offered for residents of the resort's higher-priced accommodations.

W. Bay St. (P.O. Box CB-13005), Cable Beach, Nassau, The Bahamas. © 800/SAN-DALS or 242/327-6400. Fax 242/327-6961. www.sandals.com. 403 units. Winter $1,800–$4,000 (£954–£2,120) per couple for 2 days; off season $1,600–$3,800 (£848–£2,014) per couple for 2 days. Rates include all meals, drinks, and activities. AE, DISC, MC, V. Free parking. Bus: 10. Couples only; no children allowed. **Amenities:** 8 restaurants; 9 bars; 6 outdoor pools; 2 tennis courts; health club; full-service spa; watersports equipment; nonsmoking rooms; rooms for those w/limited mobility. *In room:* A/C, TV, coffeemaker, hair dryer, iron, safe.

EXPENSIVE

Sheraton Cable Beach Hotel ⋆ *Kids*   Prominently visible in the center of Cable Beach (its best asset) this seven-story high-rise is connected by a shopping arcade to the Crystal Palace Casino. The nearby Wyndham Nassau Resort is glitzier and has better and more exclusive and extensive facilities, but the Sheraton is still one of the most desirable choices for families, as it has the best children's program in the area. Because many of its bedrooms contain two double beds, its accommodations are usually suitable for a family of four. Painted pale coral pink, the property has an Aztec-inspired facade of sharp angles and strongly defined horizontal lines, with prominent balconies. Built in a horseshoe-shaped curve around a landscaped beachfront garden, it's big, brassy, and the beneficiary of an $82-million renovation, half of which had been completed by press time for this edition and the remainder of which was scheduled for completion during the course of 2007 and early 2008. This commitment to a massive outlay of cash was concurrent with the changeover of this property's management contract from Radisson to Sheraton and the Starwood Group.

You'll think of Vegas when you see the rows of fountains in front, the acres of marble sheathing inside, the four-story lobby with towering windows, and the hotel's propensity for hosting large wedding parties, often with groups of participants flown in from the mainland U.S. Big enough to get lost in, but with plenty of intimate nooks, the hotel offers an extensive array of things to do.

Bedrooms are modern and comfortable, reflecting a lighthearted and somewhat whimsical interpretation of "Tommy Bahama" style, replete with dark-stained wood furniture, white walls, and monochromatic, understated colors completely devoid of the floral prints of yesteryear. Big windows open onto views of either the garden or the beach. Units are equipped with one king-size bed or two doubles, along with phones with voice mail. Bathrooms are tiled with tub/showers.

The hotel contains three restaurants, the most glamorous of which is the Amici (recommended separately in "Where to Dine"), serving traditional Italian cuisine in a two-story garden setting. The Outdoor Grill serves Caribbean/continental breakfast and lunch buffets. In the works at press time for this edition was a steak-and-seafood restaurant where guests are seated around a tabletop grill to prepare their own steaks, seafood, or chicken. This older but much-upgraded hotel will function as one of the most important components of a sweeping expansion of the Cable Beach hotel lineup that will be affected during 2009 and 2010. Under the supervision of the Baha Mar Development Corporation, it will be the oldest and most westerly of a massive expansion of the Cable Beach beachfront.

W. Bay St. (P.O. Box N-4914), Cable Beach, Nassau, The Bahamas. © **800/ 325-3535** or 242/327-6000. Fax 242/327-6987. www.sheraton.com/cablebeach. 694 units. Feb–Apr $249–$389 (£132–£206) double; May–Aug $219–$359

(£116–£190) double; Sept–Jan $189–$329 (£100–£174) double; Christmas/New Year's $369–$489 (£196–£259) double. AE, MC, V. Free parking. Bus: 10. **Amenities:** 3 restaurants; 3 bars; 3 outdoor pools; 2 tennis courts; gym; kid's camp (ages 4–12); shopping arcade; salon; room service; babysitting; laundry service; dry cleaning; rooms for those w/limited mobility. *In room:* A/C, TV, coffeemaker, hair dryer, iron, safe.

Westwind II *Kids* Set on the western edge of Cable Beach's hotel strip, 9.5km (6 miles) from the center of Nassau, the Westwind II is a cluster of two-story buildings that contain two-bedroom, two-bathroom timeshare units, each with a full kitchen (there's a grocery store nearby). The size and facilities of these units make them ideal for traveling families, and the accommodations are available to the public whenever they're not occupied by investors. All the diversions of the megahotels are close by and easily reached, but in the complex itself, you can enjoy a low-key, quiet atmosphere and privacy. (A masonry wall separates the compound from the traffic of W. Bay St. and the hotels and vacant lots that flank it.) Each unit has a pleasant decor that includes white tiled floors, rattan furniture, bathrooms with tub/showers, and either a balcony or a terrace. Since units are identical, price differences are based on whether the units face the beach, the pool, or the garden. The manicured grounds feature palms, flowering hibiscus shrubs, and seasonal flower beds. Don't stay here if you expect any of the luxuries or facilities of the nearby Wyndham Nassau Resort (see below). Westwind II is more for self-sufficient, do-it-yourself types.

W. Bay St. (P.O. Box CB-11006), Cable Beach, Nassau, The Bahamas. ✆ **866/369-5921** or 242/327-7019. Fax 262/327-7529. www.westwind2.com. 54 units. Winter $231–$278 (£122–£147) double; off season $194–$242 (£103–£128) double. MC, V. Bus: 10. **Amenities:** Bar; 2 pools; 2 tennis courts; babysitting; coin-operated laundry; rooms for those w/limited mobility. *In room:* A/C, TV, kitchen, fridge, coffeemaker, iron, Wi-Fi.

Wyndham Nassau Resort & Crystal Palace Casino *Kids* This big, flashy megaresort on the lovely sands of Cable Beach is so vast and all-encompassing that some of its guests never venture into Nassau during their stay on the island. The futuristic-looking complex incorporates five high-rise towers, each painted a shade of pale pink or pale lavender; a futuristic central core illuminated with sunlight streaming through massive greenhouse-style translucent domes; and a cluster of beachfront gazebos—all linked with arcades, covered passageways, and mini pavilions. Guest rooms come in several different price brackets, ranging from standard island view to ocean vista, each with private balconies. Corner suites with lots of space are the way to go, complete with wraparound balconies and king-size beds looking out onto the water through floor-to-ceiling glass. Combination bathrooms (tub/showers) most often come with dressing areas and dual basins.

At press time, management was about three-quarters through a massive $30-million renovation of the interior—which had been sorely needed, in our opinion, because the decor had tended to look a bit too jazzy, a bit too overheated and colorful, and a bit tired. This hotel will be the carefully planned centerpiece, between 2008 and 2010, of a radical expansion of the hotel lineup along Cable Beach, as envisioned by the Baha Mar Development Corporation. No other hotel on New Providence Island has been through as many changes to its self-image as this one, and thanks to the massive redevelopment of the terrain around it anticipated during the coming 3 years, it's positioning itself to give its biggest competitor, the Atlantis resort on Paradise Island, some fire-breathing competition.

Aside from a massive (and massively upgraded) casino, one of the two largest in The Bahamas, the complex contains a wide array of dining and drinking facilities. Three of its restaurants are among the best-recommended in New Providence. Newest and appealingly experimental, and a personal favorite, is Moso, an enclave of hip that assembles onto one menu the best dishes from around Asia and the Pacific Rim. Even if you're not a guest of the hotel, you might want to avail yourself of the drinking and dining options or the casino action here. As part of a deeply entrenched tradition, the hotel serves as the site for the electoral conventions of the two most powerful political parties in The Bahamas.

W. Bay St. (P.O. Box N-8306), Cable Beach, Nassau, The Bahamas. ⓒ 800/222-7466 in the U.S., or 242/327-6200. Fax 954/915-2929. www.wyndhamnassauresort.com. 850 units. Feb–Apr $325–$385 (£172–£204) double; May–Aug $295–$345 (£156–£183) double; Sept–Jan $245–$305 (£130–£1620) double; Christmas/New Year's $465–$525 (£246–£278) double. AE, DC, MC, V. Free self-parking, valet parking $5 (£2.65). Bus: 10. **Amenities:** 6 restaurants; 4 bars; outdoor pool; nearby golf course; health club; Jacuzzi; sauna; children's programs (4–12); business center; massage facilities; room service; babysitting; laundry service; dry cleaning; nonsmoking rooms; rooms for those w/limited mobility. *In room:* A/C, TV, fridge (in some), coffeemaker, hair dryer, iron, safe.

MODERATE

Orange Hill Beach Inn 𝒢 𝑭𝒊𝒏𝒅𝒔   This hotel, set on 1.4 landscaped hillside hectares (3½ acres), lies about 13km (8 miles) west of Nassau and 1.5km (1 mile) east of Love Beach, which has great snorkeling. It's perfect for those who want to escape the crowds and stay in a quieter part of New Providence Island; it's easy to catch a cab or jitney to Cable Beach or downtown Nassau. The welcoming owners, Judy and Danny Lowe, an Irish-Bahamian partnership, jokingly refer to their operation as "Fawlty Towers Nassau."

Originally built as a private home in the 1920s, this place became a hotel in 1979 after the Lowes added more rooms and a swimming pool. Rooms and apartments come in a variety of sizes, although most are small. Likewise, the bathrooms are small but well maintained. Each has a balcony or patio, and some of them have kitchenettes. Many of the guests are Europeans, especially in summer. Renovations included updated furniture in the rooms and upgraded bathrooms.

On-site is a bar serving sandwiches and salads throughout the day, and a restaurant that offers simple but good dinners. Diving excursions to the rich marine fauna found along New Providence's southwestern coast are among the most popular activities here. Management maintains free regular jitney service to and from local grocery stores, a fact that's much appreciated by clients who prepare many of their meals within their individual kitchenettes.

W. Bay St., just west of Blake Rd. (P.O. Box N-8583), Nassau, The Bahamas. © 242/327-7157. Fax 242/327-5186. www.orangehill.com. 33 units. Winter $141 (£75) double, $146 (£77) w/kitchenette; off season $123 (£65) double, $126 (£67) w/kitchenette. MC, V. Free parking. Bus: 10. **Amenities:** Restaurant; bar; outdoor pool; laundry service and coin-operated laundry; rooms for those w/limited mobility. *In room:* A/C, TV, kitchenette (in some).

4 Where to Dine

NASSAU

Nassau restaurants open and close often. Even if reservations aren't required, it's a good idea to call first just to see that a place is still functioning. European and American cuisines are relatively easy to find in Nassau. Surprisingly, it used to be difficult to find Bahamian cuisine, but in recent years, more places have begun to offer authentic island fare.

EXPENSIVE

Graycliff ℛ CONTINENTAL   Part of the Graycliff hotel, an antiques-filled colonial mansion located in the commercial core of Nassau, opposite Government House, this deeply entrenched, long-enduring restaurant retains a history and an almost palpable sense of nostalgia for the old days of The Bahamas as a colonial outpost of Britain, despite sweeping changes in both the government and the society at large. The chefs use local Bahamian products whenever available and turn them into an old-fashioned cuisine that still appeals to tradition-minded visitors, many of whom return here year after year. Young diners with more contemporary palates might head elsewhere, though, as the food has fallen off a bit of late, and the staff seems chronically overworked and just a wee bit impatient. The chefs, neither completely traditional nor regional, produce such dishes as grouper soup in puff pastry, and plump, juicy pheasant cooked with pineapples grown on Eleuthera. Lobster is another specialty, one half in *beurre blanc* and the other sided with a sauce prepared with the head of the lobster. Other standard dishes include escargots, foie gras, and *tournedos d'agneau* (lamb). The pricey wine list is usually praised as one of the finest in the country, with more than 180,000 bottles. This hotel and restaurant is managed by the same entrepreneurs who run a cigar-making facility; as such, their collection of Bahama-derived cigars is said to be the most comprehensive and varied in the world.

W. Hill St. ⒸⓉ **242/322-2796.** Reservations required. Jacket advised for men. Main courses $22–$32 (£12–£17) lunch, $37–$55 (£20–£29) dinner. AE, MC, V. Mon–Fri noon–3pm; daily 6:30–10pm. Bus: 10, 10A, or 21A.

Ristorante Villagio ⒶⒶ TUSCAN/CONTINENTAL   One of the most appealing restaurants on New Providence Island lies 3.2km (2 miles) west of Cable Beach, close enough to the posh and gated residential enclave of Lyford Cay to ensure a steady flow of upscale local residents. Set within an ochre-colored enclave of shopping and office buildings known as Caves Village at Caves Point, it's posh, a bit dilletantish, and charming. There's a cozy dining room with an open-to-view kitchen, elaborate French Empire–style crystal chandeliers, a wall with display cases devoted to a collection of colorful Murano glass, and the kind of thick-legged rustic furniture that you might have pulled out of a farmhouse in Tuscany. Even better is a sprawling covered terrace whose furniture—wrought-iron tables and deep-upholstered sofas and armchairs—seems appropriate for someone's (interior) private library. Menu items are savory and artful. Their lemon grass–poached lobster salad is fabulous, as are the trenette pasta with seafood, the linguini with clams, and the Angus beef with arugula. Veal cutlets Milanese are served with hazelnut sauce. Also delicious: their slices of black sea bass atop a bed of truffle-studded creamed potatoes, bacon-braised organic leeks, and wild mushrooms; and very slow-roasted Norfolk duckling steeped in sherry, onions, and olives, then served over braised cabbage and pancetta ham. Staff here manages to combine some almost cliché-ridden, slightly dotty English supervisors and a rather hip Bahamian and international staff. In 2007, the same administrators established a nearby, somewhat less formal bistro, Mangos, within the same shopping compound, where food is only a bit less expensive, but where service can be excruciatingly slow and serving errors are frequent.

At Caves Point, W. Bay St. at Blake Rd. ✆ 242/327-0965. Reservations recommended. Main courses $28–$48 (£15–£25). Tues–Sat 6–10pm. Bus: Western.

Sun and . . . ✹✹ INTERNATIONAL   For nearly 30 years, this restaurant, through good and bad times, has been a prominent culinary landmark in Nassau, the best of a core of locally owned restaurants valiantly holding their own against daunting competition from better-funded restaurants within the island's megaresorts. Today, under the hard-working administration of Belgium-born owner and chef Ronny Deryckere and his wife, Esther, it's better and more of an inner sanctum than ever. It occupies the premises of what was originally built in the 1930s as a private residence, Red Mill House, within an upscale, mostly residential neighborhood east of downtown Nassau. You might want a drink within the bar area, which is a distinctly separate entity all its own, before heading into one of several dining rooms, each of them arranged around a central courtyard containing tropical plants, shrubs, and a swimming pool. Some of the dishes emerging from the kitchens of this place are unique on New Providence or Paradise Islands: Examples include sweetbreads, prepared either with white wine or mushroom sauce or with a demiglaze and cognac; the best Roquefort salad in town; an absolutely fabulous version of steak tartare, served with *pommes frites;* and grilled octopus with chopped onions and a tapenade of olives. Of special note is the Bahamian fisher's platter, composed of artfully prepared fish that's entirely caught within local waters. If there's a moment during the dinner when you're not otherwise occupied, check out the photos lining the walls depicting clients of yesterday, who have included Frank Sinatra, Bob Hope, Richard Widmark, and the Duke of Windsor.

Lakeview Rd. at E. Shirley St. ✆ 242/393-1205. Reservations required. Lunch platters $11–$19 (£5.85–£10); dinner main courses $30–$40 (£16–£21). AE, DC, MC, V. Tues–Sun 11:30am–2:30pm and 6:30–9:30pm. Closed Sun June–July and Aug–Sept.

The White Door ✹ INTERNATIONAL   New, hip, and appealingly eccentric, this restaurant enjoys, almost without competition, a setting that's more historic and more closely linked to the British Colonial era than any other restaurant in The Bahamas. Set across the street from the also-recommended Graycliff, in the heart of historic Nassau, it occupies a 250-year-old masonry-and-wood Bahamian house that belonged for many years to Lord Mountbatten, the uncle of Prince Philip. As such, it once housed—within the guest cottage in back—Queen Elizabeth II. The house was acquired a few years ago by Harl Taylor, whose fans describe him as "the leading taste master, or taste maker, in The Bahamas." He's known as a crafter of women's handbags and, as such, maintains a boutique of his creations on the building's second floor. Come to this place for an inside view of an old Bahamian house, dripping with colonial charm and royal antecedents. Meals here are invariably configured as part of fixed-price menus reflecting very fresh local ingredients and a vague allegiance to someone's conception of Bahamian flair. Some recent meals have included organic salads with mango-flavored vinaigrette, grapefruit, and kumquats; seafood pot pie flavored with sherry and studded with lobster meat and shrimp; and mini rack of lamb with red wine reduction, steamed broccoli, and bok choy. Dessert service is configured tapas-style, and include guava duff, homemade coconut-mango-chocolate ice cream, and Grand Marnier crepes with coconut-flavored rum sauce.

9 West Hill St. ✆ **242/326-5925.** Reservations recommended. Set-price dinners $75 (£40) without wine; set-price Sun brunch $75 (£40) without wine. AE, DC, DISC, MC, V. Thurs–Sat 6–10:30pm (with seatings at 6:30 and 9pm); Sun 11am–3pm (with open seating). Closed Aug. Bus: 10 or 21A.

MODERATE

Café Matisse ✿ INTERNATIONAL/ITALIAN   Set directly behind Parliament House, in a mustard/beige–colored building that was built a century ago as a private home, this restaurant is on everybody's short list of downtown Nassau favorites. It serves well-prepared Italian and international cuisine to businesspeople, workers from nearby government offices, and all kinds of deal makers. There are dining areas within an enclosed courtyard, as well as on two floors of the interior, which is decorated with colorful Matisse prints. It's run by the sophisticated Bahamian-Italian team of Greg and Gabriella Curry, who prepare menu items that include calamari with spicy chili-flavored jam, served with tomatoes and fresh mozzarella cheese; a mixed grill of seafood; grilled filet of local grouper served with a light tomato and caper sauce; spaghetti with lobster; grilled rack of lamb with gravy; a perfect filet mignon in a green-peppercorn sauce; and a zesty curried shrimp with rice.

Bank Lane at Bay St., just north of Parliament Sq. ✆ **242/356-7012.** Reservations recommended. Main courses $14–$23 (£7.40–£12) lunch, $19–$40 (£10–£21) dinner. AE, DISC, MC, V. Tues–Sat noon–3pm and 6–10pm. Bus: 17 and 21.

East Villa Restaurant and Lounge CHINESE/CONTINEN-
TAL   You might imagine yourself in Hong Kong during the 1980s
in this well-designed modern house across the road from the headquarters of the Nassau Yacht Club, a short drive east from the commercial core of downtown Nassau. It's somewhat upscale and
completely devoid of the sense of bureaucracy associated with
restaurants within some of the island's larger resorts. It sometimes
attracts affluent Florida yachters to its dimly lit precincts, where
aquariums bubble in a simple but tasteful contemporary setting.
Zesty Szechuan flavors appear on the menu, but there are less spicy
Cantonese alternatives, including sweet-and-sour chicken and
steamed vegetables with cashews and water chestnuts. Lobster tail in
the spicy Chinese style is one of our favorites. Dishes can be ordered
mild, medium, or zesty hot.

E. Bay St. ℂ **242/393-3377.** Reservations required. Main courses $11–$20
(£5.85–£11) lunch, $14–$40 (£7.40–£21) dinner. AE, MC, V. Sun–Fri noon–3pm;
daily 6–10pm. Bus: 9A, 9B, 11, or 19.

Luciano's of Chicago ⍟ ITALIAN/SEAFOOD/STEAK   One of
Nassau's newer upscale restaurants opened in 2005 within a low-
slung, red-painted building that's positioned close to the northbound section of the bridge across the channel that separates New
Providence from Paradise Island. The Nassau branch of a successful
franchise that originated in Chicago, it emphasizes stiff drinks, two-
fisted portions, and a sense of macho charm. Many visitors prefer
the terrace that has tables and pergolas positioned for a view of the
towers and glittering lights of the Atlantis Resort just across the
water. In addition to the terrace (which most diners seem to prefer),
there's a smoothly upscale dining room, air-conditioned and outfitted in tones of beige and brown. In addition to a tempting roster of
two-fisted steaks, menu items include romaine lettuce topped with
basil-and-garlic-marinated sweet peppers; clay pot–roasted chicken
served with sautéed garlic and kalamata olives; country-style riga-
toni with sweet Italian sausage, pancetta ham, and a light tomato-
flavored cream sauce; and a succulent Italian stew *(giambotta)* made
with chicken, sausage, onion, roasted peppers, garlic, potatoes,
white wine, and olive oil. A soup that's particularly successful is
made from escarole, white beans, and Italian sausage.

E. Bay St., just before the northbound entrance to the Paradise Island Bridge.
ℂ **242/323-7770.** Reservations recommended. Main courses $12–$30
(£6.35–£16) lunch, $17–$44 (£9–£23) dinner. AE, DC, DISC, MC, V. Mon–Fri
11:30am–3pm; daily 6–10pm. Bus: 10.

Poop Deck BAHAMIAN/SEAFOOD   Raffish and informal, this is the older (and original) version of a restaurant that recently expanded with another branch at Cable Beach. This original is less touristy, hosting a clientele of sailors, yachtspeople, and workers from the nearby marinas and boatyards. Many of them find perches on the second-floor open-air terrace, which overlooks the harbor and Paradise Island. If you like dining with a view, you won't find a better place than this in the heart of Nassau. At lunch, you can order conch chowder (perfectly seasoned) or a juicy beef burger. The waiters are friendly, the crowd is convivial, and the festivities continue into the evening, usually with lots of drinking. Native grouper fingers served with peas 'n' rice is the Bahamian soul food dish on the menu. Two of the best seafood selections are the fresh lobster and the stuffed mushrooms with crabmeat. The creamy linguine with crisp garlic bread is another fine choice.

Nassau Yacht Haven Marina, E. Bay St. ✆ **242/393-8175**. And at Sandy Port, west of Cable Beach, on W. Bay St. ✆ **242/327-3329**. Reservations recommended for dinner, not necessary at lunch. Main courses $10–$25 (£5.30–£13) lunch, $19–$40 (£10–£21) dinner. AE, DC, DISC, MC, V. Daily noon–4:30pm and 5–10:30pm. For the branch at the Nassau Yacht Haven: bus 10, 19, or 23. For the branch on W. Bay St.: bus 10 or "the Western bus."

Shoal Restaurant and Lounge ⭐ 𝘝𝘢𝘭𝘶𝘦 BAHAMIAN   Many of our good friends in Nassau swear that this is one of the best joints for authentic local food. We rank it near the top for a dining venue that's utterly without glamour but which serves sensible down-home food at a locale far removed from the tourist path. After all, where else can you get a good bowl of okra soup these days? This may or may not be your fantasy, but to a Bahamian, it's like pot liquor and turnip greens with corn bread to a Southerner. Many diners follow an inaugural bowl of soup (either split pea or the above-mentioned okra soup) with more conch, either "cracked" or perhaps curried. But you can also order some unusual dishes, such as Bahamian-style curried mutton using native spices and herbs, stewed oxtail, or braised short ribs of beef. Peas 'n' rice almost automatically accompanies virtually everything served here.

Nassau St. near its intersection with Poinciana Dr. ✆ **242/323-4400**. Main courses $9.50–$17 (£5–£9). AE, DISC, MC, V. Sun–Thurs 7:30am–11pm. Bus: 16.

Taj Mahal NORTHERN INDIAN   This is the best and most frequently recommended Indian restaurant in Nassau. Within a room lined with Indian art and artifacts, you'll dine on a wide range of savory and zesty Punjabi, tandoori, and curried dishes. Some of the best choices are the lamb selections, although such concessions to local culture as curried or tandoori-style conch have also begun cropping up on the menu. If you don't know what to order, consider a tandoori mixed platter, which might satisfy two of you with a side dish or two. All of the *korma* dishes, which combine lamb, chicken, beef, or vegetables in a creamy curry sauce, are very successful. Takeout meals are also available.

48 Parliament St. at Bay St. ✆ **242/356-3004**. Reservations recommended. Main courses $18–$38 (£9.55–£20). AE, MC, V. Daily noon–3pm and 6:30–11pm. Bus: 10 or 17.

INEXPENSIVE

Bahamian Kitchen *(Value) (Kids)* BAHAMIAN/INTERNATIONAL Located next to Trinity Church, within one of the most congested neighborhoods of downtown Nassau, this is one of the best places for good Bahamian food at modest prices. Solid, unpretentious, and decent, it evokes the kind of restaurant you might find on a remote Bahamian Out Island. Down-home dishes include lobster Bahamian style, fried red snapper, conch salad, stewed fish, curried chicken, okra soup, and pea soup and dumplings. Most dishes are served with peas 'n' rice. You can order such old-fashioned Bahamian fare as stewed fish and corned beef and grits, all served with johnnycake. If you'd like to introduce your kids to Bahamian cuisine, this is an ideal choice. There's takeout service if you're planning a picnic.

Trinity Place, off Market St. ✆ **242/325-0702**. Lunch and dinner main courses $10–$42 (£5.30–£22). AE, MC, V. Mon–Sat 11:30am–10pm. Bus: 10.

Café Skans *(Value)* GREEK/AMERICAN/BAHAMIAN Owned and operated by a hardworking Greek family, this is a straightforward, Formica-clad diner with an open kitchen, offering flavorful food that's served without fanfare in generous portions. Set in the midst of the densest concentration of shops in Nassau, it attracts local residents and office workers from the government buildings nearby. Menu items include Bahamian fried or barbecued chicken; conch chowder; bean soup with dumplings; souvlakia or gyros in pita bread; and burgers, steaks, and various kinds of seafood platters. This is where workaday Nassau comes for breakfast.

Bay St., near the corner of Market St. ✆ **242/322-2486**. Reservations not accepted. Breakfast $4–$9 (£2.10–£4.75); sandwiches $6–$12 (£3.20–£6.35); main-course platters $6–$17 (£3.20–£9). MC, V. Mon–Thurs 8am–5pm; Fri–Sat 8am–6pm; Sun 8am–4pm. Bus: 10 or 17.

Conch Fritters Bar & Grill BAHAMIAN/INTERNATIONAL
A true local hangout with real island atmosphere, this light-hearted family-friendly restaurant changes its focus several times throughout the day. Lunches and dinners are high-volume, high-turnover affairs mitigated only by attentive staff. Guests invariably include older diners and parents with young children in tow. Live music is presented every Thursday to Saturday 7pm until 10pm. Food choices are rather standard but still quite good, including cracked conch, fried shrimp, grilled salmon, blackened rib-eye steak, burgers, sandwiches, and six different versions of chicken, including a combination platter of chicken with barbecued ribs. Specialty drinks from the active bar include a Goombay Smash.

Marlborough St. (across from the British Colonial Hilton). ℂ 242/323-8801. Burgers, sandwiches, and platters $10–$39 (£5.30–£21). AE, MC, V. Daily 11am–11pm (till midnight Fri–Sat). Bus: 10.

Double Dragon CANTONESE/SZECHUAN   The chefs at this unpretentious eatery hail from the province of Canton in mainland China, and that locale inspires most of the food here. You'll find it within an unscenic, raffish-looking waterfront neighborhood a short drive east of the showcase shopping district of downtown Nassau. If you've ever really wondered about the differences between Cantonese and Szechuan cuisine, a quick look at the menu here will highlight them. Lobster, chicken, or beef, for example, can be prepared Cantonese style, with a mild black-bean or ginger sauce; or in spicier Szechuan formats of red peppers, chiles, and garlic. Honey-garlic chicken and orange-flavored shrimp are always popular and succulent. Overall, this place is a fine choice if you're eager for a change from grouper and burgers.

E. Bay St. between Mackey St. and Williams Ct. ℂ 242/393-5718. Main courses $10–$23 (£5.30–£12). AE, DISC, MC, V. Mon–Thurs noon–10pm; Fri noon–11pm; Sat 4–11pm; Sun 5–10pm. Bus: 10, 19.

CABLE BEACH
VERY EXPENSIVE
The Black Angus Grille ⊛ STEAKS/SEAFOOD   This is a truly excellent steakhouse that's positioned amid a cluster of dining options immediately above Cable Beach's Crystal Palace Casino. Relaxed but macho-looking and undeniably upscale, it's the most consistently busy restaurant at Cable Beach—a function of its good food and also a function, in the words of its manager, of the predilection of gamblers for juicy, carnivorous steaks after a nerve-jangling

session at the gaming tables. Early in 2007, management spent a small fortune upgrading the decor of this place, adding an intricately crafted paneled ceiling and generally improving a dark, slightly over-crowded venue that might have appealed to Frank Sinatra and the Rat Pack from the 1960s.

Steaks are well prepared—succulent, juicy, and cooked to your specifications. There's prime rib, filet mignon, pepper steak, grilled tuna with a white bean salad, blackened conch filet, Caesar salad, different preparations of seafood, and an array of dessert soufflés that include versions with chocolate, praline, and orange. *Hint:* If you're absolutely fixated on steak, this is an excellent choice and indeed a seductive culinary venue. But immediately adjacent to the Black Angus are two other restaurants, the all-Italian Sole Mare, with equivalently priced and, frankly, much more creative food. There's also the less expensive yet highly imaginative nouvelle-Asian Moso, which we also prefer. Note our separate recommendations of these other contenders below.

In the Wyndham Nassau Resort, upstairs from the Crystal Palace Casino, W. Bay St. ⓒ **242/327-6200**. Reservations recommended. Main courses $27–$48 (£14–£25). AE, DC, DISC, MC, V. Daily 6–11pm. Bus: 10.

Sole Mare 𝒦𝒦 NORTHERN ITALIAN This is our top choice for elegant and stylish dining along Cable Beach, and it also serves the best Northern Italian cuisine on New Providence Island. The chefs are well trained, intuitive, and inventive, as shown by intensely creative dishes that crop up at regular intervals such as lobster maca-roni paired on a main-course platter with an herb-infused version of lamb-loin souvlakia, or deep-fried calamari stuffed with a mixture of fresh herbs and feta cheese. The fresh fish of the day is the keynote of many a delectable meal here. Many of the other ingredients have to be imported from the mainland, but the chefs still work their magic with them. A meal might begin with Castilian-style garlic soup, or jumbo shrimp sautéed in ouzo, and reach a high point with either a *piperade* (Basque stew) of lobster or a filet of halibut prepared lyonnaise style with cream, minced onions, and scalloped potatoes. Veal also appears rather delectably sautéed with endive, a dish you might enjoy in an upmarket tavern in northern Italy. The restaurant offers three different flavors of dessert soufflés: The one we prefer is the version prepared with sweet Marsala wine and fresh strawberries.

In the Wyndham Nassau Resort & Crystal Palace Casino, W. Bay St. ⓒ **242/327-6200**. Reservations required. Main courses $28–$46 (£15–£24). AE, DC, DISC, MC, V. Tues–Wed and Fri–Sun 6–11pm (hours and opening days vary with the sea-son and resort occupancy; call ahead). Bus: 10.

EXPENSIVE

Amici ☆ ITALIAN   Following a radical renovation and upgrade that was completed here during 2007, this well-recommended restaurant works hard to maintain its status as a culinary showcase for the flavorful and savory Italian cuisine that many guests crave after too long an exposure to an all-Bahamian diet. Set within the Sheraton Hotel, directly astride Cable Beach, its includes spinning ceiling fans, a big-windowed view of the beach, and the kind of dark-stained wooden furniture you might expect in a trattoria in Italy. Popular and long-enduring dishes here include scampi cocktails, Caesar salads, fettuccine Alfredo, Florentine-style breast of chicken (on a bed of spinach), zesty *gamberelli Fra Diavolo* (spicy shrimp), and braised pork shank with olive oil, hot peppers, and angel-hair pasta.

In the Sheraton Cable Beach Resort, W. Bay St. ⓒ **242/327-6000.** Main courses $23–$45 (£12–£24). AE, DC, DISC, MC, V. Daily 6–10:30pm. Bus: 10.

Capriccio ITALIAN/INTERNATIONAL   Set beside a prominent roundabout, about .5km (¼ mile) west of the megahotels of Cable Beach, this restaurant lies within a much-weathered, faux-baroque Italian building with Corinthian columns and an outdoor terrace. Inside it's a lot less formal, outfitted like an upscale luncheonette, but with lots of exposed granite, busy espresso machines, and kindly Bahamian staff who understand Italian culinary nuance. At lunch you get pretty ordinary fare such as fresh salads, sandwiches, and a few hot platters like cracked conch. But the cooks shine at night, offering dishes such as chicken breast with sage and wine sauce, veal cutlets served Milanese style or with Marsala sauce, spaghetti with pesto and pine nuts, and seafood platters.

W. Bay St. ⓒ **242/327-8547.** Reservations recommended. Lunch items $6–$22 (£3.20–£12); dinner main courses $15–$29 (£7.95–£15). MC, V. Mon–Sat 11am–10pm; Sun 5–10pm. Bus: 10 or 17.

Moso ☆☆ ASIAN   This is the newest and most experimental restaurant in New Providence, the brainchild of the owner of the rapidly expanding Baha Mar Cable Beach complex. There are many good and intriguing things about it: It deliberately prices meals here several notches below the rates charged by other "signature" restaurants within the same resort. (The more expensive, also-recommended Sole Mare and Angus Grille lie within a few steps of this place, within the same restaurant complex, just above the hotel's megacasino.) You'll quickly get the sense that this is a hipster kind of place serving hipster cuisine—in fact, every dish you've ever liked from every Asian menu you've ever looked at all seem to have found its way onto the menu. Each member of this restaurant's Bahamian waitstaff spent several months studying the preparation and context of Asian food and Asian culture, and they'll guide you through a menu composed of many different small and medium-sized dishes. These you'll compose into combinations that don't necessarily follow Western dining rituals. The best menu items might include aromatic crispy duck; Mongolian-style chicken and beef hot pot; fresh tofu stir-fried with minced pork, garlic, and chili; seared ahi tuna tataki with yazu lemon sauce; and a succulent blend of octopus and local conch with cucumbers in rice vinegar. You can also order meticulously carved portions of chicken breast, shrimp, pork tenderloin, filet mignon, lobster tail, salmon, or mahimahi prepared in any of three different ways: Cantonese, Sichuan dry-rubbed, or teriyaki style.

In the Wyndham Nassau Resort, upstairs from the Crystal Palace Casino, W. Bay St. ℂ 242/327-6200. Reservations recommended. Small plates $6–$11 (£3.20–£5.85); main courses $14–$30 (£7.40–£16). AE, DC, DISC, MC, V. Thurs–Mon 6–10:30pm (opening days vary according to the season and advance bookings); bar daily 6pm–1am. Bus: 10.

The Poop Deck at Sandy Port INTERNATIONAL/SEAFOOD

This is one of the three most imposing and most desirable restaurants west of Cable Beach, convenient for the owners of the many upscale villas and condos, including Lyford Cay, that occupy New Providence's western edge. It's set within a peach-colored concrete building that's highly visible from West Bay Street. Despite the rosy exterior, it's a bit sterile-looking on the inside. This simple island restaurant evolved from a roughneck bar that occupied this site during the early 1970s. Lunch is usually devoted to well-prepared burgers, pastas, sandwiches, and salads. Dinners are more substantial, featuring filet mignon, surf and turf (seafood and steak combo), cracked conch, and fried shrimp and fresh fish caught off the Bahamian Long Island. The house drink is a Bacardi splish-splash, containing Bacardi Select, Nassau Royal Liqueur, pineapple juice, cream, and sugar cane syrup.

Poop Deck Dr., off W. Bay St. ℂ 242/327-DECK. Reservations recommended. Main courses $16–$30 (£8.50–£16) lunch, $20–$60 (£11–£32) dinner. AE, DISC, MC, V. Tues–Sat noon–10:30pm; Sun noon–10pm. Bus: 10, or "the Western bus."

Provence ⍟ MEDITERRANEAN The best dishes in Nassau

that feature the sunny cuisine of southern France are showcased within this restaurant that's outfitted in cheerful tones of yellow. Lying near the western terminus of West Bay Street, it's extremely popular with well-heeled local residents (some of whom aren't particularly enchanted with the island's blockbuster casino hotels and their eateries). Decor includes big-windowed views of the sea and oil paintings of landscapes that conjure up the Mediterranean coast. Provence prepares its *cuisine du soleil* with superb simplicity— Atlantic salmon with citrus butter, for example—so as not to mar the natural flavor. Other dishes are heavily spiced, such as the rib-eye steak in a fire-breathing pepper sauce. The chefs also turn out a delightful bouillabaisse evocative of the type served in Marseille. Daily seafood specials are featured—our favorite being the pan-seared sea bass, or else you might order the filet of black grouper. And everybody seems to like the lobster cocktails and the rack of lamb.

Old Town Sandy Port. $\textcircled{C}$ 242/327-0985. Reservations required. Lunch main courses $9–$23 (£4.75–£12); dinner main courses $27–$45 (£14–£24). AE, DISC, MC, V. Mon–Fri 11:30am–3pm and Mon–Sat 6–10:30pm. Bus: 10, or "the Western bus."

WEST OF CABLE BEACH

Travellers Rest 𝒦 *Value* BAHAMIAN/SEAFOOD Set in an isolated spot about 2.5km (1½ miles) west of the megahotels of Cable Beach, this restaurant feels far away from it all. Its owners will make you feel like you're dining on a remote Out Island. Travellers Rest is set in a cozy cement-sided house that stands in a grove of sea-grape and palm trees facing the ocean. Because of its location close to the airport, clients whose departing flights are delayed sometimes opt to "chill out" here until the appointed departures of their flights. The restaurant was established by Winnipeg-born Joan Hannah in 1972 and since then has fed ordinary as well as famous folks like Stevie Wonder, Gladys Knight, spy novelist Robert Ludlum, Julio Iglesias, Eric Clapton, and Rosa Parks. You can dine outside, but if it's rainy (highly unlikely), you can go inside the tavern, with its small bar decorated with local paintings. In this laid-back atmosphere, you can feast on well-prepared grouper fingers, barbecued ribs, curried chicken, steamed or cracked conch, or minced crawfish. Finish with guava cake, the best on the island. The conch salad served on the weekends is said to increase virility in men.

W. Bay St., near Gambier (14km/8¾ miles west of the center of Nassau). $\textcircled{C}$ 242/327-7633. Main courses $12–$28 (£6.35–£15) lunch, $14–$40 (£7.40–£21) dinner. AE, DISC, MC, V. Daily noon–10pm. Bus: 10, or "the Western bus."

5 Beaches, Watersports & Other Outdoor Pursuits

One of the great sports centers of the world, Nassau and the islands that surround it are marvelous places for swimming, sunning, snorkeling, scuba diving, boating, water-skiing, and deep-sea fishing, as well as playing tennis and golf.

You can learn more about available activities by calling **The Bahamas Sports Tourist Office** (© **800/32-SPORT** or 954/236-9292) from anywhere in the continental United States. Call Monday through Friday from 9am to 5pm, Eastern Standard Time (EST). Or write the center at 1200 South Pine Island Rd., Suite 750, Plantation, FL 33324.

HITTING THE BEACH

In the Bahamas, as in Puerto Rico, the issue about public access to beaches is a hot and controversial subject. Recognizing this, the government has made efforts to intersperse public beaches with easy access between more private beaches where access may be impeded. Although megaresorts discourage nonresidents from easy access to their individual beaches, there are so many public beaches on New Providence Island and Paradise Island that all a beach lover has to do is stop his or her car (or else walk) to many of the unmarked, unnamed beaches that flank these islands.

The average visitor will not have a problem with beaches because most people stay in one of the large beachfront resorts where the ocean meets the sand right outside of their doors. For those hoping to explore more of the coast, here are the "no problem, man" beaches—the ones that are absolutely accessible to the public:

Cable Beach 🏖🏖   No particular beach is actually called Cable Beach, yet this is the most popular stretch of sands on New Providence Island. Instead of an actual beach, Cable Beach is the name given to a string of resorts and beaches that lie in the center of New Providence's northern coast, attracting the most visitors. This beachfront offers 6.5km (4 miles) of soft white sand, with many different types of food, restaurants, snack bars, and watersports offered by the hotels lining the waterfront. Calypso music floats to the sand from hotel pool patios where vacationers play musical chairs and see how low they can limbo. Vendors wend their way between sunblock-slathered bodies. Some sell armloads of shell jewelry, T-shirts, beach cover-ups, and fresh coconuts for sipping the sweet "water" straight from the shell. Others offer their hair-braiding services or sign up visitors for water-skiing, jet-skiing, and banana boat rides. Kiosks advertise parasailing, scuba-diving, and snorkeling trips, as well as party cruises to offshore islands. Waters can be rough and reefy, then calm and clear a little farther along the shore. There are no public toilets here because guests of the resorts use their hotel facilities. If you're not a guest of the hotel and not a customer, you are not supposed to use the facilities. Cable Beach resorts begin 4.8km (3 miles) west of downtown Nassau. Even though resorts line much of this long swath of beach, there are various sections where public access is available without crossing through private hotel grounds.

Caves Beach On the north shore, past the Cable Beach hotel properties, Caves Beach is 11km (6¾ miles) southwest of Nassau. It stands near Rock Point, right before the turnoff along Blake Road that leads to the airport. Since visitors often don't know of this place, it's a good spot to escape the hordes. It's also a good beach with soft sands. There are no toilets or changing facilities.

Delaporte Beach Just west of the busiest section of Cable Beach, Delaporte Beach is a public-access beach where you can also escape the crowds. It opens onto clear waters and boasts white sands, although it has neither facilities nor toilets. Nonetheless, it's an option.

Goodman's Bay This public beach lies east of Cable Beach on the way toward the center of Nassau. Goodman's Bay and Saunders Beach (see below) often host local fund-raising cookouts, where vendors sell fish, chicken, conch, peas 'n' rice, or macaroni and cheese. People swim and socialize to blaring reggae and calypso music. To find out when one of these beach parties is happening, ask the staff at your hotel or pick up a local newspaper. A playground is here, along with toilet facilities.

Old Fort Beach ✿ To escape the crowds on weekdays, we often head here, a 15-minute drive west of the Nassau International Airport (take W. Bay St. toward Lyford Cay). This lovely beach opens onto the turquoise waters of Old Fort Bay near the western part of New Providence. The least developed of the island's beaches, it attracts many homeowners from swanky Lyford Cay nearby. In winter, the beach can be quite windy, but in summer it's as calm as the Caribbean Sea.

Saunders Beach East of Cable Beach, this is where many islanders go on the weekends. To reach it, take West Bay Street from Nassau in the direction of Coral Island. This beach lies across from Fort Charlotte, just west of Arawak Cay. Like Goodman's Bay (see above) it often hosts local fund-raising cookouts open to the public. These can be a lot of fun. There are no public facilities.

Western Esplanade   If you're staying at a hotel in downtown Nassau, such as the British Colonial, this one (also known as Junkanoo Beach) is a good beach to patronize close to town. On this narrow strip of sand convenient to Nassau, you'll find toilets, changing facilities, and a snack bar.

BIKING

A half-day bicycle tour with **Bahamas Outdoors Ltd.** (© 242/362-1574 or 242/457-0329; www.bahamasoutdoors.com) can take you on a 5km (3-mile) bike ride along some scenic forest and shoreline trails in the Coral Harbour area on the southwestern coast of New Providence, under the tutelage and with the ongoing commentary of long-time New Providence resident Carolyn Wardle, an expert in the ecology, bird life, and history of the region. The itinerary follows a series of easy trails, usually hard-packed earth, along seashores and through pink forests. Visited en route are sleepy Adelaide Village (settled by freed slaves in the 1830s) and views, with the naked eye or with binoculars, of local birds. Shorts and a T-shirt are the recommended attire, and tours rarely include more than a half-dozen participants at a time; most are morning events that rarely last for more than 4 hours each. The cost for the tour is around $70 (£37) per person. Some of the major hotels on Paradise Beach and Cable Beach rent bikes to their guests. You can bike along Cable Beach or along the beachfront at Paradise Island, but roads through downtown Nassau are too narrow and traffic is too congested to be genuinely pleasant or even particularly safe.

BOAT CRUISES

Cruises from the harbors around New Providence Island are offered by a number of operators, with trips ranging from daytime voyages for snorkeling, picnicking, sunning, and swimming, to sunset and moonlight cruises.

Barefoot Sailing Cruises, Bay Shore Marina, on East Bay Street (© 242/393-0820; www.barefootsailingcruises.com), runs the 41-foot *Wind Dance,* which leaves for all-day cruises from this dock, offering many sailing and snorkeling possibilities. This is your best bet if you're seeking a more romantic cruise and don't want 100 people aboard. The cruises usually stop at Rose Island, a charming, picture-perfect spot with an uncrowded beach and palm trees. You can also sail on a ketch, the 56-foot *Riding High.* Cruise options are plentiful, including a half-day of sailing, snorkeling, and exploring for $65 (£34) per person for a half-day and $99 (£52) for a full day.

A 2-hour sunset cruise, departing between 5pm and 8pm two to three times a week, depending on the season, the weather forecast, and advance bookings, costs $55 (£29) per person.

Flying Cloud, Paradise Island West Dock (© 242/363-4430), is a twin-hulled sailing catamaran carrying 50 people on day and sunset trips. It's a good bet for people who want a more intimate cruise and shy away from the heavy volume carried aboard Majestic Tours catamarans (see below). Snorkeling equipment is provided free. Monday to Saturday half-day charters cost $50 (£27) per person; a 2½-hour sunset cruise goes for $60 (£32). Evening bookings are on Monday, Wednesday, and Friday. A 5-hour cruise leaves on Sunday at 10am and costs $75 (£40) per person.

Majestic Tours Ltd., Hillside Manor (© 242/322-2606), will book 3-hour cruises on two of the biggest catamarans in the Atlantic, offering views of the water, sun, sand, and outlying reefs. This is the biggest and most professionally run of the cruise boats, and it's an affordable option, but we find that there are just too many other passengers aboard. An on-board cash bar keeps the drinks flowing. The *Yellow Bird* is suitable for up to 110 passengers. It departs from Prince George's Dock in downtown Nassau, just behind the tented location of the Straw Market; ask for the exact departure point when you make your reservation. The cost is $25 (£13) per adult, half-price for children under 10 years, and snorkeling equipment is $12 (£6.35) extra. The outfitter has also added another boat, the *Robinson Crusoe,* holding 200 passengers. On Wednesday, Friday, and Sunday, there are cruises from 10am to 4:30pm, costing $50 (£27) for adults and half-price for children 10 and under. Sunset dinner cruises from 7 to 10pm on Tuesday and Friday cost $65 (£34.80) per adult, again half-price for children.

FISHING

May to August are the best months for the oceanic bonito and the blackfin tuna, June and July for blue marlin, and November through February for the wahoo found in reefy areas.

Arrangements can be made at any of the big hotels, but unfortunately, there's a hefty price tag. With equipment included for parties of between two and six, prices usually begin at around $500 (£265) for a half-day and from $1,000 (£530) for a full day's fishing.

One of the most reliable companies, **Born Free Charters** (© 242/393-4144) offers a fleet of three vessels, each between 11m and 14m (35–48 ft.) long, that can seat six comfortably; they can be rented for a half-day ($500–$700/£265–£371) or a full day

($1,000–$1,400/£530–£742). Each additional person is charged $50 (£27). Fishing choices are plentiful: You can troll for wahoo, tuna, and marlin in the deep sea, or cast in the shallows for snapper, grouper, and yellowtail. Anchoring and bottom-fishing are calmer options. We recommend this charter because Born Free offers so many types of fishing and gives you a lot of leeway regarding where you want to fish and how much time you want to spend.

Occasionally, boat owners will configure themselves and their boats as businesses for deep-sea fishing. Unless you're dealing with a genuinely experienced guide, your fishing trip may or may not be a success. John Pratt has emerged over the years as one of the most consistently reliable deep-sea fishermen. He maintains a 14m (45-ft.) fishing boat, making it available for full- or half-day deep-sea fishing excursions. It docks every night at the island's largest marina, the 150-slip **Nassau Yacht Haven,** on East Bay Street (✆ **242/ 393-8173** or 242/422-0364), where a member of the staff will direct you. Alternatively, you can call ✆ **242/422-0364** to speak to Mr. Pratt directly. It takes about 20 minutes of boat travel to reach an offshore point where dolphin and wahoo may or may not be biting, depending on a raft of complicated seasonable factors. These trips need to be booked several weeks in advance.

GOLF

Some of the best golfing in The Bahamas is found in Nassau and on nearby Paradise Island. Although "dormant," or storm-damaged courses, on the extreme western end of New Providence might one day be rejuvenated, at the time of this writing, the only functioning golf course on New Providence Island that was open to nonmembers was the **Cable Beach Golf Course** 𝕽𝕽 on West Bay Street, Cable Beach (✆ **242/327-1741**). An intricately designed 18-hole, 6,453-yard, par-71 championship golf course, it benefited from a major redesign between 2000 and 2003. The makeover reshaped the fairways, repositioned putting greens, and introduced new hazards and water-lined holes throughout two-thirds of its layout. Better year-round playing conditions were ensured by introducing a salt-tolerant grass known as paspalum that is greener, firmer, and more upright, withstanding the salty breezes and tropical heat while providing a premium putting surface. The golf course's alterations were overseen by veteran designer and consultant Fred M. Settle, Jr., of International Golf Design, Inc.

Many of the players who tee off are guests of hotels on Cable Beach. Between November and April, greens fees cost $145 (£77) for guests of Cable Beach hotels, $180 (£95) for people staying any-where else. In the off season (May–Oct), residents of the Cable Beach properties pay $95 (£50); people staying at other venues pay $120 (£64). Greens fees include the use of an electric golf cart.

HORSEBACK RIDING

Happy Trails Stables, Coral Harbour, on the southwest shore (© **242/362-1820;** www.bahamahorse.com), offers a 90-minute horseback trail ride, which is limited to a maximum of eight riders at a time, for $110 (£58). The price includes free transportation to and from your hotel. Riders must weigh less than 91kg (200 lb.). The stables are signposted from the Nassau International Airport, which is 3km (1¾ miles) away. Children must be 12 or older, and reservations are required.

SNORKELING, SCUBA DIVING & UNDERWATER WALKS

There's great snorkeling off most of the beaches on New Providence, especially **Love Beach.** Most hotels and resorts will rent or loan guests snorkeling equipment. Several of the companies mentioned above under "Boat Cruises" also offer snorkel trips, as does Bahamas Divers, below.

Our favorite site for snorkeling is **Goulding Cay,** lying off the western tip of New Providence. Underwater you'll find a field of hard corals, especially the elegant elkhorn. The clear waters here and the shallow coral heads make it ideal for filmmakers. In fact, it's been featured in many films, ranging from a number of James Bond movies to *20,000 Leagues Under the Sea.* More elkhorn coral is found to the south at **Southwest Reef,** which also has stunning star coral in water less than 2.4m (8 ft.) deep. To the north is **Fish Hotel,** which is not much on coral but is graced with large schools of fish, especially red snapper, jacks, and grunts.

There are more dive sites around New Providence than you can see in one visit, so we've included a few of our favorites. **Shark Wall** *꿈꿈* is the most intriguing, which is a diving excursion 16km (10 miles) off the coast; others include the **Rose Island Reefs,** the **Southwest Reef,** the **Razorback,** and **Booby Rock Reef.** Dive out-fitters can also lead you to many old shipwrecks off the coast, along with caves and cliffs. Wrecks include *Mahoney* and *Alcora,* plus the wreck used in the James Bond film *Never Say Never Again.* Divers also explore the airplane propeller used in another Bond film, *Thunderball.* All dive outfitters feature one or more of these sites.

Bahamas Divers, East Bay Street (© **242/393-5644**), has packages that include both a half-day of snorkeling at offshore reefs for $39 (£21) per person and a half-day scuba trip with experienced certified divers, for between $89 (£47) and $109 (£58), depending on the destination. Half-day excursions for certified divers to deeper outlying reefs, drop-offs, and blue holes can be arranged, usually for a fee of $89 (£47) for a two-tank dive and $55 (£29) for a one-tank dive. Novice divers sometimes sign up for a carefully supervised "resort course" which includes instruction with scuba equipment in a swimming pool, followed by a shallow shorefront dive, accompanied with an instructor, for a fee of $89 (£47) per person.

Participants receive free transportation from their hotel to the boats. Children must be 10 or older, and reservations are required, especially during the holiday season.

Stuart Cove's Dive Bahamas, Southwest Bay Street, South Ocean (© **242/362-4171**), is about 10 minutes from top dive sites, including the coral reefs, wrecks, and an underwater airplane structure used in filming James Bond thrillers. For the island's most exciting underwater adventure, divers head to the wreck of the *Caribe Breeze,* depicted in the film *Open Water.* Here the staff feeds reef sharks some 15m (49 ft.) below the water; from a position of safety, divers in full scuba gear can witness the show. Steep sea walls and the Porpoise Pen Reefs (named for Flipper) are also on the diving agenda. A two-tank dive in the morning costs $99 (£52); an all-day program goes for $150 (£80). All prices for boat dives include tanks, weights, and belts. An open-water certification course starts at $950 (£504). Bring along two friends, and the price drops to $490 (£260) per person. Three-hour escorted boat snorkeling trips cost $55 (£29); children under 12 are included for $30 (£16) each. A special feature is a series of shark-dive experiences priced from $145 (£77). At Shark Arena, divers kneel while a dive master feeds the toothsome predators off a long pole. On the Shark Buoy dive at about 9m (30 ft.), sharks swim among the divers while the dive master feeds them.

The outfitter has generated much excitement with its introduction of yellow "submarines," actually jet bikes called Scenic Underwater Bubbles. An air-fed bubble covers your head as these self-contained and battery-powered jet bikes propel you through an underwater wonderland. The subs are popular with nondivers, and they're viewed as safe for kids as well (that is, those older than 12). An underwater armada is escorted along to view the reefs, all for a cost of $110 (£58). The whole experience, from pickup at your hotel or cruise ship to return, takes about 3 hours.

6 Seeing the Sights

Most of Nassau can be explored on foot, beginning at Rawson Square in the center. Here is where Bahamian fishers unload a variety of produce and fish—crates of mangoes, oranges, tomatoes, and limes, plus lots of crimson-lipped conch. To experience this slice of Bahamian life, go any morning Monday through Saturday before noon.

THE TOP ATTRACTIONS

Ardastra Gardens ⊛   The main attraction of the Ardastra Gardens, almost 2 hectares (5 acres) of lush tropical planting about 1.5km (1 mile) west of downtown Nassau near Fort Charlotte, is the parading flock of **pink flamingos.** The Caribbean flamingo, national bird of The Bahamas, had almost disappeared by the early 1940s but was brought back to significant numbers through the efforts of the National Trust. They now flourish in the rookery on Great Inagua. A flock of these exotic feathered creatures has been trained to march in drill formation, responding to the drillmaster's commands with long-legged precision and discipline. The flamingos perform daily at 10:30am, 2:10pm, and 4:10pm.

Other exotic wildlife at the gardens include boa constrictors (very tame), macaws, kinkajous (honey bears) from Central and South America, peacocks and peahens, capuchin monkeys, iguanas, ring-tailed lemurs, red-ruff lemurs, margays, brown-headed tamarins (monkeys), and a crocodile. There are also numerous waterfowl to be seen in Swan Lake, including black swans from Australia and several species of wild ducks. Parrot feedings take place at 11am, 1:30pm, and 3:30pm.

You can get a good look at Ardastra's flora by walking along the signposted paths. Many of the more interesting and exotic trees bear plaques with their names.

Chippingham Rd. ⓒ 242/323-5806. www.ardastra.com. Admission $12 (£6.35) adults, $6 (£3.20) children 4–12, under 4 free. Daily 9am–4:30pm. Bus: 10.

National Art Gallery of The Bahamas ⊛   At long last, this archipelago nation has a showcase to display its talented artists. In a restored 18th-century building in the center of Nassau, the gallery features Bahamian art, which as an entity has existed for only 50 years. Museum curators claim that the present collection is only the nucleus of a long-range strategy to beef up the present number of works. Most of the paintings on exhibit are divided into a historical and a contemporary collection. Pioneering Bahamian artists are honored, as are younger and more modern painters. Among island artists, Amos Ferguson is one of the most acclaimed. See his somewhat naive yet sophisticated technique at its best in the painting *Snowbirds.* He used house paint on cardboard to create a remarkable portrait. Maxwell Taylor and Antonius Roberts are two other heavily featured Bahamian painters.

Villa Doyle, W. Hill St. in downtown Nassau. © 242/328-5800. www.nagb.org.bs. Admission $5 (£2.65) adults, $3 (£1.60) seniors and students, free for children 12 and under. Tues–Sat 10am–4pm. Bus: 10.

Seaworld Explorer ⓐ If you are curious about life below the waves but aren't a strong swimmer, hop aboard this submarine that holds about 45 passengers. Tours last 90 minutes and include 45 to 55 minutes of actual underwater travel at depths of about 3.5m (11 ft.) below the waves. Large windows allow for expansive views of a protected ecology zone offshore from the Paradise Island Airport. About 20 minutes are devoted to an above-water tour of landmarks on either side of the channel that separates Nassau from Paradise Island.

W. Bay St. at Elizabeth Ave. © 242/356-2548. Reservations required. Tours $45 (£24) adults, $23 (£12) children 2–12. Tours Tues, Wed, Fri, and Sat at 11:30am year-round; additional departure at 1:30pm Dec–June. Bus: 10.

MORE ATTRACTIONS

Balcony House The original design of this landmark house transplants late-18th-century Southeast American architecture. The pink two-story structure is named for its overhanging and much-photographed balcony. Restored in the 1990s, the House has been returned to its original design, recapturing a historic period. The mahogany staircase inside was thought to have been salvaged from a wrecked ship in the 1800s. At press time for this edition, the house was closed for renovations but might, by the time of your visit, have reopened. Call to confirm before you go.

Trinity Place and Market St. © 242/302-2621. Free admission, but donation advised. Mon–Wed and Fri 10am–4:30pm; Thurs 10am–1pm. Bus: 10.

Blackbeard's Tower These crumbling remains of a watchtower are said to have been used by the infamous pirate Edward Teach in the 17th century. The ruins are only mildly interesting—there isn't much trace of buccaneering. What's interesting is the view: With a little imagination, you can see Blackbeard peering out from here at unsuspecting ships. Blackbeard also purportedly lived here, but this is hardly well documented.

Yamacraw Hill Rd. (8km/5 miles east of Fort Montagu). No phone. Free admission. Daily 24 hr. Reachable by jitney.

What to See & Do in Nassau

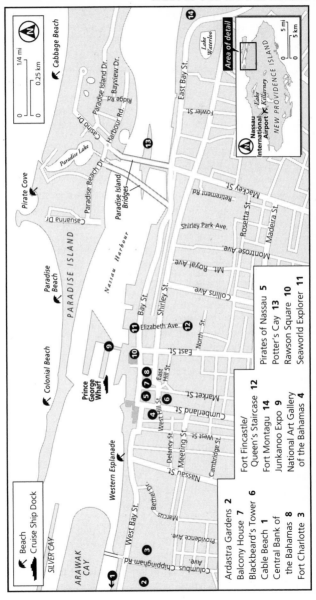

ARAWAK CAY

SILVER CAY

Beach
Cruise Ship Dock

Western Esplanade

Prince George Wharf

Colonial Beach

Nassau Harbour

PARADISE ISLAND

Paradise Beach

Pirate Cove

Paradise Lake

Casuarina Dr.

Paradise Beach Dr.

Paradise Island Bridges

Casino Dr.

Paradise Island Dr.

Ridge Rd.

Bayview Dr.

Harbour Rd.

Cabbage Beach

East Bay St.

Fowler St.

Lake Waterloo

Mackey St.

Retirement Rd.

Shirley Park Ave.

Rosetta St.

Madeira St.

Montrose Ave.

Mt. Royal Ave.

Collins Ave.

Shirley St.

Bay St.

Elizabeth Ave.

North St.

East St.

East Hill St.

Market St.

Cumberland St.

West St.

Meeting St.

Delancy St.

Cambridge St.

Nassau St.

West Bay St.

Bethel Dr.

Marcus

Providence Ave.

Columbus Ave.

Chippingham Rd.

1/4 mi
0.25 km

Area of detail

5 mi
5 km

Nassau International Airport

Lake Killarney

Lake Nassau

NEW PROVIDENCE ISLAND

Fowler St.

Ardastra Gardens **2**
Balcony House **7**
Blackbeard's Tower **6**
Cable Beach **1**
Central Bank of the Bahamas **8**
Fort Charlotte **3**

Fort Fincastle/ Queen's Staircase **12**
Fort Montagu **14**
Junkanoo Expo **9**
National Art Gallery of the Bahamas **4**

Pirates of Nassau **5**
Potter's Cay **13**
Rawson Square **10**
Seaworld Explorer **11**

87

> (*Finds*   **Hanging Out at Potter's Cay**
>
> One of the liveliest places in Nassau during the day is Pot-
> ter's Cay, a native market that thrives beneath the Paradise
> Island Bridge. From the Out Islands, fishing boats and
> heavily laden sloops arrive early in the morning to unload
> the day's catch. Spiny lobster is the most expensive
> seafood, but grouper remains king along with fresh crab,
> jack, mackerel, and other fish.
>
> Conch is arguably the Bahamian's favorite dish, and at
> dozens of stands, you can watch conch being extracted
> from its shell. You'll see chefs eagerly buying the best of
> the day's catch to inspire their menus for the day. You'll
> also find vendors selling freshly harvested vegetables,
> including the fiery hot peppers so beloved by locals, along
> with paw-paws (papaya), stalks of bananas, fresh herbs,
> various root vegetables, tomatoes, and squash along with
> an array of luscious exotic fruits. *Here's a tip:* Many of
> these vendors have a wicked sense of humor and will offer
> you a taste of the tamarind fruit, claiming it's the "sweet-
> est taste on God's earth." Invariably, tricked visitors spit it
> out. The taste is horrendously offensive.
>
> You can also see mail boats leaving and coming to this
> quay. Watching the frenetic departure or arrival of a mail
> boat is one of the more amusing scenes to be viewed on
> New Providence.

Central Bank of The Bahamas   The nerve center that governs
the archipelago's financial transactions is also the venue for a year-
round cycle of temporary exhibitions of paintings that represent the
nation's multifaceted artistic talent. The cornerstone of the building
was laid by Prince Charles on July 9, 1973, when the country
became independent from Britain. Queen Elizabeth II officially
inaugurated the bank in February 1975.

Trinity Place and Frederick St. (© **242/322-2193.** Free admission. Mon–Fri
9:30am–4:30pm. Bus: 10.

Fort Charlotte   Begun in 1787, Fort Charlotte is the largest of
Nassau's three major defenses, built with plenty of dungeons. It used
to command the western harbor. Named after King George III's

consort, it was built by Gov. Lord Dunmore, who was also the last royal governor of New York and Virginia. Its 42 cannons never fired a shot—at least, not at an invader (only seven cannons remain on-site). Within the complex are underground passages, which can be viewed on free tours. Tours at the fort are free, but guides are very happy to accept a tip.

Off W. Bay St. on Chippingham Rd. No phone. Admission $5 (£2.65). Daily 8am–4pm. Bus: 10.

Fort Fincastle   Reached by climbing the Queen's Staircase, this fort was constructed in 1793 by Lord Dunmore, the royal governor. You can take an elevator ride to the top and walk on the observation floor (a 38m-high/125-ft. water tower and lighthouse) for a panoramic view of the harbor. The tower is the highest point on New Providence. The so-called bow of this fort is patterned like a paddle-wheel steamer used on the Mississippi; it was built to defend Nassau against a possible invasion, though no shot was ever fired.

Although the ruins of the fort hardly compete with the view, you can walk around on your own. Be wary, however, of the very persistent young men who will try to show you the way here. They'll try to hustle you, but you really don't need a guide to see some old cannons on your own.

Elizabeth Ave. No phone. Free admission. Mon–Sat 8am–5pm. Bus: 10 or 17.

Fort Montagu   Built in 1741, this fort—the oldest one on the island—stands guard at the eastern entrance to the harbor of Nassau. The Americans captured it in 1776 during the Revolutionary War. Less interesting than Fort Charlotte and Fort Fincastle, the ruins of this place are mainly for fort buffs. Regrettably, this fort can be visited only from the outside, but many visitors find the nearby park, with well-maintained lawns and plenty of shade, more interesting than the fort itself. Vendors often peddle local handicrafts in this park, so you can combine a look at the fort with a shopping expedition, if you like.

Eastern Rd. No regular hours. Bus: 10 or 17.

Junkanoo Expo   This museum is dedicated to Junkanoo—the colorful, musical, and surreal festival that takes place on December 26 when Nassau explodes into sounds, festivities, celebrations, and masks. It is the Bahamian equivalent of the famous Mardi Gras in New Orleans. If you can't visit Nassau for Junkanoo, this exhibition is the next best thing. You can see the lavish costumes and floats which the revelers use during this annual celebration. The bright colors and costume designs are impressive, if for no other reason than the sheer size of the costumes themselves. Some of the costumes are nearly as big as one of the small parade floats, but they are worn and carried by one person. The Expo has been installed in an old customs warehouse at the entrance to the Nassau wharf. The Expo also includes a souvenir boutique with Junkanoo paintings and a variety of Junkanoo handicrafts.

Prince George Wharf, Festival Place. $©$ 242/323-3182. Admission $1 (55p). Mon–Sat 9am–4:30pm. Bus: 10.

Pirates of Nassau *Kids*   This museum, which opened in 2003, celebrates the dubious "golden age of piracy" (1690–1720). Nassau was once a bustling and robust town where buccaneers grew rich from gold and other goods plundered at sea. Known as a paradise for pirates, it attracted various rogues and the wild women who flooded into the port to entertain them—for a price, of course. The museum re-creates those bawdy, lusty days in exhibits illustrating pirate lore. You can walk through the belly of a pirate ship (the *Revenge*) as you hear "pirates" plan their next attack. You can smell the dampness of a dungeon, and you'll even hear the final prayer of an ill-fated victim before he walks the gangplank. It's fairly cheesy but fun for kids. Exhibits also tell the saga of Capt. Woodes Rogers, who was sent by the English crown to suppress pirates in The Bahamas and the Caribbean.

Marlborough and George sts. $©$ 242/356-3759. Admission $12 (£6.35) adults, $6 (£3.20) children 3–17, free for children 2 and under (1 child gets in free). Mon–Sat 9am–6pm; Sun 9am–12:30pm. Bus: 10.

7 Shopping

Today Nassau shopping is more upscale than in decades past. Swanky jewelers and a burgeoning fashion scene have appeared. There are still plenty of T-shirts claiming that "It's Better in The Bahamas," but in contrast, you can also find platinum watches and diamond jewelry.

The range of goods is staggering; in the midst of all the junk souvenirs, you'll find an increasing array of china, crystal, watches, and clothing from such names as Bally, Herend, Lalique, Baccarat, and Ferragamo.

But can you really save money compared to what you would pay stateside? The answer is "yes" on some items, "no" on others. To figure out what's a bargain and what's not, you've got to know the price of everything back in your hometown, turning yourself into a sort of human calculator about prices.

Don't try to bargain with the salespeople in Nassau stores as you would do with merchants at the local market. The price asked in the shops is the price you must pay, but you won't be pressed to make a purchase. The salespeople here are courteous and helpful in most cases.

There are no import duties on 11 categories of luxury goods, including china, crystal, fine linens, jewelry, leather goods, photographic equipment, watches, fragrances, and other merchandise. Antiques, of course, are exempt from import duty worldwide. But even though prices are "duty-free," you can still end up spending more on an item in The Bahamas than you would back in your hometown. It's a tricky situation.

If you're contemplating a major purchase, such as a good Swiss watch or some expensive perfume, it's best to do some research in your local discount outlets or online before making a serious purchase in The Bahamas. While the alleged 30% to 50% discount off stateside prices might apply in some cases, it's not true in others. Certain cameras and electronic equipment, we have discovered, are listed in The Bahamas at, say, 20% or more below the manufacturer's "suggested retail price." That sounds good, except the manufacturer's suggested price might be a lot higher than what you'd pay back home. You aren't getting the discount you think you are. Some shoppers even take along department-store catalogs from the States or print out online buying guides to determine if they are indeed getting a bargain.

A lot of price-fixing seems to be going on in Nassau. For example, a bottle of Chanel is likely to sell for pretty much the same price, regardless of the store.

How much you can take back home depends on your country of origin. For more details, plus Customs requirements for some other countries, refer to "Entry Requirements & Customs," in chapter 2.

The principal shopping areas are **Bay Street** and its side streets downtown, as well as the shops in the arcades of hotels. Not many street numbers are used along Bay Street; just look for store signs.

BRASS & COPPER

Brass and Leather Shop   With two branches on Charlotte Street, this shop offers English brass, handbags, luggage, briefcases, attachés, and personal accessories. Shop no. 2 has handbags, belts, scarves, ties, and small leather goods from such designers as Furla,

Tumi, HCL, and others. If you look and select carefully, you can find some good buys here. 12 Charlotte St., between Bay and Shirley sts. ✆ 242/322-3806.

CRYSTAL, CHINA & GEMS

Solomon's Mines   Evoking the title of a 1950s MGM flick, this is one grand shopping adventure. This flagship store, with many branches, is one of the largest duty-free retailers in either The Bahamas or the Caribbean, a tradition since 1908. Entering the store is like making a shopping trip to London or Paris. The amount of merchandise is staggering, from a $50,000 Patek Philippe watch to one of the largest collections of Herend china in the West. Most retail price tags on watches, china, jewelry, crystal, Herend, Baccarat, Ferragamo, Bally, Lalique, and other names are discounted 15% to 30%—and some of the merchandise and oddities here are not available in the States, such as their stunning collection of African diamonds. The selections of Italian, French, and American fragrances and skin-care products are the best in the archipelago. Bay St. ✆ 242/356-6920. Charlotte and Bay sts. ✆ 242/325-7554.

FASHION

Barry's Limited   One of Nassau's more formal and elegant clothing stores, this shop sells garments made from lamb's wool and English cashmere. Elegant sportswear (including Korean-made guayabera shirts) and blazers are sold here. Most of the clothes are for men, but women often stop in for the stylish cuff links, studs, and other accessories. Bay and George sts. ✆ 242/322-3118.

Bonneville Bones   The name alone will intrigue, but it hardly describes what's inside. This is the best men's store we've found in Nassau. You can find everything here, from standard T-shirts and designer jeans to elegant casual clothing, including suits. Bay St. ✆ 242/328-0804.

Cole's of Nassau   This boutique offers the most extensive selection of designer fashions in Nassau. Women can find everything from swimwear to formal gowns, from sportswear to hosiery. Cole's also sells gift items, sterling-silver designer and costume jewelry, hats, shoes, bags, scarves, and belts. Parliament St. ✆ 242/322-8393.

Fendi   This is Nassau's only outlet for the well-crafted Italian-inspired accessories endorsed by this famous leather-goods company. With handbags, luggage, shoes, watches, wallets, and portfolios to choose from, the selection may well solve some of your gift-giving quandaries. Charlotte St. at Bay St. ✆ 242/322-6300.

HANDBAGS

The Harl Taylor Bag Collection   Housed on the second floor of the same richly historic home that contains (the also-recommended) The White Door restaurant (see "Where to Dine"), this boutique showcases the artfully stylish, and sometimes painfully stylish, handbags of a man who's sometimes referred to as "The Bahamas' leading tastemaker," Harl Taylor. Handbags come as part of two distinctly separate lines: The Beachware Collection, where mostly straw, Bahama-made bags cost from $45 (£24) to $125 (£66) each; and the haute Collection, which focuses on bags (priced at $300–$3,000/£159–£1,590 each) like you've never ever seen carried around by the Queen of England. Open Monday to Saturday 9am to 6pm. 9 West Hill St. ℃ **242/326-5925**.

HANDICRAFTS

Sea Grape Boutique   This is one of the genuinely fine gift shops on New Providence, with an inventory of exotic decorative items that you'll probably find fascinating. It includes jewelry crafted from fossilized coral, sometimes with sharks' teeth embedded inside, and clothing, some of it made from BatikArts.com that's well suited to the sometimes-steamy climate of The Bahamas. There's a second branch of this outfit, Sea Grape Too, in the Radisson Hotel's Mall, on Cable Beach (℃ 242/327-5113). W. Bay St. (next to Travellers Restaurant). ℃ **242/327-1308**.

JEWELRY

Colombian Emeralds   Famous around the Caribbean, this international outlet is not limited to emeralds, although its selection of that stone is the best in The Bahamas. You'll find an impressive display of diamonds, as well as other precious gems. The gold jewelry here sells for about half the price it does Stateside, and many of the gems are discounted 20% to 30%. Ask about their "cybershopping" program. Bay St. ℃ **242/326-1661**.

John Bull   The jewelry department here offers classic selections from Tiffany & Co.; cultured pearls from Mikimoto; the creations of David Yurman, Carrera y Carrera; Greek and Roman coin jewelry; and Spanish gold and silver pieces. It's the best name in the business. The store also features a wide selection of watches, cameras, perfumes, cosmetics, leather goods, and accessories. It is one of the best places in The Bahamas to buy a Gucci or Cartier watch. Bay St. ℃ **242/322-4253**.

LEATHER

In addition to the stores mentioned below, another good store for leather goods is the **Brass and Leather Shop,** described under "Brass & Copper," above.

Gucci   This shop, opposite Rawson Square, is the best place to buy leather goods in Nassau. The wide selection includes handbags, wallets, luggage, briefcases, gift items, scarves, ties, evening wear for men and women, umbrellas, shoes, sandals, watches, and perfume, all by Gucci of Italy. Saffrey Sq., Bay St., corner of Bank Lane. ℂ **242/325-0561.**

Leather Masters   This well-known retail outlet carries an internationally known collection of leather bags, luggage, and accessories by Ted Lapidus, Lanvin, and Lancel of Paris; Etienne Aigner of Germany; and i Santi of Italy. Leather Masters also carries luggage by Piel and Travel Pro; leather wallets by Bosca; and pens, cigarette lighters, and watches by Colibri. Silk scarves, neckties, and cigar accessories are also featured. 8 Parliament St. ℂ **242/322-7597.**

LINENS

The Linen Shop   This is the best outlet for linens in Nassau. It sells beautifully embroidered bed linens, Irish handkerchiefs, and tablecloths. Look also for the most exquisite children's clothing and christening gowns in town. In the Ironmongery Building, Bay St., near Charlotte St. ℂ **242/322-4266.**

MAPS

Balmain Antiques   This place offers a wide and varied assortment of 19th-century etchings, engravings, and maps, many of them antique and all reasonably priced. Other outlets have minor displays of these collectibles, but this outlet has the finest. Some items are 400 years old. It's usually best to discuss your interests with Mr. Ramsey, the owner, so he can direct you to the proper drawers. His specialties include The Bahamas, America during the Civil War, and Black history. He also has a collection of military historical items. The shop now features Haitian primitive art. You'll find the shop on the second floor, three doors east of Charlotte Street. In the Mason's Building, Bay St., near Charlotte St. ℂ **242/323-7421.**

MARKETS

The **Nassau International Bazaar** consists of some 30 shops selling international goods in a new arcade. A pleasant place for browsing, the $1.8-million complex sells goods from around the globe. The bazaar runs from Bay Street down to the waterfront (near the Prince

George Wharf). With cobbled alleyways and garreted storefronts, the area looks like a European village.

Prince George Plaza, Bay Street, is popular with cruise-ship passengers. Many fine shops (Gucci, for example) are found here. When you get tired of shopping, you can dine at the open-air rooftop restaurant that overlooks Bay Street.

PERFUMES & COSMETICS

Nassau has several good perfume outlets, notably **John Bull** and **Little Switzerland,** which also stock a lot of nonperfume merchandise.

The Beauty Spot The largest cosmetic shop in The Bahamas, this outlet sells duty-free cosmetics by Lancôme, Chanel, YSL, Elizabeth Arden, Estée Lauder, Clinique, Christian Dior, and Biotherm, among others. It also operates facial salons. Bay and Frederick sts. ℭ 242/322-5930.

The Perfume Bar This little gem has exclusive rights to market Boucheron, and it also stocks the Clarins line (though not exclusively). Bay St. ℭ 242/322-7216.

The Perfume Shop In the heart of Nassau, within walking distance of the cruise ships, the Perfume Shop offers duty-free savings on world-famous perfumes. Women can treat themselves to a flacon of Eternity or Chanel. For men, the selection includes Drakkar Noir, Polo, and Obsession. Corner of Bay and Frederick sts. ℭ 242/322-2375.

8 New Providence After Dark

Gone are the days when tuxedo-clad gentlemen and elegantly gowned ladies drank and danced the night away at such famous nightclubs as the Yellow Bird and the Big Bamboo. You can still find dancing, along with limbo and calypso, but for most visitors, the major attraction is gambling.

Cultural entertainment in Nassau is limited, however. The chief center for this is the **Dundas Center for the Performing Arts,** which sometimes stages ballets, plays, or musicals. Call ℭ 242/393-3728 to see if a production is planned during your visit.

ROLLING THE DICE

As another option, you can easily head over to Paradise Island and drop into the massive, spectacular casino in the Atlantis resort. See chapter 4.

Wyndham Nassau Resort & Crystal Palace Casino This dazzling casino, radically upgraded and refined during 2007, is the only one on New Providence Island and is now run by the Wyndham Nassau Resort. During the lifetime of this edition, the gaming establishment will fall under the orbit of the new Baha Mar development group, which plans big and imaginative things for it through 2008. Thanks to constant and ongoing improvements, and the willingness of its management to restock it with some of the world's most up-to-date casino games and slot machines, it stacks up well against the major casinos of the Caribbean. Incorporating more than 3,252 sq. m (35,004 sq. ft.) into its flashy-looking premises, it's animated, bustling, and filled with the serious business of people having fun with their money and their temptations. The gaming room features hundreds of slot machines—only a few of which resemble the low-tech one-armed bandits that were in vogue 20 years ago. You'll also find blackjack tables, roulette wheels, craps tables, a baccarat table, and a hypersophisticated electronic link to Las Vegas that provides gaming odds on most of the major sporting events in the world. There's also a genuine commitment to poker, which management here defines as one of the fastest-growing and most passionate gaming sports of the millennium. W. Bay St., Cable Beach. © 242/327-6200.

THE CLUB & MUSIC SCENE

Club Fluid Set within a two-story building in downtown Nassau, this basement-level nightclub features a baby-blue-and-white interior, dozens of mirrors that are much appreciated by narcissists, two bars, and a dance floor. It attracts an animated crowd of local residents, most of them between 20 and 45, who appreciate the reggae, soca, hip-hop, and R&B music. It's open Wednesday to Saturday from 9pm to 2am. W. Bay St., near the corner of Frederick St. © 242/356-4691. Cover $12–$20 (£6.35–£11).

Rain Forest Theater Accessible directly from the Crystal Palace Casino on Cable Beach, this 800-seat theater is a major nightlife attraction. Revues tend to be small-scale, relatively restrained, and very definitely on the safe and "family-friendly" side of the great cultural divide. Fake palm trees on each side and touches of glitter set the scene for the on-stage entertainment. Hours vary with the season, the act, and the number of guests in the hotel at the time. Billboards located prominently throughout the hotel will hawk whoever is headlining at the moment. At press time for this edition, it was Jambalaya, a Caribbean/West African dance troupe, which showed tremendous verve and style. In the Crystal Palace Casino, W. Bay St., Cable Beach. © 242/327-6200. Entrance $30–$35 (£16–£19) per person. Drinks are extra.

THE BAR SCENE

Charlie's on the Beach/Cocktails 7 Dreams   The focus within this sparsely decorated club is local gossip, calypso and reggae music, and stiff drinks, all of which translates to a high-energy night out in Nassau. The setting is a simple warehouselike structure a few blocks west of the British Colonial Hilton, though management warns that during some particularly active weekends (including spring break), the entire venue might move, short term, to a larger and as yet undetermined location. Open only Wednesday and Friday to Sunday 9pm to 4am. W. Bay St. near Long Wharf Beach. ℭ 242/328-3745. Cover $10–$20 (£5.30–£11).

Señor Frog's   How can you hate a bar, restaurant, cafe, and taco joint that manages to satirize itself as richly as this one does? The interior is deliberately and somewhat claustrophobically over-crowded with references to Latino music, frogs, faux palm trees, and battered wooden tables that have hosted all kinds of food and bev-erage service—from midday salsa and chips to "Let's sample all of the best margaritas available on this menu" contests. Expect merengue music (especially on weekends, when tables are pushed aside to form an ersatz dance floor) and a menu loaded with burg-ers, fajitas, and tacos. W. Bay St., near the British Colonial Hilton. Snacks and platters $5–$15 (£2.65–£7.95). ℭ 242/323-1777.

4

Paradise Island

Located just 180m (590 ft.) off the north shore of Nassau, Paradise Island is a favorite vacation spot for East Coast Americans who flee their icy winters for the stunning white sands of Paradise Beach. In addition to its gorgeous strands, the island boasts beautiful foliage, including brilliant red hibiscus and a grove of casuarina trees sweeping down to form a tropical arcade.

Now the priciest piece of real estate in The Bahamas, this island once served as a farm for Nassau and was known as Hog Island. Purchased for $294 by William Sayle in the 17th century, it cost A&P grocery-chain heir Huntington Hartford $11 million in 1960. He decided to rename the 6.5km-long (4-mile) sliver of land Paradise before selling out his interests. Long a retreat for millionaires, the island experienced a massive building boom in the 1980s. Its old Bahamian charm is now gone forever, lost to the high-rises, condos, second homes of the wintering wealthy, and gambling casino that have taken over. The centerpiece of Paradise Island is the mammoth Atlantis Paradise Island Resort & Casino, which has become a nightlife mecca and a sightseeing attraction in its own right.

For those who want top hotels, casino action, Vegas-type revues, fabulous beaches, and a posh address, Paradise Island is the place. It's now sleeker and more upscale than Cable Beach, its closest rival, and Freeport/Lucaya. True, Paradise Island is overbuilt and overly commercialized, but its natural beauty still makes it a choice vacation spot, perfect for a quick 3- or 4-day getaway.

Paradise Island is treated as a separate entity in this guide, but it is actually part of New Providence, connected by a bridge. You can travel between the two on foot, by boat, or by car. It's easy to stay in Nassau or Cable Beach and come over to enjoy the beaches, restaurants, attractions, and casino on Paradise Island. You can also stay on Paradise Island and head over into Nassau for a day of sightseeing and shopping. So view this section as a companion to chapter 3. Refer to "Fast Facts: New Providence" on p. 50 for transportation details, nearby sights, and a wider array of sports and recreation choices.

1 Orientation

ARRIVING

Most visitors to Paradise Island arrive in Nassau and commute to Paradise Island by ground transport.

When you arrive at the Lynden Pindling International Airport (also known as the **Nassau International Airport;** see chapter 3 for information on flying into Nassau), you won't find bus service to take you to Paradise Island. Many package deals will provide hotel transfers from the airport. Otherwise, if you're not renting a car, you'll need to take a taxi. Taxis in Nassau are metered and take cash only, no credit cards. It will usually cost you $30 (£16) to go by cab from the airport to your hotel. The driver will also ask you to pay the northbound one-way $1 (55p) bridge toll (this charge will be added onto your metered fare at the end).

VISITOR INFORMATION

Paradise Island does not have a tourist office, so refer to the tourist facilities in downtown Nassau (see "Orientation," at the beginning of chapter 3). The concierge or the guest services staff at your hotel can also give you information about the local attractions.

ISLAND LAYOUT

Paradise Island's finest beaches lie on the Atlantic (northern) coastline; the docks, wharves, and marinas are located on the southern side. Most of the island's largest and glossiest hotels and restaurants, as well as the casino and a lagoon with landscaped borders, lie west and north of the roundabout. The area east of the roundabout is less congested, with only a handful of smaller hotels, a golf course, the Versailles Gardens, the cloister, the airport, and many of the island's privately owned villas.

2 Getting Around

You don't need to rent a car. Most visitors walk around Paradise Island's most densely developed sections and hire a taxi for the occasional longer haul. For information on renting a car, refer to "By Rental Car," on p. 30 in chapter 2.

The most popular way to reach nearby Nassau is to **walk across the toll bridge.** There is no charge for pedestrians.

If you want to tour Paradise Island or New Providence by **taxi,** you can make arrangements with either the taxi driver or the hotel reception desk. Taxis wait at the entrances to all the major hotels. The hourly rate is about $60 (£32) in cars or small vans.

If you are without a car and don't want to take a taxi or walk, you can take a **ferry to Nassau.** The ferry to Nassau leaves from the dock on Casino Drive every half-hour, and the 10-minute ride costs $3 (£1.60) one-way. Quicker and easier than a taxi, the ferry deposits you right at Prince George Wharf, in downtown Nassau Bay Street. Daily service is from 9am to 6pm.

Water taxis also operate between Paradise Island and Prince George Wharf in Nassau. They depart daily from 8:30am to 6pm at 20-minute intervals. Round-trip fare is $6 (£3.20) per person.

If you are a guest at one of the properties associated with Atlantis Paradise Island Resort & Casino, you can hop aboard one of the complimentary shuttle buses for drop-offs at any of the hotel accommodations within the Atlantis Resort. They depart from the Lynden Pindling International Airport at 30-minute intervals every day between 7am and 11pm, costing $6 (£3.20) per person round trip. Guests can also take a complimentary tour of the island, leaving daily at noon.

Unlike New Providence, no public buses are allowed on Paradise Island.

3 Where to Stay

In the off season (mid-Apr to mid-Dec), prices are slashed by at least 20%—and perhaps a lot more, though the weather isn't as ideal. But because Paradise Island's summer business has increased dramatically, you'll never see some of the 60% reductions that you might find at a cheaper property in the Greater Nassau area. Paradise Island doesn't have to lower its rates to attract summer business. For inexpensive accommodations, refer to the recommendations on New Providence Island (see chapter 3). Paradise Island isn't cheap!

VERY EXPENSIVE

Atlantis Paradise Island Resort & Casino ✦✦✦ *Kids*   This creatively designed megaresort, the biggest in The Bahamas, functions as a vacation destination and theme park in its own right. A blockbuster in every sense of the word, it contains the most creative interiors, the most intriguing aesthetics, and the most elaborate waterscapes of any hotel in the country. It's the most recent incarnation of a resort that originated early in the days of Paradise Island tourism, passing through rocky and sometimes less glamorous days before reaching its startling newest incarnation as a destination that appeals to adults (its gambling facilities are the largest in The Bahamas) and to ecologists (its focus on the protection of marine life adds a welcome dose of "save the planet" to an otherwise relent-lessly consumerist theme). And it exerts a potent lure for children, and the child that remains within many of us, thanks to its evocation of a "Lost Continent" whose replicated ruins evoke—you guessed it—Atlantis.

But whereas the newest of its buildings manage to conjure thoughts of both science fiction and ancient mythology at the same time (no easy feat), its older buildings still retain a whiff of the old Resorts International and Merv Griffin days of the 1980s. But thanks to skillful landscaping and the presence on-site of miles of canals whose currents carry swimmers with flotation devices on meandering runs down mythical rivers, no one seems to notice. The entire sprawling compound opens onto a long stretch of white-sand beach with a sheltered marina. Think Vegas in the Tropics, with a mythological theme and an interconnected series of lagoons, lakes, rivers, waterfalls, and water tubes thrown in, and you'll get the picture. One advantage to the place is that there's a lot of visual dis-traction and high-energy, upbeat stimulation; the downside is that it's sprawling, impersonal, and at times downright bureaucratic, and the service from the sometimes bored staff just can't keep up with the number of guests here.

Overall, however, it's an appropriate choice for a (rather expen-sive) family vacation, since the price of the resort includes direct access to endless numbers of watery gimmicks. Children's programs are widely comprehensive and well choreographed, and many par-ents simply turn their kids loose for a day onto the extensive grounds and the dozens of inland canals and water tunnels criss-crossing the flat and sand terrain on which the resorts sits, with the understanding that a battalion of lifeguards and supervisors keep the show rolling and the safety levels up to par. Singles and young cou-ples who want a lot of razzle-dazzle appreciate the place, too, though some people find it over-the-top, too expensive, and too firmly mired in the limitations of its own "lost continent" theme.

Much of the look of the place derives from its ownership by Kerzner International, a global investment company that originated in South Africa. Atlantis offers so many sports, dining, and enter-tainment options that many guests never venture off the property during their entire vacation. It's expensive, but for your money, you'll find yourself neck-deep amid many of the diversions you might have otherwise expected from a theme park. And if you opt for accommodations in one of the resort's less plush accommoda-tions, especially within the Beach Tower of the Atlantis's main core,

Where to Stay & Dine in Paradise Island

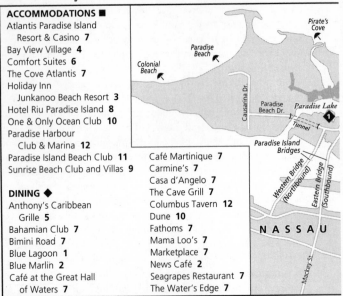

ACCOMMODATIONS ■

Atlantis Paradise Island
   Resort & Casino **7**
Bay View Village **4**
Comfort Suites **6**
The Cove Atlantis **7**
Holiday Inn
   Junkanoo Beach Resort **3**
Hotel Riu Paradise Island **8**
One & Only Ocean Club **10**
Paradise Harbour
   Club & Marina **12**
Paradise Island Beach Club **11**
Sunrise Beach Club and Villas **9**

DINING ◆

Anthony's Caribbean
   Grille **7**
Bahamian Club **7**
Bimini Road **7**
Blue Lagoon **1**
Blue Marlin **2**
Café at the Great Hall
   of Waters **7**
Café Martinique **7**
Carmine's **7**
Casa d'Angelo **7**
The Cave Grill **7**
Columbus Tavern **12**
Dune **10**
Fathoms **7**
Mama Loo's **7**
Marketplace **7**
News Café **2**
Seagrapes Restaurant **7**
The Water's Edge **7**

the cost bite won't seem quite as severe. Accommodations within The Atlantis Resort retain distinctly different levels of opulence, for the most part based on where they're located. The most opulent and most expensive accommodations lie in semisecluded annexes whose facilities are not open to the general hotel population of Atlantis. They include The One&Only Ocean Club and The Cove, a 600-unit all-suite hotel-within-the-hotel, which opened in 2007. Both of those pockets of heightened posh were conceived and designed as separate and semi-independent components within the Greater Atlantis, and each is described in separate recommendations below.

As this resort has expanded, accommodations within the central core of the Atlantis megacompound are emerging as the less expensive accommodations within the resort. And of those accommodations, the most plush lie within the Royal Towers—the tallest and most imaginative building in The Bahamas. You'll get the feeling that an army of designers labored long and hard over the interior decors, replete as they are with decorative replicas of sea horses, winged dragons, and megasize conch shells sprouting from cornices and rooflines. (Rooms in the Royal Towers' Imperial Club have a personal concierge and upgraded amenities.) The most deluxe

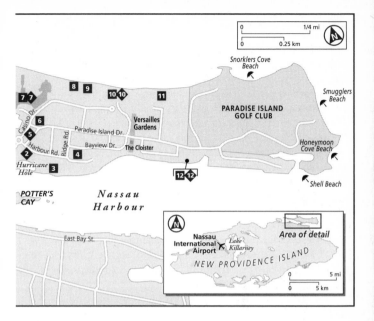

accommodation anywhere within the Atlantis fiefdom is the Bridge Suite, an architectural oddity that links, several stories above ground level, the two spires of the Royal Towers. It rents for $25,000 (£13,250) a day and during its celebrated history was occupied by Michael Jordan during his involvement with tournaments at the on-site golf course.

The casino and entertainment complex lie in an area over the watery depths of a lagoon. Less posh and less plush are rooms within the Coral Tower, and least expensive of the entire lot are accommodations within the still-serviceable but older Beach Tower, with a floor plan shaped like an airplane propeller, from the dimly remembered 1980s. But even in the older, least expensive sections, accommodations are comfortable and well accessorized, and available with the full understanding that occupants get full access to the sprawling water parks that are otherwise accessible only on a limited basis to nonresidents. Most units sport a balcony or terrace with water views, individually controlled air-conditioning, in-room movies, and voice mail and modem access, plus roomy bathrooms with tubs and showers.

Any old hotel might sport tropical gardens, but the Atlantis goes one better by featuring the world's largest collection of outdoor open-air marine habitats, each of them aesthetically stunning. A few of these were conceived for snorkelers and swimmers, but most were designed so guests could observe the marine life from catwalks above and from glassed-in underwater viewing tunnels. Even folks who don't stay here, including thousands of cruise-ship passengers, can take part in tightly orchestrated tours. These jaunts include 11 different exhibition lagoons, containing millions of gallons of water and at least 200 species of tropical fish. On-site marine habitats include a separate lagoon for sharks, for dolphins, and for stingrays, respectively, and individual habitats for lobsters, piranhas, and underwater exotica. Swimmers can meander along an underwater snorkeling trail (Paradise Lagoon) and explore a five-story replica of an ancient ziggurat-shaped Mayan temple. The temple's sides incorporate a waterslide with slippery, wet, and wild runs that feature an 18m (59-ft.) nearly vertical drop. Participants emerge from the sculpted mouths of giant Mayan gods like human sacrifices as they race giddily down the course of the waterslide.

In 2007, additional water features known collectively as Aquaventure were added to the layout, bringing the number of hectares devoted to water features at Atlantis to 39 (97 acres). The most visible monument within Aquaventure is a mythical-looking building, the Power Tower, site of another set of waterslides more imaginative even than those within the above-noted Mayan temple, each skillfully landscaped into the surrounding vegetation. Aquaventure, its labyrinth of meandering streams and waterfalls, is accessible, without charge, for residents of any of the accommodations within the Atlantis complex but otherwise is strictly off-limits to the general public.

One major entertainment venue within the Paradise Island layout includes the Marina Village. It was inspired by an old Bahamian harborfront in "the good old days" with a string of clapboard-sided houses (think historic Key West, Florida, but with a lot more money). Flanking a marina that draws some of the most spectacular yachts in the world, it's a self-enclosed venue, within the orbit of Atlantis, for dozens of shops, bars, and restaurants, replete with gazebos and live musicians. Along with the casino and an arcade of shops, it is one of the areas open to the general public: The water park and many of the grounds surrounding this place are strictly reserved only for hotel guests of the resort.

Tips Wandering Through "The Lost Continent"

Regrettably for casual walk-through visitors, the marine habitats, gardens, and other attractions here are open only to guests at the Atlantis Resort, or to nonguests who sign up for a guided tour of the resort. The cost of this "Discover Atlantis" tour is $29 (£15) per person, with children under 12 getting in for half-price. For information on participating in one of these guided tours, call the Atlantis Resort (✆ 242/363-3000).

If you want to visit Atlantis on your own the general public has unrestricted access to the casino, the nightclubs, the shopping arcade, and the shops and restaurants of Marina Village. But access to Aquaventure, the waterslides, and most of the waterscapes is strictly off-limits to nonresidents.

The focal point of this extravagance is the massive **Paradise Island Casino,** the best-designed and—at the time of this writing—most imaginatively conceived casino in The Bahamas. The casino alone contains four separate bars and two separate restaurants. Within the diverse and scattered elements of this extended resort, you'll find around 38 separate food and beverage outlets, some of which open, close, and are reconfigured at occasionally dizzying rates. (For detailed descriptions of the most intriguing, see "Where to Dine" and "Paradise Island After Dark," later in this chapter.) None of them comes cheap: You should expect to pay a lot to dine or drink in most of them.

Casino Dr. (P.O. Box N-4777), Paradise Island, The Bahamas. ✆ **800/ATLANTIS** in the U.S., or 242/363-3000. Fax 242/363-6300. www.atlantis.com. 2,900 units. Winter $420–$785 (£223–£416) double; from $940 (£498) suite. Off-season $380–$715 (£201–£379) double; from $715 (£379) suite. Package deals available. AE, DC, DISC, MC, V. Self-parking $12 (£6.35) per day, valet parking $14 (£7.40) per day. **Amenities:** 20 restaurants within the Atlantis subsection of the resort; 18 lounges and clubs; 17 outdoor pools interspersed with 39 hectares/97 acres of waterscape; golf course; 5 tennis courts; health club; spa; sauna; watersports equipment/rentals; children's programs (ages 4–12); salon; room service; massage; babysitting; laundry service; dry cleaning; nonsmoking rooms; rooms for those w/limited mobility. *In room:* A/C, TV, minibar, hair dryer, iron, safe, in-room fridge available for $15 per day.

The Cove Atlantis ✦✦✦ Housed within a handsome, newly built turquoise-and-coral-colored tower whose fanciful detailing matches the mythical theme of the other showcase designs of the Atlantis Resort, this hotel was configured as a semiprivate hideaway.

Don't expect anything conventional about this place: It contains only suites and an adult-oriented venue that takes pains to dilute a growing perception that The Atlantis has placed too heavy an emphasis on family fun, hordes of short-term cruise-ship passengers, and the ongoing daycare and amusement of teeny-boppers from the North American mainland. Inaugurated in the spring of 2007, it boasts an avant-garde design that's a combination of the best of minimalist Japan and ultra-high-end postmodern Florida. Every accommodation is luxurious, some of presidential proportions (including a duplex with a total of more than 372 sq. m/4,000 sq. ft.), with personal butlers and every imaginable electronic and service-related amenity. Most of the units, however, are spacious but not obscenely oversized, ranging in square footage from 62 to 158m (672–1,700 sq. ft.), and each manages to be opulent, postmodern, summery, and tasteful. The social centerpiece of the hotel is a 2,700m (9,000-ft.) rectangular "ultrapool" which is strictly off-limits to anyone under 18. It is ringed with 22 private cabanas, which can be rented by the day for sybaritic adults seeking seclusion from the family-with-children crowds. On the premises is the Mandara Spa, whose design was inspired by the architecture of Bali, with rampant use of stone, bamboo, and tropical hardwoods. Although it hadn't opened before press time for this edition, a branch of Bobby Flay's Mesa Grill had carved out space for itself on the ground floor of this hotel-within-a hotel.

Casino Dr. (P.O. Box N-4777), Paradise Island, The Bahamas. ⓒ **800/ATLANTIS** in the U.S., or 242/363-3000. Fax 242/363-6300. www.atlantis.com. 600 suites. Winter $735–$1,510 (£390–£800) suite; off-season $625–$1,415 (£331–£750) suite. **Amenities:** 2 restaurants; 2 bars; 3 pools; access to an 18-hole golf course; access to 5 tennis courts; health club; spa; steam room; shuttle to the One&Only Ocean Club; access to the Atlantis casino; room service; babysitting; laundry service; dry cleaning; nonsmoking rooms. *In room:* A/C, TV, minibar, hair dryer, iron, safe, butler service.

One&Only Ocean Club 🏆🏆🏆   Tranquil, secluded, and intimate, this is the most exclusive address on Paradise Island, with sky-high prices that match the refined ambience and pampering service (the best in The Bahamas). Although it's owned by the same entity that controls the much larger Atlantis Resort nearby, huge efforts are expended to separate it from the clients at the less personalized, more family-friendly, theme-oriented Atlantis. In fact, although the facilities of the Atlantis are open and available to the residents of the One&Only Ocean Club, that same privilege does not extend in the opposite direction. As such, you'll find a boutique-style hotel with a highly visible security force that, to a large degree, is cloistered from the larger and much splashier "upscale mass market" venue nearby. This is one of the best-developed tennis resorts in The Bahamas, and the white-sand beach adjacent to the hotel is the finest in the Nassau/Paradise Island area.

The spacious and elegantly furnished rooms are plushly comfortable, with king-size beds, gilt-framed mirrors, and dark-wood armoires. The marble bathrooms in the suites are massive, and each contains a bidet, twin basins, and both a tub and a shower.

The real heart and soul of the resort lies in the surrounding gardens, which were designed by the island's former owner, Huntington Hartford II, heir to the A&P grocery fortune. This resort, in fact, was once the site of his private home. Formal gardens surround a rebuilt medieval French cloister set on 14 hectares (35 acres) of manicured lawns. (Bought by newspaper mogul William Randolph Hearst during one of his trips through France and later sold to Huntington Hartford, it was disassembled and rebuilt on this site as part of a major drama that's more fully explained later within this chapter.) The graceful 12th-century arcades of the cloister are visible at the crest of a hill, across a stretch of terraced waterfalls, fountains, a stone gazebo, and rose gardens. Larger-than-life statues dot the vine-covered niches on either side of the gardens. Begin your tour of the gardens at the large swimming pool, which feeds a series of reflecting pools that stretch out toward the cloister. A new addition is the child-friendly family pool, replete with aqua toys and a waterfall.

Arguably the best dining on Paradise Island can be found at the resort's Dune restaurant, creation of culinary legend Jean-Georges Vongerichten. See "Where to Dine," later in this chapter, for a review.

Ocean Club Dr. (P.O. Box N-4777), Paradise Island, The Bahamas. ② **800/321-3000** in the U.S., or 242/363-2501. Fax 242/363-2424. www.oneandonlyresorts.com. 106 units, 3 private villas. Winter $750–$1,250 (£398–£663) double; from $1,330 (£705) suite; from $7,500 (£3,975) villa. Off-season $490–$1,190 (£260–£631) double; from $805 (£427) suite; from $7,000 (£3,710) villa. AE, MC, V. Free parking. **Amenities:** 2 restaurants; 3 bars; 2 pools; 18-hole golf course; 6 tennis courts; health club; spa; steam room; shuttle to Atlantis casino; room service; babysitting; laundry service; dry cleaning; nonsmoking rooms. *In room:* A/C, TV, kitchenette (in some), minibar, hair dryer, iron, safe, butler service.

EXPENSIVE

Holiday Inn Junkanoo Beach Resort ⟨☆⟩ ⟨Kids⟩   This older 12-floor property adjacent to the waters of Nassau Harbour opens onto a marina with very little beach but a good-size swimming pool. It was rescued from oblivion in the late 1990s when a Florida-based investment group, Driftwood Ventures, renovated it. This group turned it into an all-inclusive resort, which lies just a short stroll away from the popular Atlantis and all its attractions. Bedrooms are midsize with twin or king-size beds, plus well-maintained bathrooms with tub/showers. The decor is comfortable, airy, and sunny, and outfitted with tropically inspired colors and upholstery. All third-floor rooms and select units on the fourth floor are designated for nonsmokers only. The food served at the restaurants is palatable but needs much improvement, and service is very slow, so be duly warned. However, there are nightly live shows to spice up the lackluster meal offerings, including fire dancing and Bahamian bands.

Harbour Dr. (P.O. Box SS-6249), Paradise Island, The Bahamas. ⓒ **800/HOLIDAY** in the U.S., or 242/363-2561. Fax 242/363-3803. www.paradiseislandbahama.com. 246 units. Winter $303–$413 (£161–£219) double; $520 (£276) suite; off season $238–$388 (£126–£206) double, $470 (£249) suite. Rates are all-inclusive. AE, DC, DISC, MC, V. **Amenities:** 3 restaurants; 2 bars; pool; 2 tennis courts; health club; Jacuzzi; watersports equipment/rentals; children's programs; car rental; massage; nonsmoking rooms; rooms for those w/limited mobility. *In room:* A/C, TV, fridge, beverage maker, hair dryer, iron, safe.

Hotel Riu Paradise Island ⓚ *Kids*

Opening onto a 5km (3-mile) stretch of beach, this is the newest addition to the beachfront. In December 2004, the Riu Hotels chain refurbished the old Sheraton Grand here into an all-inclusive megaresort. Renovations included enlarging the pool, adding a restaurant, and generally enhancing rooms. This 14-story ecru-colored high-rise offers some of the most comfortably appointed bedrooms on Paradise Island. It's more understated than the Atlantis, a lot cheaper, and more user-friendly and manageable in terms of size and layout. Your kids would be happier with all the spectacular events at the Atlantis, but the Riu is a viable runner-up for the family trade. Guests can leave the shelter of the poolside terrace and settle almost immediately onto one of the waterside chaise longues at the beach. The hotel is within walking distance of the casino, restaurants, and nightlife facilities of the Atlantis Paradise Island Resort & Casino properties.

Welcoming drinks are served while you relax on comfortable chairs in the lobby bar amid palm trees and tropical foliage. All the spacious accommodations here are deluxe and tastefully decorated, and equipped with medium-size bathrooms containing tub/showers. Many have spacious balconies that afford sweeping water views or luxurious terraces.

For an extra charge, you can skip the all-inclusive dinner fare and dine at Tengoku, a Japanese-themed restaurant. Other choices available to jaded buffet-goers include Atlantic Restaurant, serving some of Paradise Island's finest steaks and featuring a nonsmoking section, plus a terrace; and Sir Alexander, which is Riu's gourmet a la carte restaurant, featuring highly refined, mainly continental gourmet cuisine with first-rate ingredients. Live entertainment is available 6 nights a week.

6307 Casino Dr. (P.O. Box SS-6307), Paradise Island, The Bahamas. ℂ **888/666-8816** in the U.S., or 242/363-3500. Fax 242/363-3900. www.riu.com. 379 units. Winter $438–$454 (£232–£241) double, from $522 (£277) suite; off season $424–$444 (£225–£235) double, from $484 (£257) suite. Rates are all-inclusive. AE, MC, V. **Amenities:** 3 restaurants; 2 bars; pool; 4 tennis courts; gym; spa; Jacuzzi; sauna; kids' club; watersports equipment; salon; room service; massage; babysitting; laundry service; dry cleaning; nonsmoking rooms; rooms for those w/limited mobility. *In room:* A/C, TV, minibar, hair dryer, safe, ceiling fan.

Paradise Island Beach Club ℛ   This two- and three-story time-share complex is set near the eastern tip of Paradise Island, adjacent to a relatively isolated strip of spectacular beachfront. Managed by Marriott, it's more of a self-catering condo complex than a full-fledged resort. Many guests cook at least some meals in their own kitchens and head elsewhere, often to bigger hotels, for restaurants, watersports, gambling, and entertainment. Views from the bedrooms are usually ocean panoramas; overall, the setting is comfortable and, at its best, even cozy. You'll feel like you have your own Florida apartment, with easy access to the beach. Accommodations have two bedrooms (a maximum of six persons), with wicker and rattan furnishings, and nice touches that include double basins in each bathroom, plus a tub and shower.

On the premises are both a round and a triangular swimming pool, one with a simple snack bar that's open only at lunchtime, except on Monday and Wednesday, when there's a Bahamian buffet. The entertainment and casino facilities of the more densely developed sections of Paradise Island are just a short walk away. The major drawback here is the service, which is very laissez-faire.

Ocean Ridge Dr. (P.O. Box N-10600), Paradise Island, The Bahamas. ℂ **242/363-2523.** Fax 242/363-2130. www.pibc-bahamas.com. 44 units. Winter $534 (£283) 2-bedroom apt; off season $422 (£224) 2-bedroom apt. AE, MC, V. **Amenities:** Pool bar; 2 pools; exercise room; salon; massage; coin-operated laundry service; limited mobility rooms. *In room:* A/C, TV, kitchen, hair dryer, iron, safe.

Sunrise Beach Club and Villas ℛ ℳ ⁣ *Kids*   This cluster of Spanish-inspired low-rise town houses occupies one of the most desirable stretches of beachfront on Paradise Island. Midway between the Riu Hotel and the One&Only Ocean Club, it's a short walk from the casino and a variety of sports and dining options. Accommodations are clustered within five separate groupings of red-roofed town houses, each with access to the resort's two swimming pools (one of which has a waterfall) and a simple snack bar. The hotel is usually full of Germans, Swiss, and Austrians, many of whom stay for several weeks. Guests can prepare most of their own meals, since units have kitchens. Expect pastel colors, summery-looking furniture, and a private patio or veranda, plus king-size beds and floor-to-ceiling mirrored headboards, as well as average-size bathrooms with tub and shower. The best units are the three-bedroom apartments, situated directly on the beach. This is a good bet for "quieter" families who want a more subdued and relaxed vacation, and who want to avoid the circus at the Atlantis.

P.O. Box SS-6519, Paradise Island, The Bahamas. ℂ 800/451-6078 or 242/363-2234. Fax 242/363-2308. www.sunrisebeachclub.com. 100 units. Winter $315–$350 (£167–£186) 1-bedroom unit, $551–$612 (£292–£324) 2-bedroom unit; off season $210–$243 (£111–£129) double, $441 (£234) 2-bedroom unit. AE, MC, V. **Amenities:** Restaurant; bar; 2 pools; babysitting; coin-operated laundry; nonsmoking rooms; rooms for those w/limited mobility. *In room:* A/C, TV, kitchen, hair dryer, iron, safe, beverage maker.

MODERATE

Bay View Village ℛ   More than 20 kinds of hibiscus and many varieties of bougainvillea beautify this 1.6-hectare (4-acre) condo complex. The accommodations here are near the geographic center of Paradise Island and also only a 10-minute walk to either the harbor or Cabbage Beach (the complex has no beach of its own). The restaurants, nightlife, and casino of Atlantis are only a few minutes away, although the modest Terrace restaurant here is nothing to be ashamed of.

We particularly recommend rooms near the center of the resort because they are closest to the three swimming pools and laundry facilities. Each accommodation has its own kitchen with dishwasher, plus a patio or balcony and daily maid service. A shopping center is only 3 minutes away. Some units open onto views of the harbor. A full-time personal cook can be arranged on request. The units come in a wide variety of sizes; the largest can hold up to six. Rates are slightly less for weekly rentals. Penthouse suites contain roof gardens with views of the harbor. Bedrooms come with king-, queen-, or twin-size beds. Bathrooms are medium in size, well maintained, and equipped with tub/showers.

Bayview Dr. (P.O. Box SS-6308), Paradise Island, The Bahamas. ℂ 242/363-2555. Fax 242/363-2370. 75 units. www.bwbayviewsuites.com. Winter $248 (£131) 1-bedroom suite, $385 (£204) town house (for 4 persons), from $405 (£215) villa; off season $187 (£99) 1-bedroom suite, $290 (£154) town house (for 4 persons), from $300 (£159) villa. AE, DC, MC, V. **Amenities:** Restaurant; bar; 3 pools; tennis court; babysitting; coin-operated laundry; nonsmoking rooms; rooms for those w/limited mobility. *In room:* A/C, TV, kitchen, coffeemaker, hair dryer, iron, safe.

Comfort Suites *(Value* A favorite with honeymooners and a good value, this three-story all-suite hotel is across the street from the Atlantis. If the mammoth Atlantis seems too overpowering, Comfort Suites is a nice alternative. You get the splash and wonder of the Atlantis, but you don't have to stay there all night or when the cruise-ship crowds descend. Although Comfort Suites has its own pool bar and restaurant, guests are also granted signing privileges at the nearby Atlantis for its drinking-and-dining spots, as well as the pool, beach, and sports facilities. Accommodations are priced by their views: over the island, the pool, or the garden. The medium-size bathrooms have beach towels and ample vanities. Bedrooms are standard motel size, with two double beds or one king.

Paradise Island Dr. (P.O. Box SS-6202), Paradise Island, The Bahamas. © 877/ 424-6423 in the U.S. or Canada, or 242/363-3680. Fax 242/363-2588. www. comfortsuites.com. 227 units. Winter $195–$315 (£103–£167) double; off season $264–$314 (£140–£166) double. Rates include continental breakfast. AE, DISC, MC, V. **Amenities:** Restaurant; bar; pool; tennis court; health club; babysitting; laundry service and coin-operated laundry; nonsmoking rooms; rooms for those w/limited mobility. *In room:* A/C, TV, fridge, hair dryer, iron, safe (in some), beverage maker.

INEXPENSIVE

Paradise Harbour Club & Marina The noteworthy thing about this place is its sense of isolation, despite being on heavily developed Paradise Island. Built in 1991 near the island's extreme eastern tip, it's just a few steps from the also-recommended Columbus Tavern (see review later this chapter). It's pale pink, with rambling upper hallways, terra-cotta tile floors, and clean, well-organized bedrooms with tub/showers in the bathrooms. If available, opt for one of the top-floor accommodations so you can enjoy the view. Some of its quaint amenities, all free, include a water taxi to downtown Nassau, a beach shuttle (albeit in a golf cart), snorkeling gear, and bikes.

Paradise Island Dr. (P.O. Box SS-5804), Paradise Island, The Bahamas. © 242/ 363-2992. Fax 242/363-2840. www.phc-bahamas.com. 23 units. Winter $150 (£80) double, $210 (£111) junior suite, $275 (£146) 1-bedroom unit; off season $120 (£64) double, $180 (£95) junior suite, $250 (£133) 1-bedroom unit. MC, V. **Amenities:** Restaurant; bar; pool; exercise room; Jacuzzi; watersports equipment/ rentals; golf cart shuttle to the beach; room service; babysitting; coin-operated laundry; rooms for those w/limited mobility. *In room:* A/C, TV, kitchen (in some), minibar, coffeemaker, hair dryer, iron, safe (in some).

4 Where to Dine

Paradise Island offers an array of the most dazzling, and the most expensive, restaurants in The Bahamas. If you're on a strict budget, cross over the bridge into downtown Nassau, which has far more reasonably priced places to eat. Meals on Paradise Island are often expensive but unimaginative. (Surf and turf appears on many a menu.) Unfortunately, you may not get what you pay for.

The greatest concentration of restaurants, all near the casino, is owned by Kerzner International. There are other good places outside this complex, however, including Dune at the One&Only Ocean Club, which is that hotel's showcase restaurant.

EXPENSIVE

Bahamian Club *&&* STEAKS   With an upscale British colonial–era feel and an aura that's like that of a posh, elegant, and somewhat macho-looking country club, this is a big but civilized and clubby spot, with spacious vistas, mirrors, gleaming mahogany, and forest-green walls. The excellent food is served in two-fisted portions. Meat is king here, all those old favorites from roasted prime rib to Cornish hen, plus the island's best T-bone, along with a selection of veal and lamb chops. The retro menu also features the inevitable Dover sole, lobster thermidor, and grilled salmon. All of these dishes are prepared with top-quality ingredients from the mainland. Appetizers also hearken back to the good old days, with fresh jumbo shrimp cocktail, baby spinach salad with a blue-cheese dressing, and onion soup. Try the Bahamian conch chowder for some local flavor. Side dishes are excellent here, especially the penne with fresh tomato sauce and the roasted shiitake mushrooms. Proper attire required—no jeans or sneakers.

In the Atlantis Paradise Island Resort's Coral Towers, Casino Dr. ⓒ **242/363-3000.** Reservations required. Main courses $38–$50 (£20–£27). AE, DC, DISC, MC, V. Wed–Mon 6–11pm.

Blue Lagoon *&* SEAFOOD   Views of the harbor and Paradise Lake, along with music from a one-man band, complement your candlelight meal here—a nice escape from the casino's glitter and glitz. Many of the fish dishes, including stone crab claws and the Nassau conch chowder, are excellent. The chef even whips up a good Caesar salad for two. The ubiquitous broiled grouper almondine is on the menu, as are dishes such as steak au poivre with a brandy sauce and duck à l'orange. Yes, you've probably had better versions of these dishes elsewhere, but they are competently prepared and served here, even though the meats are shipped in frozen.

In the Club Land'or, Paradise Dr. © **242/363-2400.** Reservations required. Main courses $29–$75 (£15–£40). AE, DISC, MC, V. Mon–Sat 5–10pm.

Café at the Great Hall of Waters 🐟 (Kids) INTERNATIONAL

Speaking to us confidentially, a staff member of the Atlantis said that this was probably its most underappreciated dining spot. After a close second look, we've upgraded our evaluation of the place, recommending it highly to anyone except agoraphobics, who might be frightened by its soaring ceiling and relative lack of intimacy. If you prefer to dine in a monumental setting ringed with the most "marine habitats" of any restaurant in the world, the place might be for you. You actually feel like an underwater diver as rainbow-hued fish float past the huge plate-glass windows and the illuminated underwater "ruins" of Atlantis, while rows of lobsters parade through the sand. With a ceiling that seems miles above you, the Café's dining areas are located on the lower floor of the Royal Towers. There's a kids' menu, and little ones love taking walks along the edges of the marine habitats between courses. In such a watery setting, the food becomes almost secondary, although it's quite good. The chef imports top-quality ingredients for such dishes as rack of lamb with an arugula pesto. Lobster is a specialty, and you can also order well-prepared versions of smoked salmon with lemon grass and jumbo lump Andros crab cakes. Desserts are uniformly delicious.

Royal Towers, Atlantis Paradise Island Resort, Casino Dr. © **242/363-3000.** Reservations required. Main courses $30–$50 (£16–£27). AE, DC, MC, V. Thurs–Mon 7–11am, 11:30am–2:30pm, and 6–10pm.

Café Martinique 🐟🐟🐟 FRENCH

The most elegant and upscale restaurant on Paradise Island lies within the Marina Village restaurant and shopping compound that's associated with the Atlantis Paradise Island. It occupies a replica of the kind of town house that might belong to a billionaire who happened to live, say, in Martinique and happened to have imported art and antiques from Belle Epoque Paris. This mixture of haute Paris with a French Colonial twist is enormously appealing and especially visible, for example, within the wrought-iron "bird cage" elevator that brings you and your party upstairs to the dining room. We propose that you begin your meal in the supremely comfortable bar area—the kind of place where Charles de Gaulle might have been feted during one of his official visits to his *departements d'outre-mer*. The carved mahogany antiques are pure French Caribbean, the uphol-steries scream "upscale Paris," and the food items communicate "luxe." In the tastefully posh dining area, masses of flowers, cheese and dessert trolleys, and the cuisine of superchef Jean-Georges Von-gerichten await your pleasure. This is one of the very few dining areas at Atlantis where men are asked to wear jackets, but in consideration of the upscale nature of the place and the air-conditioned environ-ment, no one seems to object. Begin with such delectable items as foie gras or caviar, perhaps smoked salmon. The main courses are limited, but each dish is sublime, especially the lobster thermidor and the Dover sole meunière. The chefs are known for their grills, everything from prime rib for two to a succulent veal chop.

In the Marina Village at the Atlantis Paradise Island, Casino Dr. ℂ 242/363-3000. Reservations required. Main courses $31–$75 (£16–£40). AE, DC, DISC, MC, V. Daily 6–11pm.

Casa d'Angelo ℛ ITALIAN   Posh, plush, richly upholstered, and lined with art and art objects reflecting the tastes of Old World Italy, Paradise Island's premier Italian restaurant offers classic dishes pre-pared with skill, served with flair, and evocative of the kind of elegant manicured food you'd expect from a topnotch Italian restaurant in Florida. Some of the best main courses include sautéed "Fra Diavolo–style" calamari and clams served over crostini bread; carpac-cio of tuna with spinach, olives, and artichoke hearts with orange sauce; risotto with porcini mushrooms, truffle oil, goat cheese, and thyme; wood oven–roasted free-range chicken with roasted garlic and Tuscan potatoes; and grilled swordfish steak with garlic, white wine, tomatoes, capers, black olives, onions, and fresh oregano.

In the Coral Tower at the Atlantis Paradise Island Resort, Casino Dr. ℂ 242/363-3000. Reservations required. Main courses $32–$60 (£17–£32). AE, DC, MC, V. Daily 6–10pm.

Dune ℛℛℛ INTERNATIONAL   One of the most sophisticated and cutting-edge restaurants on Paradise Island is in the west wing of the lobby level of the One&Only Ocean Club. It has a charcoal gray and black decor that looks like it was plucked from a chic enclave in Milan, a sweeping view of the ocean, a teakwood floor that evokes that aboard a yacht, and very attentive service. Near the restaurant's entrance is a thriving herb garden from which many of the culinary flavorings are derived. The chefs here invariably select the very finest ingredients, which are then handled with a razor-sharp technique. Every dish has a special something, especially shrimp dusted with orange powder and served with artichokes and arugula. A splendid choice is tuna spring rolls with soybean salsa. Also charming to the palate is a chicken and coconut-milk soup served with shiitake cakes. The goat cheese and watermelon salad is an unexpected delight. Filet of grouper—that standard throughout The Bahamas—is at its savory best here when served with a zesty tomato sauce.

In the One&Only Ocean Club, Ocean Club Dr. ℂ **242/363-2501**, ext. 64739. Reservations required. Main courses $22–$40 (£12–£21) lunch, $42–$60 (£22–£32) dinner. AE, DC, DISC, MC, V. Daily 7–11am, noon–3pm, and 6–10:30pm.

Fathoms ✦ SEAFOOD   You'll feel as if you're dining under the sea in this very dark seafood palace. The grotto-themed decor, depending on your tastes, might be either mystical or a bit spooky. Illuminating its glossy, metallic interior and four enormous plate-glass windows, sunlight filters through the watery marine habitats that surround the Dig, Atlantis's re-creation of an archaeological excavation of the underwater ruins of the Lost Continent.

At first you'll think the best appetizer is a selection of raw seafood in season. But then you're tempted by the blackened sashimi flavored with red ginger as it passes by. The lobster gazpacho is terrific, and you can also dig into a bowl of steamy black mussels flavored with chardonnay, garlic, and tomato. The wood-grilled yellowtail appears perfectly cooked with a wasabi potato mash and caviar, and the grilled Atlantic salmon becomes extra inviting with its side dish of Parmesan garlic fries, a first for many diners. The meat devotee will find a wide selection here. Save room for dessert, and make it a light, feathery soufflé—a different one is served every night.

In the Royal Towers of the Atlantis Paradise Island, Casino Dr. ℂ **242/363-3000**. Reservations recommended. Main courses $27–$50 (£14–£27). AE, DC, MC, V. Daily 5:30–10pm.

Mama Loo's ✦ ASIAN   Many people come here just to hang out in the bar of this engaging and stylish restaurant. But if you're in the mood for a good Chinese meal, you'll be ushered to a table in a circular dining room with a ceiling draped with peach-colored fabric that evokes a plushly decorated tent. Sophisticated and with a decor that seems to encourage both your sense of humor and your sense of camp, it suggests Shanghai during the British colonial age. The menu includes dishes from the Szechuan, Cantonese, Polynesian, and Caribbean repertoire. The best dish on the menu is Mama Loo's Shanghai lobster broiled with Asian spices and served with broccoli flavored with ginger. Two specialties we also like are shrimp in spicy chile sauce with a peanut sauce on the side, and deep-fried chicken filets with honey-garlic sauce. Even their spicy conch salad puts an Asian twist on an otherwise local Bahamian staple.

In the Coral Tower, Atlantis Paradise Island, Casino Dr. ✆ **242/363-3000.** Reservations recommended. Main courses $26–$45 (£14–£24). AE, DC, DISC, MC, V. Tues–Sat 6–10pm.

Marketplace ★ (Value) BUFFETS/INTERNATIONAL Unless you're hopelessly jaded or blasé, you won't leave here without feeling amazement at how abundant and elaborate the buffets at a casino-themed resort can really be. Decorated with old vases and terra-cotta tiles, it evokes a sprawling market where all the food just happens to be beautifully prepared, elegantly displayed, and showcased in breathtaking variety and quantity—the best buffet on Paradise Island. Before you start loading things onto your plate, browse your way past the various cooking stations and do some strategic planning. From fresh fruit to made-as-you-watch omelets, you can make breakfast as light or as heavy as you want. At lunch and dinner, you'll find everything from fresh seafood and made-to-order pastas to freshly carved roast beef and lamb. No intimate affair, this place seats some 400 diners. Sit inside or on the patio overlooking a lagoon.

In the Royal Towers, Atlantis Paradise Island Resort, Casino Dr. ✆ **242/363-3000.** Reservations not needed. Breakfast buffets $25 (£13) per person; lunch buffets $28 (£15) per person; dinner buffets $53 (£28) per person. AE, DC, MC, V. Daily 7–11am, noon–3pm, and 5:30–10pm.

Nobu ★★★ JAPANESE/ASIAN In its way, it's the most talked-about, hip, and sought-after restaurant within the Atlantis resort, thanks to massive publicity, stylish and avant-garde Asian food, and an association with an ongoing round of celebrities. It's the culinary statement of Japanese chef Nobu Matsushisa, whose branch in New York City caused a sensation among the glitterati there when it opened in the '90s. Don't expect a conventional meal here, as dishes appeal as much to the intellect as they do to the stomach. The kitchen staff here is as finely tuned as their New York or London counterparts. Some diners prefer to start with Nobu's special cold dishes, including lobster ceviche. But since conch is queen in The Bahamas, you might opt instead for conch ceviche. The best appetizer we've sampled in this array is the yellowtail sashimi with jalapeño. If you prefer your dishes hot, try the rock shrimp tempura with a creamy spicy sauce or else Chilean sea bass with black bean sauce. Many of the dishes, such as a whole fish, emerge from a wood-fired oven. The tempura selection is vast, ranging from pumpkin to shiitake. Most patrons order pieces of sushi or sashimi, and the selection here is wide, including some exotica such as "live" conch, sea urchins, or freshwater eel. Of course, you can also order well-prepared standards which include tuna, octopus, and salmon, as well as snow crab or king crab. A wide selection of sushi rolls is also offered, including a lobster roll. If you want the most lavish and exotic menu on Paradise Island, you can request the chef's signature fixed-price meal, which he calls "Chef's Choice Omakase Menu."

In the Atlantis Paradise Island Resort's Royal Towers, Casino Dr. ℃ 242/363-3000. Reservations required. Main courses $15–$70 (£7.95–£37); sushi or sashimi $4–$15 (£2.10–£7.95); sushi or sashimi dinner $49 (£26); chef's special menu $150 (£80). AE, DC, DISC, MC, V. Daily 6–11pm.

Water's Edge ℞ BUFFETS/SEAFOOD   Frankly, we prefer the buffet station at the also-recommended Marketplace, but if you're looking for a buffet venue where ongoing displays of seafood are the main appeal, this fits the bill. Three 4.5m (15-ft.) waterfalls splash into an artificial lagoon just outside the dining room's windows. Huge chandeliers illuminate the room, which has views of an open kitchen where a battalion of chefs create a nightly seafood buffet. And if you're in the mood for pasta and pizza, they're here, but for the most part garnished with (guess what?) seafood. Depending on the night, some of the dishes are better than others, but almost universally, the lavish displays of fresh shellfish from the raw bar will include 6-ounce lobster tails, stone crab claws, more shrimp than you can cope with, and, when they're in season, fresh raw oysters. The main problem here is that the food has a hard time competing with the ambience. If you've already sampled the Marketplace, you might have already had enough buffets, at least for a while.

In the Coral Towers at the Atlantis Paradise Island, Casino Dr. ℃ 242/363-3000. Reservations recommended. Seafood buffet $45 (£24). AE, DC, DISC, MC, V. Daily 5:30–10pm.

MODERATE
Bimini Road ℞ BAHAMIAN/INTERNATIONAL   The name Bimini Road refers to a mysterious underwater rock formation off the coast of Bimini that resembles a ruined triumphal boulevard that might have been designed by the ancient Romans or, more appropriately, the ancient Atlanteans. Partly because of its relatively reasonable prices and partly because it showcases the cuisine of The Bahamas more proudly than any other restaurant at the Atlantis Paradise Island, this eatery is among the most consistently popular and crowded dining spots on Paradise Island. Some aspects of the place,

especially the red leatherette banquettes and Formica tables, evoke a Goombay version of a brightly painted diner somewhere in the Out Islands. Yet a second glance will reveal a sophisticated-looking and hysterically busy open kitchen (entertainment in its own right), and walls covered with tropical murals, some of them influenced by the Junkanoo festival. The kitchen constantly chugs out food items that include lobster and beef rib-eye. You might start with such special-ties as a scorched conch salad or else Rum Bay boiled fish in a cit-rus broth. Other island favorites include the catch of the day, which can be grilled, blackened, or fried island style. A tasty dish is chicken mojo—boneless breast with spices and a lime mojo sauce that is charcoal-roasted and served over native rice. The only problem with this place involves an inconvenient crowd of expectant diners who cluster, somewhat uncomfortably, near the entrance waiting for an empty table. A phone call in advance for information about wait times might help you avoid this inconvenience.

In the Marina Village at the Atlantis Paradise Island, Casino Dr. © **242/363-3000.** Reservations accepted only for parties of 6 or more. Main courses $24–$40 (£13–£21). AE, DISC, MC, V. Daily noon–3pm and 6–11pm.

Blue Marlin ⭐ *Finds* BAHAMIAN/SEAFOOD   With a name like Blue Marlin, you expect and get fish and seafood dishes, although there are other choices as well. The catch always tastes fresh, and it's well prepared. If you've never had cracked conch, this place provides a good introduction to that famous Bahamian dish (it's like breaded veal cutlet). Lobster thermidor is a popular choice here, and the chef always fashions a linguine studded with morsels of fresh seafood. For the poultry or meat fancier, choices include Eleuthera coconut chicken and tender spare ribs basted with guava. Some nights at 7:30pm, a limbo show is presented along with a slightly gruesome live glass-eating act. You have a choice of dining inside or out.

Hurricane Hole Plaza. © **242/363-2660.** Reservations recommended. Main courses $12–$25 (£6.35–£13). AE, DISC, MC, V. Daily 5pm–10pm.

Carmine's ITALIAN   A lot of the signals that emanate from this place communicate "family." Here we're talking about a large, loud, and in-your-face Italian family who work out their emotional conflicts with gusto, verve, and platters piled high with an amazing amount of food. Set at the most distant point of the Marina Village from the casino, this is the local branch of a restaurant that will always be asso-ciated with the Little Italy or the outer boroughs of New York City.

Even though it was custom-built, you'll get the idea that a team of decorators gentrified this boathouse, with its installation of many square yards of mahogany bar tops, terra-cotta tiles, and monumental wine racks. This place prides itself on serving portions that could feed a party of four to six diners. As such, it's at its best when family members or friends gather together and order several platters for consumption by the entire table. If you're a single diner or a couple, head instead for other dining haunts such as the Café Martinique or Bahamian Club.

In the Marina Village at the Atlantis Paradise Island, Casino Dr. © 242/363-3000. Reservations accepted only for parties of 6 or more. Main courses $30–$36 (£16–£19). AE, DC, DISC, MC, V. Daily 6–11pm.

Columbus Tavern ✦ *Finds* CONTINENTAL/BAHAMIAN Far removed from the glitz and glamour of the casinos, the tavern seems relatively little known, even though Freddie Lightbourne of the Poop Deck restaurant has been running it for years now. It deserves to be discovered because it serves good food at reasonable (for Paradise Island) prices. The tavern has the typical nautical decor (don't come here for the setting), with tables placed both inside and outside overlooking the harbor. The bar is worth a visit in itself, with its long list of tropical drinks. You can go local by starting off with the conch chowder, or opt for cheese-stuffed mushrooms with foie gras. Even though it's imported frozen, the rack of lamb is flawless. You can also order tamarind chicken and a quite good filet of grouper with a tantalizing lobster and shrimp sauce.

In the Paradise Harbour Club Resort, Paradise Island Dr. © 242/363-5923. Reservations required for dinner. Main courses $11–$26 (£5.85–£14) lunch, $20–$48 (£11–£25) dinner. AE, MC, V. Daily 9am–10:30pm.

INEXPENSIVE

Anthony's Caribbean Grill AMERICAN/CARIBBEAN Its owners think of this place as an upscale version of Bennigan's or T.G.I. Fridays. But the decor is thoroughly Caribbean, thanks to psychedelic tropical colors, underwater sea themes, and jaunty maritime decorative touches. A bar dispenses everything from conventional mai tais to embarrassingly oversize 48-ounce "sparklers"—with a combination of rum, amaretto, vodka, and fruit punch that is about all most serious drinkers can handle. Menu items include burgers, pizzas capped with everything from lobster to jerk chicken, barbecued or fried chicken, ribs with Caribbean barbecue sauce, and several meal-size salads.

In the Paradise Island Shopping Center, at the junction of Paradise and Casino drives. © 242/363-3152. Lunch $10–$15 (£5.30–£7.95); dinner $10–$39 (£5.30–£21). AE, DISC, MC, V. Daily 7:30am–11pm.

News Café DELI Low-key and untouristy, this spot has a Formica-clad decor that's a far cry (and, to some people, a welcome change from) the unrelenting glossiness of other parts of Paradise Island. This is where you'll find most of the island's construction workers, groundskeepers, and hotel staff having breakfast and lunch. The eatery maintains a stack of the day's newspapers, so you can have something to read as you sip your morning cappuccino or latte. You can also stock up here on sandwiches for your beach picnic.

In the Hurricane Hole Plaza, Paradise Island. ℂ **242/363-4684.** Reservations not accepted. Breakfast, lunch sandwiches, and platters $7–$12 (£3.70–£6.35); assorted coffees $2–$4 (£1.05–£2.10). AE, DC, DISC, MC, V. Daily 24 hr.

Seagrapes Restaurant (Kids) BUFFET/INTERNATIONAL Buffet lunches and dinners are the specialty of this pleasantly decorated tropical restaurant. This is the most affordable and family-oriented choice in the Atlantis Paradise Island, offering Cuban, Caribbean, and Cajun dishes. It's pretty straightforward fare, but you get a lot of food for not a lot of money—a rarity on pricey Paradise Island. The restaurant, which can seat 200 to 300 diners at a time, overlooks the lagoon and has a marketplace look, with buffet offerings displayed in little stalls and stations. Every Thursday, Friday, and Saturday between 6 and 9pm, the place goes absolutely gaga over children. During those hours, a battalion of clowns, jugglers, and magicians transform the place into a circuslike venue replete with cotton candy and popcorn stands (bad for appetites), and a face-painting station. Depending on how family-centered you like your dining to be, you'll be either charmed or annoyed by this—just know in advance.

In the Atlantis Paradise Island, Casino Dr. ℂ **242/363-3000.** Breakfast and lunch buffet $19 (£10); dinner buffet $32 (£17). AE, DC, DISC, MC, V. Daily 7–11am, noon–2:30pm, and 5:30–10pm.

5 Beaches, Watersports & Other Outdoor Pursuits

Visitors interested in something more than lazing on the beaches have only to ask hotel personnel to make the necessary arrangements. Guests at the **Atlantis Paradise Island** (ℂ **242/363-3000**), for example, can have access to a surprising number of diversions without so much as leaving the hotel property. They can splash in private pools; play tennis, Ping-Pong, and shuffleboard; ride the waves; snorkel; or rent Sunfish, Sailfish, jet skis, banana boats, and catamarans from contractors located in kiosks.

HITTING THE BEACH

On Paradise Island, **Cabbage Beach** (also known in some circles as **West Beach**) 🏖️🏖️ is the real showcase. Its broad white sands stretch for at least 3km (1¾ miles). Casuarinas, palms, and sea grapes border it. It's likely to be crowded in winter, but you can find a little more elbowroom by walking to the northwestern stretch of the beach. You can reach Paradise Island from downtown Nassau by walking over the bridge, taking a taxi, or boarding a ferryboat at Prince George Dock. Cabbage Beach does not have public facilities, but you can patronize one of the handful of bars and restaurants nearby and use their facilities. Technically, to use the facilities, you should be a customer—even if that means buying only a drink. Note that during the construction of the Atlantis Paradise Island's new waterfront hotel and timeshare accommodations, access to some sections of Cabbage/West Beach might be off-limits.

Our other favorite beach in this area is the white-sand **Paradise Beach** 🏖️🏖️. The beach is used mainly by guests of The Cove Atlantis (p. 105), as it lies at the far western tip of the island. (Sunsets viewed from its sands are particularly beautiful.) If you're not a resident, access is difficult. If you're staying at a hotel in Nassau and want to come to Paradise Island for a day at the beach, it's better to go to Cabbage Beach (see above).

GOLF

Ocean Club Golf Club 🏖️🏖️, on Paradise Island Drive (© **242/ 363-3000;** www.oneandonlyresorts.com), at the east end of the island, is an 18-hole championship golf course designed by Tom Weiskopf that overlooks both the Atlantic Ocean and Nassau Harbour. Attracting every caliber of golfer, the par-72 course is known for its hole 17, which plays entirely along the scenic Snorkelers Cove. Greens fees include use of a golf cart. They range from $190 to $260 (£101–£138) per player, without reductions for guests at any individual hotels. Rental clubs and shoes are available.

Golfers who want more variety will find one other course on New Providence Island (see "Beaches, Watersports & Other Outdoor Pursuits," in chapter 3).

SNORKELING & SCUBA DIVING

For more scuba sites in the area, see "Snorkeling, Scuba Diving & Underwater Walks," in chapter 3.

Bahamas Divers, in the Yachthaven Marina, on East Bay Street (© **242/393-5644;** www.bahamadivers.com), is the best all-around center for watersports on the island, specializing in scuba diving and snorkeling. A two-tank morning dive goes for $89 to $109 (£47–£58), whereas a single-tank afternoon dive costs $55 (£29). A half-day snorkeling trip is only $39 (£21), and dive packages are also offered.

6 Seeing the Sights

Most of the big hotels here maintain activity-packed calendars, especially for that occasional windy, rainy day that comes in winter. Similar to life aboard a large-scale cruise ship, the resorts offer activities (some of them age-specific) that include water-volleyball games, bingo, fish-feeding demonstrations, and movie screenings. And that doesn't include the disco parties for teens and preteens that tend to be scheduled for late afternoon or very early evenings. To an increasing degree, hotels such as the Atlantis have configured themselves as destinations in their own right.

Atlantis Paradise Island Resort & Casino 𝒦𝒦   Regardless of where you're staying—even if it's at the most remote hotel on New Providence—you'll want to visit this lavish theme park, hotel, restaurant complex, casino, and entertainment center. It's Paradise Island's biggest attraction. You could spend all day here—and all night, too—wandering through the shopping arcades; sampling the international cuisine of the varied restaurants; or gambling at the roulette wheels, slot machines, poker tables, and blackjack tables. And once you're here, don't even think about leaving without a walk along the Marina or a visit to The Dig, a theme-driven marine attraction that celebrates the eerie and tragic legend of the lost continent of Atlantis. During the day, you can wear casual clothes, but at night you should dress up a bit, especially if you want to try one of the better restaurants.

The most crowded time to visit Atlantis is between 9am and 5pm on days when cruise ships are berthed in the nearby harbor. (That's usually every Tues, Fri, and Sat from 9am to around 5pm.) The most crowded time to visit the casino is between 8 and 11pm any night of the week. There is no cover to enter: You pay just for what you gamble away (and that could be considerable), eat, and drink. Ironically, it's illegal for Bahamian citizens or residents to gamble. That restriction, however, most definitely does not apply to visitors from offshore. Except for the price of the liquor, entertainment within the bars is free. That usually includes live salsa, Goombay, and calypso music provided by local bands.

Casino Dr. ℭ **242/363-3000.** Free admission. Daily 24 hr.

The Cloister ✿   Located in the Versailles Gardens of the One&Only Ocean Club, this 12th-century cloister built by Augustinian monks in southwestern France was reassembled here stone by stone. Huntington Hartford, the A&P heir, purchased the cloister from the estate of William Randolph Hearst at San Simeon in California. Regrettably, after the newspaper czar originally bought the cloister, it was hastily dismantled in France for shipment to America. However, the parts had not been numbered—they all arrived unlabeled on Paradise Island. The reassembly of the complicated monument baffled most conventional methods of construction until artist and sculptor Jean Castre-Manne set about to reassemble it piece by piece. It took him 2 years, and what you see today, presumably, bears some similarity to the original. The gardens, which extend over the rise to Nassau Harbour, are filled with tropical flowers and classic statues. Although the monument retains a timeless beauty, recent buildings have encroached on either side, marring Huntington Hartford's original vision.

In the gardens of the One&Only Ocean Club, Ocean Club Dr. ✆ **242/363-2501.** Free admission. Daily 24 hr.

7 Shopping

For serious shopping, you'll want to cross over the Paradise Island Bridge into Nassau (see chapter 3). However, many of Nassau's major stores also have shopping outlets on Paradise Island.

The Shops at the Atlantis, in the Atlantis Paradise Island Resort (✆ **242/363-3000**), is the largest concentration of shops and boutiques on Paradise Island, rivaling anything else in The Bahamas in terms of size, selection, and style. The boutiques are subdivided into two different sections that include the well-appointed Crystal Court Arcade corridor that meanders between the Royal Tower and the Coral Tower, and that encompasses 3,252 sq. m (35,004 sq. ft.) of prime high-traffic retail space. Newer, and usually with entrances that open directly to the outside air, are boutiques within the resort's waterfront **Marina Village.** An additional handful of emporiums is scattered randomly throughout other sections of the resort, as noted below. It's all about flagrantly conspicuous consumption that's sometimes fueled by the gaming frenzy in the nearby casino. So if you want to do more than browse, bring your platinum card and remain alert that in a high-ticket venue like this, maxing out your credit cards might be easier, and happen sooner, than you might ever have believed.

The resort contains two separate branches of **Colombian Emeralds** (one in the Marina Village, another within the Atlantis Paradise Island's Beach Tower), where the colored gemstones far outnumber the relatively limited selection of diamonds. Individual purveyors on-site include **Lalique,** the France-based purveyor of fine crystal and fashion accessories for men and women; **Cartier; Versace,** the late designer to the stars (this boutique also has a particularly charming housewares division); **Façonnable,** a youthful, sporty designer for young and beautiful club-hoppers; **Bulgari,** purveyor of the most enviable jewels in the world, as well as watches, giftware, and perfumes; and **Gucci** and **Ferragamo,** in case you forgot your dancing shoes. And if you want a bathing suit, **Coles of Nassau** sells swimwear by Gottex, Pucci, and Fernando Sanchez. Finally, **John Bull,** known for its Bay Street store in Nassau and as a pioneer seller of watches throughout The Bahamas, also has an interesting assortment of watches, jewelry, and designer accessories at this outlet.

One of our favorite shops, **Doongalik Studios** (② 242/394-1886), in the Marina Village compound, doesn't sell the predictably upscale roster of gemstones and fashion that you might have had your fill of by now. At the time of this writing, it's the only art gallery within Marina Village. Owned and operated by the architect and art connoisseur who designed Marina Village itself (Jackson Burnside), it positions itself as a bastion of Bahamian culture within the glittering row of shops otherwise devoted to luxury goods. Come here for insight into who is creating contemporary art in The Bahamas. Oil paintings by locally famous artists (including John Cox, John Paul, Jessica Colebrooke, and Eddie Minnis) range from $800 to $2,000 (£424–£1,060) each; prints—sometimes of works by the same artists—go for between $15 and $100 (£7.95–£53) each. Sculptures can be especially interesting, with some crafted from gnarled driftwood.

8 Paradise Island After Dark

Paradise Island has the best nightlife in The Bahamas, and most of it centers on the Atlantis.

The Atlantis Paradise Island Resort's Casino and Discothèque

There's no other spot in The Bahamas, with the possible exception of the Crystal Palace complex on Cable Beach, with such a wide variety of after-dark attractions, and absolutely nothing that approaches its inspired brand of razzle-dazzle. Even if you stay in Nassau or Cable Beach, you'll want to drop into this artfully decorated self-contained temple to decadence, even if gambling isn't really your passion. Love it or hate it, this place is simply a jaw-dropper.

The casino is the most lavishly planned, most artfully "themed" casino this side of Vegas. The only casino in the world built above a body of water, it was designed in homage to the lost continent of Atlantis, and it appears to have risen directly from the waters of the lagoon. The gaming area is centered on buildings representing a Temple of the Sun and a Temple of the Moon, with a painted replica of the zodiac overhead. Rising from key locations are four of the most elaborate sculptures in the world. Massive and complex, they were crafted by teams of artisans spearheaded by Dale Chihuly, the American-born resident of Venice whose glass-blowing skills are the most celebrated in the world. Other than the decor, the casino's gaming tables, open daily from 10am to 4am, are the main attraction in this enormous place, and about a thousand whirring and clanging slot machines operate 24 hours a day.

Recent additions to this blockbuster casino include a lineup of poker tables and the **Pegasus Race and Sports Book,** with an illuminated and computerized display that lists the odds for many of the world's upcoming sporting events. Thanks to instantaneous communications with a centralized betting facility in Las Vegas, the staff here will make odds on a staggering number of sports events, both professional and college, as well as horseracing and greyhound racing. This facility also contains a mini amphitheater with plush armchairs and views over a battery of TV screens, each displaying one of the sporting and/or racing events for which odds are being calculated and money is changing hands. One side of the casino contains **Aura,** a club that manages to attract a few local hipsters as well as guests of the Atlantis. Come here anytime during casino hours for a drink. A sweaty, flirty crowd parties all night on the dance floor. Often you can catch some of the best live music in The Bahamas, as bands take to the stage that's cantilevered above the dance floor. The club gets going around 9pm nightly, with a cover charge of $30 (£16) required from all nonguests of the Atlantis. (Note that the entrance charge is usually waived for women.) Ringing the casino are at least 3,252 sq. m (35,004 sq. ft.) of retail shopping space, with even more located nearby in the Marina Village (see "Shopping," above) and an impressive cluster of hideaway bars and restaurants.

Also in the same Atlantis complex, **Joker's Wild** is the only real comedy club in The Bahamas, with a talented company of funny people who work hard to make you laugh. Show times are Tuesday through Sunday at 9:30pm. At least two comedians will appear on any given night, most of them hailing from The Bahamas, with occasional appearances of performers from London and New York. Midway between the Beach Tower and the Coral Tower, Casino Dr. ✆ **242/363-3000.** No cover charge for casino, but a cover charge of $20–$25 (£11–£13) applies for entrance to individual clubs and discos, depending on the night of the week, the season, and occupancy levels at the resort. Cover charges apply to both guests and nonguests.

THE BAR SCENE

Bimini Road   The joint is always jumping at the Marina Village at the Atlantis. This bar and restaurant are imbued with a Junkanoo theme with wall-sized murals. At many bars at this sprawling resort, the bartenders seem to ignore you. Not here. They are a lively bunch, slinging drinks with names like the Fountain of Youth. A specialty is a sour apple–flavored mixture known as Gussie Mae. The place is especially popular with yachties, who tie up at the nearby marina. A costumed dance troupe performs 4 nights a week (times vary), and live bands pump out island music for most of the night. Even patrons get in on the act with conga lines. The restaurant serves food daily from 11am to 10pm, including conch fritters and cracked lobster tail. The bar itself is open from 11am to 1:30pm daily. Marina Village, Atlantis Resort, Casino Dr. ✆ **242/363-3000.**

Dune Bar   This luxe dining room is also the setting for the island's most elegant and sophisticated lounge; it's becoming increasingly popular as a plush and appealing meeting spot for singles. The action centers around a translucent white marble bar skillfully illuminated from behind, and its outdoor terrace can be undeniably romantic. At the One&Only Ocean Club, Ocean Club Dr. ✆ **242/363-2501.** Call for open hours, which can vary.

Plato's Lounge   This is the most popular bar at the Atlantis Paradise Island, a sensual spot where you can escape the din of the slot machines and relax within an upscale environment that's flanked with replicas of Greek-language texts that might have been hand-lettered in ancient times by Plato himself. (Presumably, the framed ancient Greek papyrus texts on the wall are copies of what Plato wrote about Atlantis.) Sofas are deep and plushly comfortable, a pianist sets the mood during cocktail hour and early evening, and you'll invariably get the sense here that you're right in the heart of everything. In the morning, the site doubles as a cafe, serving pastries and snacks from 6am until 4pm. It's open around the clock daily. On the lobby level of the Royal Towers, Atlantis Resort, Casino Dr. ✆ **242/363-3000.**

5

Grand Bahama (Freeport/Lucaya)

Fabulous beaches and relatively affordable prices continue to make Grand Bahama Island a year-round destination. Weather also enhances its continued popularity. Even though the island sits in the Atlantic Ocean, the forever-warm waters of the Gulf Stream make the beaches, particularly at the western tip, desirable even in winter. The Little Bahama Bank protects the island from the storms that roar in from the northeast. Grand Bahama Island is also convenient to reach, lying only 81km (50 miles) east of Palm Beach, Florida.

Despite some cutting-edge architectural development in the late 1990s near Lucaya Beach, the island may never return to its high-roller days with the gloss and glitz of the '60s. In that era, everybody from Howard Hughes to Frank Sinatra and Rat Packers showed up to feud, play, act out, maneuver, manipulate, and overindulge. However, recent improvements in Port Lucaya and massive redevelopment on the island's West End have brought a smile back to its face, which had grown wrinkled and tired over the latter part of the 20th century. But downtown Freeport is "blighted" by the closure, and continuing decay, of a megaresort that once flourished as its centerpiece, the Crowne Plaza. That scar has, regrettably, extended into the island's once-largest and once-fabled shopping mall, the International Bazaar. Due to the lack of business and "the morgue" (that is, the sprawling, storm-damaged corpse of the nearby Crowne Plaza Resort), the shopping area remains in a lackluster state of decay and decline.

The second-most-popular tourist destination in The Bahamas (Nassau/Cable Beach/Paradise Island ranks first), Grand Bahama lies just 81km (50 miles) and less than 30 minutes by air off the Florida coast. The island is the northernmost and fourth-largest landmass in The Bahamas (118km/73 miles long and 6.5–13km/4–8 miles wide).

Freeport/Lucaya was once just a dream. Wallace Groves, a Virginia-born financier, saw the prospect of developing the island into a minia-ture Miami Beach. Almost overnight in the 1950s, the low-lying pine forest turned into one of the world's major resorts. Today, although the island's center of gravity has firmly shifted from Freeport to Lucaya, Groves's dream has at least been partially realized.

The Lucaya district was developed 8 years after Freeport, as a resort center along the coast. It has evolved into a blend of residential and tourist facilities. As the two communities grew, their identities became almost indistinguishable. But elements of their original purposes still exist today. Freeport is the downtown area and attracts visitors with its commerce, industry, and own resorts. Meanwhile, Lucaya is called the "Garden City" and pleases residents and vacationers alike with its fine beaches.

Grand Bahama is more than an Atlantic City clone, however. If you don't care for gambling in the island's only casinos or if shopping and fun-in-the-sun is not your scene, try one of the alternatives. Because the island is so big, most of it remains relatively unspoiled. You can commune with nature at plenty of quiet places, including the Rand Nature Centre. Lucayan National Park—with its underwater caves, forest trails, and secluded beach—is another major attraction. Just kilometers from Freeport/Lucaya are serene places where you can wander in a world of casuarina, palmetto, and pine trees. During the day, you can enjoy long stretches of beach, broken by inlets and fishing villages.

The reviews of Grand Bahama Island are definitely mixed. Some discerning travelers who could live anywhere have built homes here; others vow never to set foot on the island again, finding it, with the exception of Port Lucaya, "tacky" or "uninspired." Judge for yourself.

1 Orientation

For a general discussion on traveling to The Bahamas, refer to chapter 2.

ARRIVING

A number of airlines fly to Grand Bahama International Airport from the continental United States, including **American Airlines** (© 800/433-7300; www.aa.com) and **Bahamasair** (© 242/377-3218; www.bahamasair.com), both with daily flights from Miami. **Gulfstream Continental Connection** (© 800/231-0856; www.gulfstreamair.com) flies to Freeport from Miami and West Palm Beach once daily, and from Fort Lauderdale five times daily. **US Airways** (© 800/428-4322; www.usairways.com) flies once daily from Charlotte, North Carolina.

Grand Bahama Island

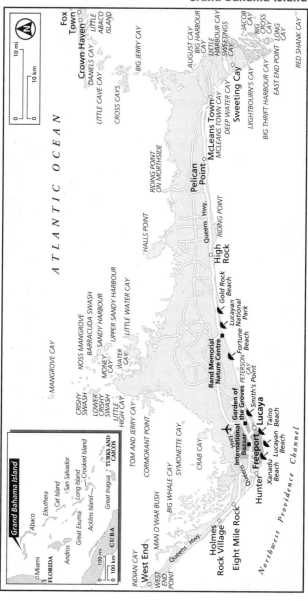

Other competing airlines include **AirTran** (© 800/247-8726; www.airtran.com), flying nonstop from Atlanta (daily) as well as Baltimore (Thurs–Mon). **Delta Connection** (© 800/221-1212) flies daily from Atlanta.

Many visitors arrive in Nassau, then hop on one of the five daily Bahamasair flights to Freeport. These 30-minute hops run $135 to $200 (£72–£106) round-trip.

No buses run from the airport to the major hotel zones. But many hotels will provide airport transfers, especially if you've bought a package deal. If yours does not, no problem; taxis meet arriving flights and will take you from the airport to one of the hotels in Freeport or Lucaya for about $12 to $22 (£6.35–£12). The ride shouldn't take more than about 10 minutes.

Discovery Cruise Lines (© 800/937-4477 or 242/351-1339; www.discoverycruiseline.com) offers daily passage between the Fort Lauderdale Seaport and Grand Bahama Island. Frankly, the Discovery vessels making this 89km (55-mile) jaunt haven't been the newest or glitziest cruise ships sailing in the past 3 or 4 decades, but they are shipshape and fit the bill. The trip over from Florida takes about 5 hours, and they have the required pool deck and bar, along with a casino, bar show lounge, and dining facilities. They do feed passengers very well. A round-trip fare runs $180 to $200 (£95–£106) per person, and you can make reservations online.

VISITOR INFORMATION

Assistance and information are available at the **Grand Bahama Tourism Board,** International Bazaar in Freeport (© 242/352-6909; www.grand-bahama.com). Two other information booths are located at the **Freeport International Airport** (© 242/352-2052) and at the Port Lucaya Marketplace (© 242/373-8988). Hours for all three branches are 9am to 5pm Monday to Saturday, and the branches at the airport and at the Port Lucaya Marketplace are also open on Sunday 9am to 5pm.

ISLAND LAYOUT

Other than the perhaps unexpected novelty of driving on the left, getting around Freeport/Lucaya is fairly easy because of its flat terrain. Although Freeport and Lucaya are frequently mentioned in the same breath, newcomers should note that Freeport is a landlocked collection of hotels and shops rising from the island's center, while the better-maintained and more appealing Lucaya, about 4km (2½ miles) away, is a bustling waterfront section of hotels, shops, and restaurants clustered next to a saltwater pond on the island's southern shoreline.

Freeport lies midway between the northern and southern shores of Grand Bahama Island. Bisected by some of the island's largest roads, it was originally conceived as the site of the biggest hotels and what until a few years ago was one of the most-visited attractions in the country, the International Bazaar shopping complex. Now in a dismaying state of disrepair, it's a theme-oriented retail mall that has seen better days, now a depressing remnant of its former glory. Immediately adjacent is the local straw market, where you can buy inexpensive souvenirs and Bahamian handicrafts.

To reach **Port Lucaya** from Freeport, head east from the International Bazaar along East Sunrise Highway, then turn south at the intersection with Seahorse Road. The intersection—actually an over-size roundabout—is marked with a prominent stone marker saying PORT LUCAYA. From that roundabout, less than a mile later, you'll find yourself within the heart of the Lucaya complex. Know in advance that the shops and restaurants on the marina side of Seahorse Road are identified as being within the "Port Lucaya" subdivision of the Lucaya Complex. Conversely, the Westin and the Sheraton hotels, their restaurants and shops, and the Isle of Capri Casino, all of which are clustered on the landward side of Seahorse Road, are identified as the "Our Lucaya" subdivision of the Lucaya complex.

The architectural centerpiece of Port Lucaya is **Count Basie Square,** named for the great entertainer who used to have a home on the island. A short walk east or west of the square, most of the hotels in the Lucaya Complex rise above the narrow strip of sand that separates the sea from a saltwater pond.

Life on Grand Bahama Island doesn't get more glamorous after you leave the Lucaya Complex. To the west of Freeport and Lucaya, the West Sunrise Highway passes grim and impersonal-looking industrial complexes which include The Bahamas Oil Refining Company. Once you pass the built-up waterfront sprawl of Freeport's western end, you can take Queen's Highway northwest all the way to **West End,** a distance of some 45km (28 miles) from the center of Freeport. Along the way you pass the unpicturesque wharves of Freeport Harbour, where cruise ships dock. Just to the east lies Hawksbill Creek, a not-particularly-interesting-looking village that houses some of the workers at the nearby port facilities.

Much less explored is the isolated **East End** of Grand Bahama. Its most distant tip lies about 72km (45 miles) from the center of Freeport and is reached via the Grand Bahama Highway. Despite its name, the route is bumpy and potholed in some spaces and—along extensive stretches of its central area—either is blocked by piles of sand, rock, and fallen trees or is not-as-yet-completed. For access to the most distant reaches of the East End from Freeport or Lucaya, allow about 2 hours of driving time. First you pass the **Rand Nature Centre,** about 5km (3 miles) east of Freeport. About 11km (6¾ miles) on is **Lucaya National Park,** and 8km (5 miles) farther lies the hamlet of **Free Town;** east of Free Town is **High Rock,** known for its Emmanuel Baptist Church. From here, the road becomes considerably rougher until it ends in **MacLean's Town,** which celebrates Columbus Day with an annual conch-cracking contest. From here, it's possible to take a water taxi across Runners Creek to the exclusive Deep Water Cay club, catering to serious anglers.

In Freeport/Lucaya, but especially on the rest of Grand Bahama Island, you will almost never find a street number on a hotel or a store. Sometimes in the more remote places, including underpopulated areas on the outskirts of Lucaya itself, you won't even find signs identifying the names of the streets. In lieu of numbers, locate places by their relation to nearby hotels, beaches, or landmarks.

2 Getting Around

BY TAXI

The government sets the taxi rates, and the cabs are metered (or should be). Metered rates are $3 (£1.60) for the first .3km (quarter-mile) and 40¢ each additional 1.6km (1 mile). Additional passengers over the age of 2 are $3 each. If there's no meter, agree on the price with the driver in advance. You can call for a taxi, although most taxis wait at the major hotels or the cruise-ship dock to pick up passengers. One major taxi company is **Freeport Taxi Company,** Logwood Road (© **242/352-6666**), open 24 hours. Another is **Grand Bahama Taxi Union,** at the Freeport International Airport, Old Airport Road (© **242/352-7101**), also open 24 hours. *Note:* Typical taxi rates are as follows. From the Cruise Ship Harbour to: Xanadu Beach Hotel, $17 (£9); Port Lucaya Marketplace, $24 (£12.70); Flamingo Beach Resort/The Ritz, $24 (£12.70); Viva Fortuna Beach, $29 (£15.35). From the airport to: anywhere in Port Lucaya or Our Lucaya, $19 (£10); Viva Fortuna, $20 (£11); Royal Oasis, $11 (£5.85); Xanadu, $14 (£7.40).

BY BUS

Public bus service runs from the International Bazaar and downtown Freeport to the Lucaya area. The typical fare is $1 (55p) for adults, 50¢ (25p) for children. Check with the tourist office (see "Visitor Information," above) for bus schedules. There is no number to call for information.

BY CAR

If you plan to confine your exploration to the center of Freeport with its International Bazaar and Lucaya with its beaches, you can rely on public transportation. However, if you'd like to branch out and explore the rest of the island (perhaps finding a more secluded beach), a rental car is the way to go. Terrain throughout Grand Bahama Island is universally flat, a fact that's appreciated by drivers trying to conserve gasoline. Try **Avis** (© **800/331-1212** or 242/332-4062; www.avis.com) or **Hertz** (© **800/654-3131** or 242/352-9250; www.hertz.com). Both of these companies maintain offices in small bungalows near the Freeport International Airport. From inside the terminal, an employee of either company will contact a colleague, who will direct you to the curb outside the luggage pickup point. There someone from the rental car company will arrive in a car or van to drive you to their pickup location.

One of the best companies is **Dollar Rent-a-Car,** Old Airport Road (© **242/352-9325;** www.dollar.com), which rents everything from a new-style Kia Sportage to a VW Jetta. Rates range from $60 (£32) per day manual or from $49 (£26) for an automatic, with unlimited mileage, plus another $12 (£6.35) per day for a CDW (Collision Damage Waiver; $500 (£265) deductible). Gas costs around $6.50 (£3.45) per gallon. Remember to drive on the left as British rules apply.

BY SCOOTER

A scooter is a fun way to get around, as most of Grand Bahamas is flat with well-paved roads. Scooters can be rented at most hotels or, for cruise-ship passengers, in the Freeport Harbour area. Helmets are required and provided by the outfitter. You can find dozens of stands along the road in Freeport and Lucaya, and also in the major parking lots, charging rates ranging from $40 to $55 (£21–£29) a day.

ON FOOT

You can explore the center of Freeport or Lucaya on foot, but if you want to venture into the East End or West End, you'll need to rent a car, hire a taxi, or try Grand Bahama's erratic public transportation.

FAST FACTS: Grand Bahama

Banks   In Freeport/Lucaya, banks are open from 9:30am to 3pm Monday to Thursday, and 9:30am to 4:30pm on Friday. Most banks here have ATMs that accept Visa, MasterCard, American Express, and any other bank or credit card on the Cirrus, Honor, Novus, and PLUS networks.

Climate   See "When to Go," in chapter 2.

Currency Exchange   Americans need not bother to exchange their dollars into Bahamian dollars because the currencies are on par. However, Canadians and Brits will need to convert their money, which can be done at local banks or sometimes at a hotel, though hotels tend to offer less favorable rates.

Doctors   For the fastest and best service, head to Rand Memorial Hospital (see "Hospitals," below).

Drugstores   For prescriptions and other pharmaceutical needs, go to Mini Mall, 1 West Mall, Explorer's Way, where you'll find **L.M.R. Drugs** (① **242/352-7327**), next door to Burger King. Hours are Monday to Saturday 8am to 8pm and Sunday 8am to 3pm.

Embassies & Consulates   See "Fast Facts: The Bahamas," in chapter 2.

Emergencies   For all emergencies, call ① **911,** or dial 0 for the operator.

Eyeglass Repair   The biggest specialist in eyeglasses and contact lenses is the **Optique Shoppe,** 7 Regent Centre, downtown Freeport (① **242/352-9073**).

Hospitals   If you have a medical emergency, contact the government-operated, 90-bed **Rand Memorial Hospital,** East Atlantic Drive (① **242/352-6735** or 242/352-2689 for ambulance emergency).

Internet Access   Visit the **Cybercafe at the Port Lucaya Marketplace** (① **242/559-0111**), open Monday to Saturday 9am to 8pm.

Information   See "Visitor Information," earlier in this chapter.

Laundry & Dry Cleaning   Try **Jiffy Cleaners Number 3,** West Mall at Pioneer's Way (① **242/352-7079**), open Monday 8am to 1pm, Tuesday to Saturday 8am to 6pm.

Newspapers & Magazines   *The Freeport News* is a morning newspaper published Monday through Saturday except holidays. The two dailies published in Nassau, the *Tribune* and the *Nassau Guardian,* are also available here, as are some New York and Miami papers, especially the *Miami Herald,* usually on the date of publication. American news magazines, such as *Time* and *Newsweek,* are flown in on the day of publication.

Police   In an emergency, dial ⓒ **911.**

Post Office   The main post office is on Explorer's Way in Freeport (ⓒ **242/352-9371**).

Safety   Avoid walking or jogging along lonely roads. There are no particular danger zones, but stay alert: Grand Bahama is no stranger to drugs and crime.

Taxes   All visitors leaving The Bahamas from Freeport must pay a departure tax, but because it's factored into the cost of your airline or cruise ship ticket, very few visitors even realize that it's even being charged. Hotel bills are saddled with a 12% tax regardless of the category of room you occupy. But other than that, as an encouragement to shoppers, no other sales taxes are charged.

Taxis   See "Getting Around," earlier in this chapter.

Weather   Grand Bahama, in the north of The Bahamas, has temperatures in winter that vary from about 60°F to 75°F (16°C–24°C) daily. Summer variations range from 78°F to the high 80s (26°C to the low 30s Celsius). In Freeport/Lucaya, phone ⓒ **915** for weather information.

3 Where to Stay

Your choices are the Freeport area (near the Bahamia Casino and the International Bazaar) or Lucaya (closer to the beach).

Remember: In most cases, a resort levy of 8% and a 15% service charge will be added to your final bill. Be prepared, and ask if it's already included in the initial price you're quoted.

FREEPORT
EXPENSIVE

Island Seas Resort   A three-story timeshare property that's open to nonmembers and painted a tone of peach, this resort opens onto a secluded beach positioned midway between downtown Freeport

Where to Stay & Dine in Freeport/Lucaya

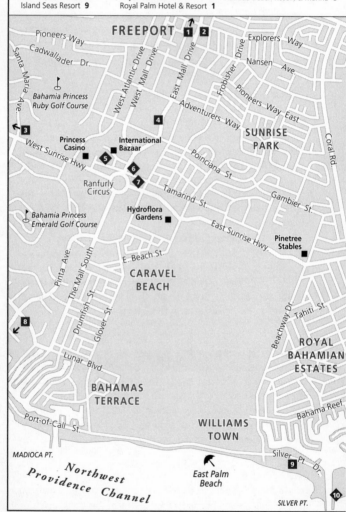

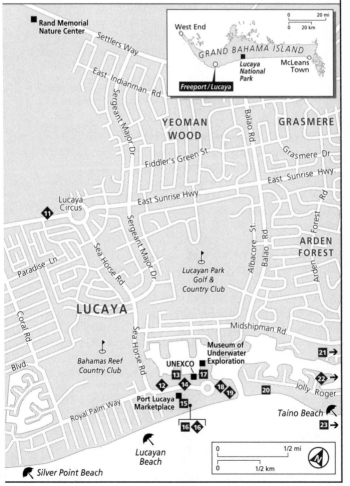

and Port Lucaya. The resort also offers its own water fun with its pool, hot tub, and waterfall. Also on-site is a tiki-hut restaurant and bar. The location is convenient for the Port Lucaya Market and the Lucaya Golf and Country Club. Depending on their individual owners, each condo is furnished with a decor that's different from that of its immediate neighbor. Floor plans include both one- and two-bedroom suites. Each contains a full bathroom with tub/shower, plus a full kitchen and balcony. Although technically they're not associated with the hotel in any way, many watersports outfitters are located right on the beach.

William's Town (P.O. Box F-44735), Freeport, Grand Bahamas, The Bahamas. © 242/373-1271. Fax 242/373-1275. www.islandseas.com. 197 units Year-round $109–$129 (£58–£68) double; $129–$149 (£68–£79) 2-bedroom suite. AE, DISC, MC, V. **Amenities:** Restaurant; bar; pool; tennis court; gym/exercise facilities; bike rentals; on-site car-rental kiosk; massage. *In room:* A/C, TV, fully equipped kitchen, iron, safe.

INEXPENSIVE

Best Western Castaways Resort & Suites *Kids*   Castaways is a modest and unassuming hotel that's almost immediately adjacent to the International Bazaar in downtown Freeport. A mix of vacationers and business travelers stay here because of its clean, well-maintained motel-style rooms and its moderate prices. Pink-walled, green-shuttered rooms surround a quartet of landscaped courtyards, creating shelter from the traffic outside. It's not on the water, but a free shuttle will take you to nearby Williams Town Beach. Surrounded by gardens, the four-story hotel has an indoor/outdoor garden lobby with a gift shop and on-site kiosks selling island tours and water sports venues. Cheerful bedrooms are outfitted in your basic motel/tropical resort style. The Flamingo Restaurant features Bahamian and American dishes daily from 7:30am to 10pm; it also serves one of the island's best breakfasts. There's a swimming pool area with a wide terrace and a pool bar serving sandwiches and cool drinks. A children's playground adjoins the pool.

E. Mall Dr. (P.O. Box F-42629), Freeport, Grand Bahama, The Bahamas. © 800/780-7234 in the U.S., or 242/352-6682. Fax 242/352-5087. www.bestwestern.com. 118 units. Winter $155 (£82) double, $180 (£95) suite; off season $130 (£69) double, $165 (£87) suite. Children under 12 stay free in parent's room. AE, MC, V. **Amenities:** Restaurant; 2 bars; pool; babysitting; self-service laundry; nonsmoking rooms; rooms for those w/limited mobility. *In room:* A/C, TV, hair dryer, iron, safe.

Island Palm Resort *Value*   Set within the commercial heart of Freeport, this simple three-story motel consists of four buildings separated by parking lots and greenery. An easy walk to virtually everything in town, and 2km (1¼ miles) from the International

Bazaar, it offers good value in no-frills, eminently serviceable rooms with well-kept bathrooms equipped with tub/showers. Complimentary shuttle-bus service ferries anybody who's interested to nearby Williams Town Beach (also called Island Seas Beach), where you can use the seaside facilities (including jet skis and snorkeling equipment) of its sibling resort, a timeshare unit known as Island Seas.

E. Mall Dr. (P.O. Box F-44881), Freeport, Grand Bahama, The Bahamas. ② 242/352-6648. Fax 242/352-6640. 143 units. Winter $89 (£47) double; off season $79 (£42) double. Extra person $15 (£7.95). AE, DISC, MC, V. **Amenities:** Bar; pool; non-smoking rooms; rooms for those w/limited mobility. *In room:* A/C, TV.

Royal Islander   This hotel was built during an unfortunate Disney-style period in Freeport's expansion during the early 1980s. Its improbable-looking pyramidal roofs inspired by a trio of Mayan pyramids were rendered somewhat less obvious in 2004 when they were resheathed with dark gray metal. Inside it's tasteful and hospitable, with rooms arranged around a verdant courtyard that seems far removed from the busy traffic and sterile-looking landscape outside. Rooms on the street level have white-tile floors, while those upstairs have wall-to-wall carpeting. Bathrooms are a bit on the small side, with sinks and tub/showers. Throughout, the motif is Florida/tropical, with some pizzazz and rates that tend to be cheaper than at the Best Western across the street. There's a family link between the owners of this place and the owners of the more opulent and famous Xanadu (see separate recommendation). A bus shuttles about every hour between this hotel and Xanadu beach.

There's a coffee-shop-style snack bar and a small restaurant on the premises, but other than that, you'll have to wander a short distance, perhaps to the International Bazaar just across the street, to find diversions and dining.

E. Mall Dr. (P.O. Box F-42549), Freeport, Grand Bahama, The Bahamas. ② 242/351-6000. Fax 242/351-3546. www.bahamasvacationguide.com/royalislander.html. 100 units. Year-round $90 (£48). Children under 14 stay free in parent's room. AE, MC, V. **Amenities:** Restaurant; snack bar; bar; pool; Jacuzzi; self-service laundry; nonsmoking rooms; children's playground. *In room:* A/C, TV, safe.

Royal Palm Hotel & Resort   Don't confuse this hotel with some of its competitors, whose names and amenities are roughly equivalent. The staff here commented to us about how often a taxi will arrive with passengers whose reservations are at other hotels with similar names that included the Royal Islander, the Island Palm, and the relatively more expensive Island Seas, each of which is also recommended. This particular choice is a well-maintained, cost-effective motel that's the closest property to the airport on Grand

Bahama Island. It's set behind a hot-pink two-story facade which, while inland from the beach, nonetheless provides an oasis of resort-style living, thanks to the way its wings wrap on three sides around a swimming pool. This is an especially good bet, thanks to its radical renovation that was completed during the winter of 2005. Without any extra charge, rooms are suitable for up to four occupants each. Each is outfitted like you'd expect at a motel-style tropical resort—with tile floors, simple but tasteful furniture, and flower-patterned upholsteries. Although it's usually a bit more expensive than either the Royal Islander or the Island Palm, its repeat clientele—about 50% of whom are on-island for business reasons—don't seem to mind.

East Mall at Settlers' Way (P.O. Box F-44900), Freeport, The Bahamas. (©) 242/352-3462. Fax 242/352-5759. www.royalpalmsuites.com. 48 units. $129–$149 (£68–£79) double. AE, DC, MC, V. **Amenities:** Restaurant; Internet cafe; poolside bar (Conch Juice Corner); tennis court; gift shop; shuttles approximately every hour to Xanadu Beach; children's playground. *In room:* A/C, TV, kitchenette, fridge, coffeemaker, hair dryer, microwave.

LUCAYA
EXPENSIVE
Westin Grand Bahama Island at Our Lucaya Resort & Sheraton Grand Bahama Island at Our Lucaya Resort 𝒦𝒦 (Kids)
This massive $400-million resort is one of the largest in The Bahamas—and by far, it's the finest, most appealing, and best-accessorized property on Grand Bahama Island. The resort is set beside one of the best white strands in The Bahamas—Lucaya Beach. Although the area had been losing tourist business to Paradise Island, it got a big boost in 1999 when this sprawling metropolis opened its doors.

Guests of any of the subdivisions of this resort usually get more than they bargained for. The first of the three sections was completed late in 1998 as the **Sheraton Grand Bahama Island at Our Lucaya Resort.** With a vague South Beach Art Deco design, it's laid out like a massive open-sided, stone-trimmed hexagon. About half of the rooms face the beach and the swimming pool, the other half look toward the gardens. The 513-room resort is contemporary but relaxed; the developers have created a young vibe that draws a high number of families. Bedrooms are whimsical and fun, thanks to fabric designs you'd expect on a loud Hawaiian shirt from the Elvis era and maple-veneered furniture, all put together with artful simplicity.

In 2000, two newer, more upscale, and more cutting-edge subdivisions of Our Lucaya opened immediately next door. The smaller and somewhat more private of the two is **Westin Lighthouse Pointe,** a 322-unit low-rise condo and timeshare complex that focuses on an adult clientele. Its larger counterpart—and, frankly, the one we find the most appealing and intriguing—is the 536-unit **Westin Breakers Cay.** This grand 10-story, white-sided tower has edges that bend in a postmodern S-curve beside the beach. Each of this complex's three subsections stretch like pearls in a necklace along a narrow strip of beachfront, allowing guests to drop into any of the bars, restaurants, and gardens that flank its edges. Also on-site, in a two-story compound flanking the sea, The Lanai is composed of just 23 sprawling two-bedroom suites. Each is richly furnished, melding Colonial Caribbean style with 21st-century decor.

A complex this big contains an impressive array of restaurants, each designed with a different theme and ambience. The most interesting of the resort's dining venues will be reviewed under "Where to Dine," later in this chapter. And consistent with the broad themes, each of the subdivisions has a dramatic and/or unconventional swimming pool. For example, the Sheraton at Our Lucaya's pool seems to flow around a replica of a 19th-century sugar mill, complete with an aqueduct that might be worthy of the ancient Romans. And the Westin at Our Lucaya is separated from the powder-white sands of Lucaya Beach by a trio of lap pools, each 15m (49 ft.) long and 1.2m (4 ft.) deep, with edges that replicate the sinuous S-shape of the hotel's footprint. Lap swimmers especially appreciate these spans of water, each of which has a subtly different temperature. The pools culminate in a watery crescent whose "invisible edge" seems to merge directly into the waters of the Atlantic. In particular, the swim-up bar and hot tubs seem perfect for wedding celebrations after the ceremony.

A spa and fitness center, a quartet of tennis courts, a convention center, a state-of-the-art casino (The Isle of Capri—at press time, the only functioning casino on Grand Bahama Island), and an upscale shopping mall have all also been added in recent years. There's also an increasing emphasis on golf, thanks to the opening of the spectacular Reef Course (p. 164). An innovative feature for tennis players is the Fast Grand Slam of Tennis, which features replicas of the world's best-known court surfaces—red clay at the French Open, manicured grass at Wimbledon, Rebound Ace at the Australian Open, and DecoTurf at the U.S. Open.

Children aged 2 to 12 can be amused and entertained throughout daylight hours every day at The Bahamas' best-run children's venue, Camp Lucaya.

Royal Palm Way (P.O. Box F-42500), Lucaya, Grand Bahama, The Bahamas. ⓒ 877-OUR-LUCAYA in the U.S., or 242/373-1333. Sheraton fax 242/373-8804; Westin fax 242/350-5060. www.ourlucaya.com. 1,260 units. Sheraton year-round $149–$220 (£79–£117) double; from $480 (£254) suite; $30 (£16) extra per day for 3rd and 4th occupants. Westin Lighthouse Pointe or Breakers Cay year-round $210–$279 (£111–£148) double; from $730 (£387) suite; $30 (£16) extra per day for 3rd and 4th occupants. 2-bedroom Lanai suites $1,600–$3,000 (£848–£1,590) per night year-round for up to 6 occupants. AE, DC, DISC, MC, V. **Amenities:** 10 restaurants; 10 bars; 5 pools; 2 18-hole golf courses; 4 tennis courts; health club; spa; watersports equipment/rentals; kids' camp and children's programs; business center; salon; room service; babysitting; laundry service; dry cleaning; nonsmoking rooms; rooms for those w/limited mobility. *In room:* A/C, TV, kitchenette (in suites), minibar, iron, safe.

MODERATE

Pelican Bay at Lucaya ⟨★★⟩   Here's a good choice for travelers with champagne tastes and beer budgets, a hotel with more architectural charm than any other small property on Grand Bahama. It's built on a peninsula jutting into a labyrinth of inland waterways, with moored yachts on several sides. Pelican Bay evokes a Danish or Dutch seaside village with rows of "town houses," each painted a different color and sporting whimsical trim, and each overlooking the harbor. The hotel opened in the fall of 1996 and later expanded with another wing in 1999, and refurbished in 2005 into the kind of venue you might expect from an upscale decorating magazine. Its location couldn't be better, immediately adjacent to Port Lucaya Marketplace, where restaurants and entertainment spots abound. Lucaya Beach, one of the best stretches of white sand on the island, lies within a 5-minute walk. Taíno Beach, with equally good sands, lies immediately to the east of the hotel, on the opposite side of a saltwater channel with hourly ferryboat service. UNEXSO, which provides some of the best dive facilities in The Bahamas, is next door. If that's not enough, the extensive amenities of Our Lucaya (see previous listing) are available for use.

Accommodations—especially the suites—are about as stylish and high-fashion as you'll find on Grand Bahama Island, rivaled only by the Westin/Sheraton compound at Our Lucaya, located a very short walk away. Each has either a veranda or a balcony, usually with water views, and floors of buffed, tinted concrete with a scattering of rustic art objects and handicrafts from all over the world. The hotel has one main restaurant, the Ferry House, which specializes in imaginative international cuisine and serves lunch Monday to Saturday and dinner daily. The Yellow Tail Pool Bar offers drinks, salads, and sandwiches throughout the day.

Seahorse Rd. (P.O. Box F-42654), Lucaya, Grand Bahama, The Bahamas. ✆ 800/
600-9192 in the U.S., or 242/373-9550. Fax 242/373-9551. www.pelicanbay
hotel.com. 183 units. Winter $259–$319 (£137–£169) double, $379 (£201) suite;
off season $159–$229 (£84–£121) double, $319 (£169) suite. Rates include break-
fast. AE, MC, V. **Amenities:** Restaurant; bar; 3 pools; Jacuzzi; business center;
babysitting; nonsmoking rooms. *In room:* A/C, TV, minibar (in suites), minifridge, coffeemaker, hair dryer, iron, safe.

Port Lucaya Resort & Yacht Club 🍴   Comfortable, cost-conscious, unpretentious, and convenient, this resort opened in 1993 in
the heart of the Port Lucaya restaurant, hotel, and nightlife complex.
Many guests are drawn to the nautical atmosphere of the resort and
its proximity to Port Lucaya Marketplace. It was designed as a compound of pastel-colored two-story structures that guests reach either
on foot or (if they're transporting luggage) via golf cart after checking
in. They're scattered in rows that wind around a horseshoe-shaped
courtyard, very close to a marina and within a very short walk from
the restaurants, bars, shops, and nightlife options of the marketplace
at Port Lucaya. The wings of guest rooms separate the piers—home
for some very expensive marine hardware—from a verdant central
green space with a gazebo-style bar and a swimming pool. Although
set inland on a waterway (Lucayan Harbour), this resort lies within a
few minutes' walk of Lucaya Beach, one of the island's finest, and is
also close to Taíno Beach. Even though it's not right on the beach, it's
such an easy walk that no one seems to complain.

The medium-size rooms have tile floors and are attractively and
comfortably furnished with rattan pieces and big wall mirrors. The
rooms are divided into various categories, ranging from standard to
deluxe, and open onto the marina (preferred by yachting guests),
the Olympic-size swimming pool, or the well-landscaped garden. (If
you don't want to hear the sounds coming from the lively marketplace, request units 1–6, which are more tranquil and distanced
from the noise.) Bathrooms are tidy but not overly large, with
tub/showers and a layout like what you might get at a middle-
bracket motel in south Florida.

Bell Channel Bay Rd. (P.O. Box F-42452), Lucaya, Grand Bahama, The Bahamas.
✆ 800/LUCAYA-1 or 242/373-6618. Fax 242/373-6652. www.portlucayaresort.com.
160 units. Winter $112–$162 (£59–£86) double, $196–$280 (£104–£148) suite; off
season $90–$134 (£48–£71) double, $214–$224 (£113–£119) suite. Extra person
$28 (£15) per day. Children 12 and under stay free in parent's room. AE, DISC, MC, V.
Amenities: 2 bars; pool; Jacuzzi; babysitting; nonsmoking rooms. *In room:* A/C, TV,
hair dryer, iron, fridge available for $10 (£5.30) extra per day.

INEXPENSIVE

Bell Channel Inn This is the best resort choice for scuba divers, lying as it does near the Port Lucaya and close to the ocean. Much of it looks like a moderately priced motel in Florida, opening onto a solar-heated pool. The inn offers its own full-service dive shop and a private boat. You don't come here for luxurious bedrooms, but each unit is spacious, well furnished, and comfortable. Most of them contain small refrigerators as well, and each comes with a private balcony with a view over the channel and Port Lucaya. The hotel maintains its own free shuttle to the beach. If you're a diver, ask about the various dive packages available when booking a room; some of the best dive sites lie only a 5- to 10-minute boat ride from the dive center. The on-site Seafood Restaurant & Bar specializes in the fresh catch of the day.

Kings Rd., Lucaya, Grand Bahama Island, The Bahamas. © **242/373-1053**. Fax 242/373-2886. www.bellchannelinn.com. 32 units. $85 (£45) double; $107 (£57) triple; $129 (£68) quad. AE, MC, V. **Amenities:** Restaurant; bar; outdoor pool; laundry service; babysitting; nonsmoking rooms; dive shop; Wi-Fi in lobby. *In room:* A/C, TV, hair dryer, coffeemaker, fridge (in some).

TAÍNO BEACH
MODERATE

Ritz Beach Resort 🎇 (Kids) Not associated in any way with the Ritz Hotels in London or Paris, this hotel lies across a saltwater canal from the grounds of the Westin & Sheraton at Our Lucaya. It's also located adjacent to Taíno Beach, the "sister beach" of the better-known Lucaya Beach. Enveloped by semitropical gardens, but without the posh and cutting-edge glamour of the Westin and Sheraton hotels, it dates back to 1995, when construction began on what eventually evolved into a three-phase construction program. All the bedrooms are in concrete buildings, each painted a shade of coral. Units start with efficiencies, studios, and one-bedroom suites, and go on up to elaborate villa and penthouse accommodations. The bedrooms are spacious and well furnished and handsomely maintained, with a tub/shower in the efficiency rooms and a walk-in shower in the studios.

The quality and size of your accommodation and amenities depends on how much you want to pay. Penthouses (on the fourth floor) include a multilevel studio with its own sun deck and private pool. On the premises, two separate restaurants serve international cuisine; there's a scattering of bars whose number (a maximum of five) varies with the occupancy level of the hotel and the season. Although the scale of this compound was diminished after the 2004 hurricanes (one of the hotels next door, Taíno Beach, is still closed from the storms of that year), it's still a worthwhile hotel for a holiday on the beach. The hotel maintains a ferry service that makes frequent trips across the canal to a dock associated with the Westin & Sheraton at Our Lucaya ($2.50/£1.30) per person each way, free for infants under 2). From the Westin's dock, the restaurants, shops, and bars of the Port Lucaya Marketplace and access to Grand Bahama's only casino, the Isle of Capri, lie within a 10-minute walk.

Jolly Roger Dr. (P.O. Box F-43819), Taíno Beach, Lucaya, Grand Bahama Island, The Bahamas. ✆ **888/311-7945** or 242/373-9354. Fax 242/373-4421. www.timetravel corp.com. 110 units. Year-round $220 (£117) efficiency; $320 (£170) studio; $535 (£284) penthouse. Children 12 and under stay free in parent's room. AE, MC, V. **Amenities:** Restaurant; pool bar; pool; tennis court; babysitting; laundry service; nonsmoking rooms (all); rooms for those w/limited mobility. *In room:* A/C, TV, hair dryer, iron, beverage maker.

INEXPENSIVE

Flamingo Bay Yacht Club & Marina Hotel   Unlike the Ritz Beach Resort (its nearby sibling resort), which sits directly astride Taíno Beach, this hotel is set back from the water, about a 5-minute walk from a highly appealing length of white sand. Built of painted concrete, with three stories, it offers midsize, unpretentious, and uncomplicated bedrooms that are comfortable and attractively furnished in a Caribbean motif. Each has a well-maintained bathroom with tub/shower, and either two double beds or a king-size bed. Each comes with such extras as a microwave and toaster. From a nearby 20-slip marina, a water taxi runs hourly across a narrow saltwater canal to a pier operated by the Westin hotel. From here, it's a short walk to the Isle of Capri casino and the center of the Lucaya district, with its multiple bars, shops, restaurants, and entertainment options. (The fee for transportation either way is $2.50/£1.30 per person, free for infants under 2.) Although amenities are sparse, customers are permitted to use the plentiful options at the Ritz Beach Resort.

Jolly Roger Dr., Taíno Beach, Lucaya, Grand Bahama Island, The Bahamas. ✆ **800/824-6623** or 242/373-4677. Fax 242/373-4421. www.timetravelcorp.com. 58 units. Year-round $100–$130 (£53–£69) double. Children 12 and under stay free in parent's room. AE, DISC, MC, V. **Amenities:** Coin-operated laundry; nonsmoking rooms. *In room:* A/C, cable-connected TV, kitchenette, beverage maker.

AT XANADU BEACH

Xanadu Beach Resort and Marina ✿   Permeated with one of the most quirky and idiosyncratic histories of any hotel in The Bahamas, and now painted a cheerful shade of yellow, this hotel is radically different from the way it was when it housed the reclusive billionaire Howard Hughes. Despite storm damages in 2004 and 2005, and all kinds of setbacks, Xanadu is back, soaring triumphantly above a scrub-dotted landscape that's crisscrossed with canals, mysteriously upscale villas, and reminders of the hurricane damages of the past several years. You'll get the sense here of a brave and valiant hotel that has struggled to provide service and comfort to visitors, despite negative fortunes and a hotel scene that has shifted to an increasing degree away from Freeport and toward Port Lucaya. Much of the allure of Xanadu today is the result of the hard work and devotion of the Donato family. It benefited in 2005 from a big influx of cash that reconfigured the lobby area into a Spanish baroque fantasy. Macho-looking and elegant, it evokes a private club where billionaires of the stature of Hughes himself might feel at home. Regrettably, however, there's a sense that this place is still barely clinging to economic viability. Damaged rooflines and some of the balustrades remain in need of repair. Nevertheless, bedrooms are comfortable and the nearby beach is still alluring, even though many of the shoreline structures need rebuilding. Is the ghost of Howard Hughes still lurking in the penthouse? Perhaps. Members of the staff, particularly the ultracharming and very capable general manager, Ms. Toni Donato, have a lot to say about that, if you're able to pin them down.

P.O. Box F-42438, Freeport, Grand Bahama Island, The Bahamas. © 242/352-6783. Fax 242/352-6299. www.xanadubeachhotel.com. 186 units, plus 3 1-bedroom waterfront villas. Year-round $145 (£77) double; $245–$400 (£130–£212) suites; $450 (£239) villas per day for up to 4 occupants. AE, DC, MC, V. **Amenities:** Pool; 2 tennis courts; gym; gift shop; babysitting; full-service PADI dive shop; watersports concessions. *In room:* A/C, TV, minibar.

ON GRAND BAHAMA ISLAND'S WEST END
EXPENSIVE
Old Bahama Bay 🏝🏝 One of the most dramatic real estate developments in The Bahamas is unfolding at this outpost on the island's extreme western tip. Here descendents of local residents of the West End, each educated and trained in the U.S., are organizing and repairing, after the 2005 hurricanes, one of the most ambitious and upscale development projects in the country. Built on a site that in the early 1980s was the setting for an unsuccessful Jack Tar Village, the project centers on a cluster of upscale hotel units, a state-of-the-art 72-slip marina, and a palm-flanked beach. It's also the venue for some ambitious development plans for the very near future, including a radical reconfiguration of the coastline through

the dredging of all-new saltwater lagoons and a redesign of the (man-made) docking facilities and harborfront.

Don't expect to find any evidence of former developments on this site. Virtually everything that had been here previously was demolished to make way for the new construction. The core of the resort consists of nine two-story beach houses, each with between four and six living units inside. Spacious and breezy living quarters, they're outfitted in a Caribbean colonial/tropical country club style. Bathrooms are sheathed in marble, and each contains a shower/whirlpool tub combination and deluxe toiletries. A pair of restaurants—the Dockside Grille and Aqua—serve well-prepared Bahamian and international dishes on a rotating basis that will be determined by the season and the number of residents on-site.

Though the hotel's appealing, it's the homesites and plans for new marinas to be dredged out of the low-lying scrubland that has the real estate community buzzing. During the lifetime of this edition, we expect interesting big-scale development on this 89-hectare (220-acre) site that's ready and able to catch the real estate boom as it spills over from the Florida mainland. This resort encompasses much more than just hotel accommodations. Its owners envision it as an entire village-in-the-making, relentlessly upscale and dotted with celebrity references. There's even an airplane landing strip within a quarter-mile of this resort. Plans call for the expansion of the marina and an improvement of the beachfronts. Building sites range in price from $400,000 to $1 million each; most are already sold, we were told. Investors have included John Travolta, who presently owns four of the beachfront hotel units. Celebrity sightings here have included *Sex and the City* star Chris Noth, Geraldo Rivera, and Jack Nicklaus.

West End (P.O. Box F-42546), Grand Bahama Island, The Bahamas. ✆ **800/ 444-9469** in the U.S. or 242/350-3500. Fax 242/346-6546. www.oldbahamabay. com. 73 units. Winter $330–$575 (£175–£305) suite; from $790 (£419) 2-bedroom suite; off season $235–$395 (£125–£209) suite; from $560 (£297) 2-bedroom suite. Breakfast and dinner $115 (£61) per person extra per day. AE, MC, V. **Amenities:** 2 restaurants; 2 bars; pool; 2 tennis courts; fitness center; watersports equipment/ rentals; room service; massage; babysitting; laundry service; nonsmoking rooms (all). *In room:* A/C, TV, kitchenette, minifridge, hair dryer, iron, safe, beverage maker.

Viva Wyndham Fortuna Beach ✿ (Kids   While Grand Bahama Island has sprawling, undeveloped tracts of land to the east of this property, this is the easternmost resort on the island. Some visitors argue that the beachfront here is even better than the more extensively developed strands at Port Lucaya. The swimming pool, however, packs a lot less drama than those associated with the Westin & Sheraton at Our Lucaya. This place has made a name for itself by surviving more than one destructive hurricane. During the midsummer months, the staff welcomes an almost exclusively Italian clientele, the result of an exclusive arrangement with a tour operator. Because of that arrangement, you might have difficulty getting a room here between May and September. Throughout the rest of the year, a mostly North American clientele vacations here, and the property is promoted as an all-inclusive venue where all meals, drinks, lodgings, and most watersports are included as part of one price.

The setting is a sprawling compound of 10 hectares (25 acres) of remote and breezy beachfront property, loaded with sports activities that are covered by the price. Established in 1993, Viva Fortuna lies 9.5km (6 miles) east of the International Bazaar along the southern coast of Grand Bahama Island, amid an isolated landscape of casuarinas and scrubland. Comfortably furnished, stylish, and midsize bedrooms lie in a colorful group of two-story outbuildings, some of which are technically classified as timeshares but which are added to the resort's rental pool whenever they're not occupied. About three-quarters have ocean views; the others overlook the surrounding scrublands. Most have a private balcony and two queen-size beds; a small bathroom offers a shower stall but no tub in almost every unit. Singles are charged 40% more than the per-person double-occupancy rate.

All meals, which are included in the rates, are served buffet-style in any of three separate restaurants. In addition to an ongoing series of buffets, you'll find an Italian restaurant and an Asian restaurant, the latter centered on an appealing statue of Buddha. Know in advance that if you stay here, you'll find yourself far from Port Lucaya and its bustle (although a shuttle bus brings guests to the International Bazaar in downtown Freeport twice per day). For clients who appreciate the all-inclusive format where there's not a lot of incentive for straying very far from the property, it's a worthwhile choice.

1 Doubloon Rd. (P.O. Box F-42398), Freeport, Grand Bahama, The Bahamas. © 800/ 898-9968 or 242/373-4000. Fax 242/373-5555. www.wyndham.com. 276 units. Winter $140 (£74) per person double occupancy, $65 (£34) extra person; off season $251 (£133) per person double occupancy, $78 (£41) extra person. Rates are all-inclusive. AE, DC, MC, V. **Amenities:** 4 restaurants; 4 bars; disco; pool; 2 tennis courts; gym; sauna; Jacuzzi; watersports equipment/rentals; kids' club; babysitting; nonsmoking rooms; rooms for those w/limited mobility. *In room:* A/C, TV, fridge, coffeemaker, hair dryer, iron, safe.

4 Where to Dine

Foodies will find that the cuisine on Grand Bahama Island doesn't match the more refined fare served at dozens of places on New Providence (Nassau/Paradise Island). However, a few places in Grand Bahama specialize in fine dining; others get by with rather standard fare. The good news is that the dining scene is more affordable here.

FREEPORT
MODERATE

Silvano's ✦ ITALIAN   This 80-seat restaurant with its Mediterranean decor serves a worthy but not exceptional cuisine. A competently prepared repertoire inspired by the culinary favorites of Italy is presented here with quality ingredients, most of them shipped in from the United States. Service is polite and helpful. The grilled veal steak is one of the genuinely commendable dishes, along with the homemade pastas served with a variety of freshly made sauces. The chef also works his magic with fish and fresh shrimp. Other traditional Italian dishes round out the menu.

Ranfurley Circle. ✆ 242/352-5111. Reservations recommended. Lunch specials $7–$14 (£3.70–£7.40); main courses $16–$42 (£8.50–£22). AE, DISC, MC, V. Daily noon–3pm and 5–11pm.

INEXPENSIVE

Beckey's Restaurant BAHAMIAN/AMERICAN   Set near a busy landlocked traffic artery midway between Port Lucaya and downtown Freeport, this unpretentious yellow-and-white restaurant offers authentic Bahamian cuisine prepared in the time-tested style of the Out Islands. Owned and operated by long-time entrepreneurs Beckey and Berkeley Smith, the place offers a welcome dose of down-to-earth noncasino reality to local Bahamians and to off-island visitors who appreciate local, nonglittery lifestyles. Breakfasts are either all-American or Bahamian and are available all day. Also popular are minced lobster, curried mutton, fish platters, baked or curried chicken, and conch salads. Stick to the local specialties instead of the lackluster American dishes.

E. Sunrise Hwy. and E. Beach Dr. ✆ 242/352-5247. Breakfast $5–$11 (£2.65–£5.85); main courses $9–$25 (£4.70–£13). AE, MC, V. Daily 7am to between 8pm and 10pm, depending on the season and on business.

Geneva's BAHAMIAN/SEAFOOD   If you want to eat where the locals eat, head for this unpretentious local venue, where food is made the old-fashioned way. This restaurant is one of the best places to sample conch, which has fed and nourished Bahamians for centuries. The Monroe family will prepare it for you stewed, cracked, or fried, or as part of a savory conch chowder that makes an excellent starter. Grouper also appears, prepared in every imaginable way. The bartender will get you into the mood with a rum-laced Bahama Mama.

Kipling Lane and E. Mall, at W. Sunrise Hwy. ✆ **242/352-5085.** Lunch sandwiches and platters $6–$12 (£3.20–£6.35); dinner main courses $9–$27 (£4.75–£14). DISC, MC, V. Daily 7am–11pm.

The Pepper Pot BAHAMIAN   This might be the only place on Grand Bahama that focuses exclusively on takeout food in the Bahamian style. It's popular throughout the day and evening, but it's especially mobbed on weekends after midnight, when nightclubbers descend upon it for after-bar, after-disco munchies. (It's the only 24-hr. eatery we know of on Grand Bahama Island.) Don't expect glamour, as it's set in a cramped and very ordinary-looking modern building that's within a shopping center that's a 5-minute drive east of the International Bazaar, beside the road leading to Port Lucaya. You can order takeout portions of the island's best guava duff (a dessert specialty of The Bahamas that resembles a jelly roll), as well as a savory conch chowder; pork chops; fish dishes, usually deep-fried and served as part of "fish and chips"; chicken souse (an acquired taste); cracked conch; sandwiches and hamburgers; and an array of daily specials. The owner is Ethiopian-born Wolansa Fountain.

E. Sunrise Hwy. (at Coral Rd.). ✆ **242/373-7655.** Breakfast $3–$6 (£1.60–£3.20); main courses $11–$15 (£5.85–£7.95); vegetarian plates $5–$6 (£2.65–£3.20). No credit cards. Daily 24 hr.

The Pub on the Mall INTERNATIONAL   Located on the same floor of the same building and under the same management, three distinctive eating areas lie across the boulevard from the International Bazaar and attract many locals. The **Prince of Wales** serves such Olde English staples as shepherd's pie, fish and chips, platters of roast beef or fish, and real English ale. One end of the room is devoted to the **Red Dog Sports Bar,** with a boisterous atmosphere and at least four TV screens (including one that's a whopping 96 in. wide) blasting away for dedicated fans. **Silvano's** (see above) is an Italian restaurant serving lots of pasta, usually with verve, as well as veal, chicken, beefsteaks, seafood, and such desserts as tiramisu. A final venue which may or may not be open, depending on the plans of its staff, is Bahamian-themed **Islander's Roost,** which has a bright tropical decor and a balcony overlooking the bazaar.

Throughout this place, food is good if not great; the main platters are a good value, usually very filling and satisfying.

Ranfurley Circle, Sunrise Hwy. © 242/352-5110. Reservations recommended. Main courses $7–$36 (£3.70–£19). AE, DISC, MC, V. Prince of Wales and Red Dog daily noon–midnight; Silvano's daily noon–3pm and 5–11pm; Islanders' Roost usually, depending on business, Mon–Sat 5–11pm.

IN THE INTERNATIONAL BAZAAR
INEXPENSIVE

Café Michel BAHAMIAN/AMERICAN   The name implies that you've found an authentic French bistro amid the bustle of the International Bazaar. In reality, this place is rather akin to a tropical, vaguely Rastafarian version of a coffee shop and bar. Nonetheless (and the place has declined, like the rest of the International Bazaar, in recent years), it provides a funky and sometimes amusing option for refueling when you're shopping the cracked and dusty byways of the bazaar. Beneath a once bright, now faded red awning (inspired, one suspects, by Maxim's in Paris) are clusters of cramped, somewhat claustrophobic cafe tables, displays loaded with conch shell souvenirs, and chalkboards listing the food that's available that day. Local shopkeepers know to come here for coffee, platters, salads, and sandwiches throughout the day, or perhaps a drink after cruise ship passengers have gone for the day. Both American and Bahamian dishes are served, including seafood platters, steaks, lobster tail, and, of course, grouper.

International Bazaar. © 242/352-2191. Reservations recommended for dinner. Main courses $7–$42 (£3.70–£22). AE, MC, V. Mon–Sat 9am–5pm. Closed Sept.

China Temple CHINESE   This battered-looking Chinese joint—and don't expect more than just that—also does takeout. Over the years it's proved to be the dining bargain of the bazaar, surviving in a venue that hasn't been profitable for many of its (now-defunct) competitors. The menu is familiar, standard, and a bit shopworn: chop suey, chow mein, and sweet-and-sour chicken. It's certainly not gourmet Asian fare, but it's cheap, and it might hit the spot when you're craving something different.

International Bazaar. © 242/352-5610. Lunch $7–$9 (£3.70–£4.80); main courses $10–$14 (£5.30–£7.40). AE, MC, V. Mon–Sat 10:30am–10pm.

AT OUR LUCAYA & TAÍNO BEACH
EXPENSIVE

China Beach ☆ ASIAN FUSION   Within its own separate stone-and-stucco building on the seafronting grounds of the Westin & Sheraton at Our Lucaya, this restaurant offers a culinary passport to the Pacific Rim. Exotic delights include the spicy hot cuisines of Vietnam and Thailand, with calls at Korea, Indonesia, and Malaysia. The menu changes every month, but some dishes appear with regularity. Our favorites among these are a savory Hong Kong roast duckling and a zesty Thai chicken. The beef marinated in soy sauce is served with fresh spring onion, and the grouper filet appears with fresh ginger and scallions. Other Far East specialties include a seafood teppanyaki and stir-fry conch. The decor of this place is particularly imaginative, with scarlet parasols doubling as ceiling chandeliers, and an architecture that seems to float above one of the resort's serpentine-shaped swimming pools.

At the Westin & Sheraton at Our Lucaya resorts, Royal Palm Way. ✆ 242/373-1444. Reservations recommended. Main courses $21–$36 (£11–£19). AE, DC, DISC, MC, V. Tues–Sat 6–11pm, with occasional variations in hours based on occupancy of the surrounding resort.

Churchill's 🐟🐟 AMERICAN   One of the island's most elegant and formal restaurants, it's imbued with a sense of the faded grandeur of what used to be known as the British Empire. Surpassed only, we believe, by the Ferry House and Luciano's, both of which are recommended below, Churchill's lures diners from other parts of Grand Bahama Island to a dining room that opens onto the lobby of the Westin Hotel at Our Lucaya. The venue includes a British-colonial bar with dark-wood floor and trim, potted plants, ceiling fans, a grand piano, and big-windowed views over the sea. The island's best chophouse, it features both succulent steaks flown over from the mainland and locally caught seafood. The manor house setting is an appropriate foil for the finely honed service and top-quality ingredients, deftly prepared. Regrettably, it's open less frequently than we'd have liked, sometimes operating only on weekends during low and shoulder season.

At the Westin & Sheraton at Our Lucaya resorts, Royal Palm Way. ✆ 242/373-1444. Reservations required. Main courses $27–$65 (£14–£34). AE, DC, DISC, MC, V. Usually Mon–Sat 6–11pm, but during off season, hours vary according to occupancy levels of the hotel.

Iries 🐟 CARIBBEAN   This is one of the newest restaurants at the Westin & Sheraton at Our Lucaya. As such, a team of food and beverage experts threw tons of money and research into developing the appropriate blend of Caribbean tradition and postmodern sales and marketing. The result will remind you of the dining room of a massive colonial Caribbean (probably Jamaican) manor house. Decor is replete with replicas of pineapples (the region's traditional symbol of hospitality), Rastafarian-inspired paintings, and elaborately carved mahogany furniture similar to what might have graced the home of a 19th-century Caribbean planter. You'll get a sense of spaciousness and old-fashioned dignity and restraint. Menu items include lobster and grilled corn bisque, cracked conch with spicy Pick-a-Pepper sauce and sweet potato wedges, grilled sirloin steak with cumin and thyme, Caribbean-inspired shrimp scampi, blackened grouper with fire-roasted peppers and pineapple sauce, and tamarind-glazed hen. On your way in, check out the Bahamian Junkanoo costume, which hangs like a permanent exhibition in a museum. Replete with sequins and mystical references, it's one of the most elaborate, most outrageous, and most costly examples of its kind. The Bahamian staff here is genuinely proud of it.

The Westin & Sheraton at Our Lucaya resorts, Royal Palm Way. ✆ **242/373-1444.** Main courses $27–$50 (£14–£27). AE, MC, V. Sat–Wed 6–11pm, but hours vary according to the season and occupancy levels of the hotel which contains it.

The Stoned Crab ✿ SEAFOOD   Tired of frozen seafood shipped in from the mainland? Come to this independent (that is, not associated with any hotel) restaurant for sweet stone crab claws and the lobster, both caught in Bahamian waters. There's none better on the island. You can't miss this place—a triple pyramid (ca. 1968) whose isolated, four-story wood-and-steel framework is strong enough to withstand any hurricane. Swiss-born Livio Peronino is the manager and chef, preparing a seafood platter with everything on it, including grouper, conch fritters, and varied shellfish. The best pasta on the menu is linguine al pesto with lobster and shrimp. For starters, try the zesty conch chowder. Have a lobster salad with your meal and finish with Irish coffee.

At Taíno Beach, Lucaya. ✆ **242/373-1442.** Reservations recommended. Main courses $8–$18 (£4.25–£9.55) lunch, $22–$34 (£12–£18) dinner. AE, MC, V. Tues–Sun 11am–3pm; daily 5–10pm.

MODERATE

Prop Club AMERICAN/INTERNATIONAL   Set within its own low-slung building on the grounds of the Westin & Sheraton at Our Lucaya, this is the kind of place that raffish-looking crew members from charter yachts search out during their time in port. It evokes a battered airplane hangar where mail planes might have been repaired during World War II. When the weather's right, large doors open to bring the outdoors inside, and the party overflows onto the beach. Dig into a "mountain of ribs," or else savor the blackened grouper. Ever had a grilled margarita chicken sandwich? You can order juicy oversize burgers, fajitas, spicy conch chowder, and the like.

At the Westin & Sheraton at Our Lucaya resorts, Royal Palm Way. © 242/
373-1444. Main courses $14–$32 (£7.40–£17). AE, DC, MC, V. Restaurant daily
11:30am–10pm; bar Sun–Thurs 11:30am–1am; Fri–Sat noon–2am.

INEXPENSIVE
Willy Broadleaf ☆ INTERNATIONAL   Set on the street level
of the Westin at Our Lucaya, facing one of its S-curved swimming
pools, this imaginatively decorated restaurant focuses on one of the
most lavish buffet breakfasts we've ever seen in The Bahamas. The
decor fits the cuisine, with various sections evoking a courtyard in
Mexico, a marketplace in old Cairo, the dining hall of an Indian
maharajah (including tables that are partially concealed from neigh-
bors with yards of translucent fabric), even an African village. There
are food stations here for both cold and hot breakfast foods, lavish
buffet spreads, and separate chefs preparing omelets, eggs, pancakes,
and French toast (the best version of which is laced with coconut)
at state-of-the-art cook stations.

The Westin & Sheraton at Our Lucaya resorts, Royal Palm Way. © 242/373-1444.
Breakfast buffets $12 (£6.35) for cold foods, $20 (£11) for both hot and cold foods.
AE, DC, DISC, MC, V. Daily 6:30–11am and 6–11pm.

AT PORT LUCAYA MARKETPLACE
EXPENSIVE
Ferry House ☆☆ *(Finds)* CAJUN/SEAFOOD   This restaurant
serves the most celebrated, the most elaborate, and the most "fussed
over" cuisine on Grand Bahama Island. Much of its excellence
derives from the hard work and talent of its Iceland-born owner.
Designed to look like the mostly brown interior of a wood-trimmed
ferryboat, it faces the ocean, just at the edge of Bell Channel, the
waterway that funnels boats from the open sea into the sheltered
confines of the Port Lucaya Marina. Lunches are relatively simple
affairs, consisting of pastas, catch of the day, and meal-size salads.
Dinner might feature a seafood platter laden with calamari, fish, and
shrimp; a delectable filet mignon with potatoes and vegetables; fresh
salmon with hollandaise sauce; and savory grilled rack of New
Zealand lamb. But our favorite meal here is the seared yellowfin
tuna steak with vegetable couscous. Many of the herbs used here are
grown in the restaurant's own garden. Dessert might include a melt-
in-your-mouth chocolate cake, one of the best we've ever tasted.

Beside Bell Channel, Port Lucaya. © 242/373-1595. Reservations recommended
for dinner. Lunch platters $10–$19 (£5.30–£10); set-price lunch $25 (£13); dinner
main courses $33–$40 (£17.50–£21). AE, MC, V. Mon–Fri noon–2:30pm; Tues–Sun
6–9pm.

Luciano's ⓕ FRENCH/CONTINENTAL With its tables usually occupied by local government officials and deal makers, Luciano's is the grande dame of Freeport restaurants, with a very European atmosphere. It's the only restaurant in Port Lucaya offering caviar, foie gras, and oysters Rockefeller, all served with a flourish by a formally dressed waitstaff (who, fortunately, have a very definite sense of charm and humor). There's a bar inside and elegantly decorated tables set in the kind of socially correct dining rooms you might find in Paris. Additional seating on a breezy upstairs veranda overlooks the marina. Lightly smoked and thinly sliced salmon makes a good opener, as does a seafood crepe or snails in garlic butter. Fresh fish and shellfish are regularly featured and delicately prepared, allowing their natural flavors to shine through without heavy, overwhelming sauces. A good example includes local grouper topped with toasted almonds and a lemon-flavored butter sauce, or broiled Bahamian lobster tail. Steak Diane is one of Luciano's classics, along with an especially delectable veal medallion sautéed with shrimp and chunks of lobster.

Port Lucaya Marketplace. ⓒ 242/373-9100. www.portlucaya.com/lucianos. Reservations required in winter. Main courses $25–$44 (£13–£23). AE, MC, V. Daily 5:30–9:45pm (last order).

MODERATE

Fatman's Nephew ⓕ BAHAMIAN In another location, "Fatman" became a legend on Grand Bahama Island. Although he's no longer with us, the Fatman must have left his recipes and cooking skills to another generation of cooks. Today the place, which used to cater mainly to locals, has gone touristy, but much of the same traditional fare is still served with the same unflagging allegiance to Bahamian ways. The restaurant overlooks the marina at Port Lucaya from an eagle's-nest position on the second floor. You can enjoy drinks or meals inside, but we like to head out to an outdoor covered deck to watch the action below. At least 10 different kinds of game fish—including both wahoo and Cajun blackened kingfish—plus curried chicken, mutton, turtle steak (lightly breaded and pan-fried), or beef are usually offered. Bahamian-style shark soup, made from the flesh of either nurse sharks (they're especially flavorful because they feed primarily on lobsters) or hammerheads ("little tender ones," according to the chef), is sometimes featured on the menu. Most dishes, except for expensive shellfish, fall at the lower end of the price scale. Beware, as the local staff can be flighty.

Port Lucaya Marketplace. ⓒ 242/373-8520. Main courses $10–$40 (£5.30–£21). AE, DISC, MC, V. Mon–Sat 11am–10pm.

Giovanni's Cafe ✦ ITALIAN/SEAFOOD   Tucked into one of the pedestrian thoroughfares of Port Lucaya Marketplace, this cream-colored clapboard house provides the setting for a charming 38-seat Italian trattoria. The chefs (including head chef Giovanni Colo) serve Italian-influenced preparations of local seafood, highlighted by seafood pasta (usually prepared only for two diners) and a lobster special. Giovanni stamps each dish with his Italian verve and flavor, whether it be Bahamian conch, local seafood, or scampi. Dishes show off his precision and rock-solid technique, exemplified by sirloin steak with fresh mushrooms, delectable shrimp scampi, and fattening but extremely good spaghetti carbonara.

Port Lucaya Marketplace. ✆ 242/373-9107. Reservations recommended. Main courses lunch $9.50–$15 (£5–£7.95), dinner $15–$38 (£7.95–£20). AE, MC, V. Mon–Sat 8:30am–10pm; Sun 5–10pm.

The Harbour Room ✦✦ (Kids) EUROPEAN/CARIBBEAN   The only member of the prestigious *Chaîne des Rotisseurs* on Grand Bahama Island, this is one of the best restaurants in Port Lucaya. It offers a definite continental flair; a creative kitchen; a polite, hard-working staff; and a sense of *gemütlichkeit* in the tropics. Tucked away into one corner, its bar area is the most lavish part, with esoteric liquors and liqueurs, and an upscale and stylish decor that recalls a chic hideaway in Berlin. The dining room is simpler. Designed as a counterpart for the cuisine, and not an architectural statement in its own right, it's outfitted with dark-wood trim and a nautical decor that's especially charming when the Atlantic winds outside blow hard and cold. Its owners are not shy about publicizing their culinary ambitions. They serve one of the few white (that is, New England–style) conch chowders we've seen in The Bahamas. Jumbo cheeseburgers are appropriately juicy, but more appealing might be the Delmonico steaks, veal chops with Provençal herbs, and shrimp Alfredo with marinara-flavored pasta. Chilean sea bass poached in Irish butter and chardonnay sauce is a specialty, as is "lobster St. Jacques," wherein chunks of lobster are spooned over a bed of garlic-flavored mashed potatoes, covered with cheese, and broiled.

In the Port Lucaya Marketplace. ✆ 242/374-4466. Reservations recommended. Main courses $16–$34 (£8.50–£18); children's platters $5–$9 (£2.65–£4.80). AE, MC, V. Wed–Sun 5–11pm; Sun brunch 11am–4:30pm.

La Dolce Vita ✦ ITALIAN   Next to the Pub at Lucaya (see listing below), this small upscale Italian trattoria has a modern decor and traditional food. Enjoy freshly made pastas on a patio overlooking the marina or in the 44-seat dining room. Start with portobello mushrooms, fresh mozzarella with tomatoes, and a vinaigrette, or else carpaccio with arugula and spices. Homemade ravioli appears with fillings such as cheese, lobster, or spinach. An excellent risotto flavored with black squid ink is served, or else you can order roast pork tenderloin or a crisp and aromatic rack of lamb.

Port Lucaya Marketplace. © 242/373-8652. Reservations recommended. Main courses $21–$38 (£11–£20). AE, MC, V. Daily 5–11pm. Closed Sept.

Mediterranean Restaurant & Bar (Le Med) ® (*Value* FRENCH/ GREEK/BAHAMIAN   This is a simpler and more cost-effective version of the also-recommended Luciano's, with which it shares the same management and similar location (on the second floor of a building almost immediately next door). The decor includes a hard-working, almost indestructible combination of sand-colored floor tiles and refrigerated display cases loaded with pastries and salads. Devoid of linen, tables are so simple and angular-looking that they might have appeared within a coffee shop/diner. Don't let this simplicity fool you: The place serves well-flavored and surprisingly sophisticated food that attracted many of the actors filming the sequel to *Pirates of the Caribbean,* as well as rock star Bon Jovi and a gaggle of hangers-on. The place is crowded during the breakfast hour, when omelets (including a feta cheese and spinach–laden version of a Greek omelet), eggs and bacon, and Bahamian stewed fish and steamed conch are crowd-pleasers. Lunch and dinner feature assorted Greek and Turkish-style *mezes* and Iberian-style tapas that include both marinated octopus and grilled calamari. Crepes, priced at $8 to $10 (£4.25–£5.30) each, come in both sweet and savory versions. Other tempters include a seafood combo piled high with lobster, shrimp, conch, fish, and mussels; Delmonico-style steaks; *shashlik* (marinated kabobs redolent with herbs); and braised lamb shank cooked in red wine.

Port Lucaya Marketplace. © 242/374-2804. Breakfast $6–$10 (£3.20–£5.30); main courses $15–$25 (£7.95–£13). AE, DC, MC, V. Daily 8am–11:30pm

Pisces ® INTERNATIONAL   This ranks high among our favorites among the many restaurants in the Port Lucaya Market-place, and we're seconded by the locals and sailors who pack the place every weekend. The place is outfitted with a quirky mixture of nautical accessories and dark-varnished wood, with a prominent bar where more and more gossip is exchanged as the evening progresses. Tabletops contain laminated samples of seashells, fake gold coins, and sand. The place has a charming all-Bahamian staff outfitted in black and white. Pizzas are available and come in 27 different varieties, including a version with conch, lobster, shrimp, and chicken, as well as one with Alfredo sauce. Dinners are more elaborate, with a choice of curries (including a version with conch); lobster in cream, wine, and herb sauce; all kinds of fish and shellfish; and several kinds of pasta.

Port Lucaya Marketplace. © 242/373-5192. Reservations recommended. Pizzas $12–$28 (£6.35–£15); dinner main courses $9–$30 (£4.75–£16). AE, DISC, MC, V. Mon–Sat 5pm–1:30am.

Pub at Lucaya ENGLISH/BAHAMIAN   Opening onto Count Basie Square, and reminiscent of the days when the Royal Navy might have hauled some of its sailors out to The Bahamas from a home base in, say, Liverpool, this restaurant and bar lies near the center of the Port Lucaya Marketplace. Returning visitors might remember the joint when it was called Pusser's Pub, named after that popular brand of rum.

Many patrons visit just for the drinks, especially rum-laced Pusser's Painkillers. You can order predictable pub grub such as shepherd's pie or steak-and-ale pie. Juicy American-style burgers are another lure. There's also a scattering of more substantial Bahamian fare, especially Bahamian lobster tail, cracked conch, chicken breast with herbs, or the fresh grilled catch of the day. The tables outside overlooking the water are preferred, or else you can retreat inside under a wooden beamed ceiling, where the rustic pinewood tables are lit by faux Tiffany-style lamps.

Port Lucaya Marketplace. © 242/373-8450. Sandwiches and burgers $8–$11 (£4.25–£5.85); main courses $13–$40 (£6.90–£21). AE, MC, V. Daily 11am–11pm (bar until 1am).

Shenanigan's Irish Pub IRISH/INTERNATIONAL   Dark and beer-stained from the thousands of pints of Guinness, Harp, and Killian's that have been served and spilled here, this pub and restaurant is the premier Irish or Boston-Irish hangout on Grand Bahama Island. Many visitors come just to drink, sometimes for hours at a time, soaking up the suds and perhaps remembering to eventually order some food. If you do get hungry, the menu here recently took a noticeable swing toward the more upscale. They still serve steak-and-kidney pie, burgers, and surf and turf, but newer items include French-style rack of lamb for two, seafood Newburg, and "chicken Connemara" drenched in whiskey sauce

Port Lucaya Marketplace. © 242/373-4734. Main courses $10–$49 (£5.30–£26). AE, DISC, MC, V. Mon–Thurs 5pm–midnight; Fri–Sat 5pm–2am (last order at 9:45pm).

INEXPENSIVE

Georgie's BAHAMIAN/AMERICAN   This laid-back, informal restaurant provides a harborside perch at Port Lucaya for breakfast, lunch, or dinner. It gets particularly busy at late afternoon happy hour, when prices on drinks are reduced. Service shows more effort than polish, but dishes do arrive and they are quite flavorful time-tested recipes, a repertoire of old favorites like cracked conch (similar to breaded veal cutlet) served with tasty coleslaw. The catch of the day is usually pan-fried grouper or snapper served with peas 'n' rice. The chef almost daily prepares hot roast beef, serving it with mashed potatoes and mixed vegetables; for lunch, try one of the island's better chef's salads, loaded with turkey, ham, fresh tomatoes, cheese, and other good things. Other favorites here include fresh lobster, conch fritters, and barbecue chicken.

Port Lucaya Marketplace. ☏ **242/373-8513.** Breakfast $5–$7 (£2.65–£3.70); main courses lunch $8–$11 (£4.25–£5.85), dinner $9–$23 (£4.75–£12). DC, MC, V. Thurs, Fri, Mon–Tues 10am–8pm; Sat–Sun 8am–9pm.

Outrigger's Native Restaurant/White Wave Club BAHAMIAN Cement-sided and simple, with a large deck extending out toward the sea, this restaurant was here long before construction of the Port Lucayan Marketplace, which lies only 4 blocks away. The restaurant is the domain of Gretchen Wilson, whose kitchens produce a rotating series of lip-smacking dishes such as lobster tails, minced lobster, steamed or cracked conch, pork chops, chicken, fish, and shrimp, usually served with peas 'n' rice and macaroni. Every Wednesday night, from 5pm to 2am, the restaurant is the venue for Outrigger's Famous Wednesday Night Fish Fry, when as many as a thousand diners will line up for platters of fried or steamed fish ($10–$15/£5.30–£7.95 each) which are accompanied by a DJ and dancers. Almost as well attended are the establishment's Bonfire Nights, where set-price all-you-can-eat barbecued dinners, in addition to the a la carte offerings, go for $30 (£16) per person every Tuesday and Thursday evening. If you pay for the Bonfire night at Outrigger's, the price for the bonfire is $30 (£16); however, booking through your hotel may cost you an extra $20 (£11). Drinks are served within the restaurant, but you might consider stepping into the nearby ramshackle bar, the White Wave Club, which serves only drinks.

Smith's Point. ☏ **242/373-4811.** Main courses $10–$16 (£5.30–£8.50). No credit cards. Sun–Fri 4pm–10pm; Sat 1–9pm.

Zorba's *Value* BAHAMIAN/GREEK   If you've ever been captivated by "the Greek experience," this place might bring back happy memories, as well as providing some of the best food value at the Port Lucaya Marketplace. There's a narrow outside veranda with a relatively uninteresting view over the all-pedestrian alleyway outside, and a pale-blue-and-white Formica-clad interior that might remind you of a diner, with a TV set blasting out a Greek-language news broadcast. Big photos of Alan Bates and Anthony Quinn (playing Zorba, get it?) dancing on a beach add a touch of nostalgia for ouzo and retsina. The cuisine is a quirky and idiosyncratic mixture of Greek and Bahamian, and if you don't remember exactly what *taramasalata* or baklava is, the good-looking Bahamian staff will rattle off the ingredients like Peloponnesian pros. First thing in the morning, you'll see locals standing in line for the Bahamian breakfasts served at Zorba's, with dishes that include chicken souse, corned beef and grits, and an array of pancakes, waffles, and omelets. Lunch could be a fat gyro, burgers and salads, or a souvlakia kabob. Dinner can begin with a Greek salad and then move on to moussaka, grilled chicken on a bed of spinach, or any of several different pasta dishes, and end with baklava (honey and nut-studded pastries) for a sweet finish. We won't pretend the food here is a substitute for a trip to the Greek isles, but it's satisfying and filling.

Port Lucaya Marketplace. ✆ **242/373-6137.** Main courses lunch $4–$17 (£2.10–£9), dinner $16–$28 (£8.50–£15). AE, DISC, MC, V. Daily 7am–10:30pm.

5 Beaches, Watersports & Other Outdoor Pursuits

HITTING THE BEACH

Grand Bahama Island has enough beaches for everyone. The best ones open onto Northwest Providence Channel at Freeport and sweep east for some 97km (60 miles) to encompass Xanadu Beach, Lucaya Beach, Taíno Beach, and others, eventually ending at such remote eastern outposts as Rocky Creek and McLean's Town. Once you leave the Freeport/Lucaya area, you can virtually have your pick of white-sandy beaches all the way east. Once you're past the resort hotels, you'll see a series of secluded beaches used mainly by locals. If you like people, a lot of organized watersports, and easy access to hotel bars and rest rooms, stick to Xanadu, Taíno, and Lucayan beaches.

Though there's fine snorkeling offshore, you should book a snorkeling cruise aboard one of the catamarans to see the most stunning reefs.

Xanadu Beach ⭐⭐ is one of our favorites, immediately east of Freeport and the site of the famed Xanadu Beach Resort. The 1.6km-long (1-mile) beach may be crowded at times in winter, but that's because of those gorgeous, soft, powdery white sands, which open onto tranquil waters. The beach is set against a backdrop of coconut palms and Australian pines. In theory, at least, you can hook up here with an assortment of watersports, including snorkeling, boating, jet-skiing, and parasailing. But many of the beachfront concessions were damaged by hurricanes during the autumn of 2005, so it's a good idea to phone the Xanadu Resort in advance of your arrival to find out which purveyors have returned after the storm devastation.

Immediately east of Xanadu is **Silver Point Beach,** a little beach, site of a timeshare complex where guests are out riding the waves on water bikes or playing volleyball on the beach. You'll see horseback riders from Pinetree Stables (see below) taking beach rides along the sands.

Despite the allure of other beaches on Grand Bahama Island, most visitors will be found at **Lucaya Beach,** right off Royal Palm Way and immediately east of Silver Point Beach. This is one of the best strands in The Bahamas, with long stretches of white sand. In the vicinity of the Westin and Sheraton hotels, you'll also encounter a worthy scattering of beach bars. At any of the hotel resorts along this beach, you can hook up with an array of watersports or get a frosty drink from a hotel bar. It's not for those seeking seclusion, but it's a fun beach-party scene.

Immediately to the east of Lucaya Beach, and separated from it with a saltwater canal, **Taíno Beach** is a family favorite and a good place for watersports. This, too, is a fine wide beach of white sands, opening onto generally tranquil waters.

Another choice not too far east is **Gold Rock Beach,** a favorite picnic spot with locals on weekends, although you'll usually have this beach to yourself on weekdays. Gold Rock Beach is a 19km (12-mile) drive from Lucaya. At Gold Rock you are at the doorstep to the **Lucayan National Park** (see below), a 16-hectare (40-acre) park filled with some of the longest, widest, and most fabulous secluded beaches on the island.

BIKING

A guided bike trip is an ideal way to see parts of Grand Bahama that most visitors miss. Starting at **Barbary Beach,** you can pedal a mountain bike along the southern coast parallel to the beach. Stop for a snack, lunch, and a dip. Finally, you reach **Lucayan National Park,** some 19km (12 miles) away. Explore the cave where the Indians buried their dead in the days when Grand Bahama was theirs, centuries before the coming of Columbus. Crabs here have occasionally come up through holes in the ground carrying bits of bowls once used by the Lucayans. Grand Bahama Nature Tours (also known as **Kayak Nature Tours;** (℃) **242/373-2485;** www.GrandBahama NatureTours.com) runs these trips and transports you home to your hotel by van, so you don't have to exhaust yourself in the heat cycling back. The same company offers variations on this itinerary, with more time spent on kayaking and snorkeling and less time on bicycling. All versions of the tour last about 5 hours and cost $79 (£42) for adults, half-price for children under 12. All equipment, sustenance, and round-trip transportation from your hotel are included.

BOAT CRUISES

Ocean Wonder, Port Lucaya Dock ((℃) **242/373-5880**), run by Reef Tours, is a gargantuan 18m (59-ft.) Defender glass-bottom boat. Any tour agent can arrange for you to go out on this vessel. You'll get a panoramic view of the beautiful underwater life off the coast of Grand Bahama. Cruises depart from Port Lucaya behind the Straw Market on the bay side at 9:30am, 11:15am, 1:15pm, and 3:15pm, except Friday, when only two tours leave at 9:30 and 11:15am. The tour lasts 1½ hours, costs $25 (£13) for adults and $15 (£7.95) for children 6 to 12, and is free for children 5 and under. During high season (that is, midwinter), arrange for reservations a day or two in advance, as the boat does fill up quickly.

   Superior Watersports (P.O. Box F-40837, Freeport; (℃) **242/373-7863;** www.superiorwatersports.com), offers trips on its *Bahama Mama,* a two-deck, 22m (72-ft.) catamaran. Its Robinson Crusoe Beach Party is offered four times a week and costs $59 (£31) per adult and $39 (£21) for children under 12. Schedules vary with the seasons: from 11am to 4pm from October through March, but from noon to 5pm from April through September. There's also a shorter sunset booze cruise that goes for $45 (£24). (April–Sept, these cruises are on Tues, Thurs, and Sat night 6:30–8:30pm, and Oct–Mar the same nights, but 6–8pm.) Call for information about how to hook up with this outfitter.

   For an underwater cruise, try the company's quasisubmarine, the *Seaworld Explorer.* The sub itself does not descend; instead, you walk down into the hull of the boat and watch the sea life glide by. The "semisub" departs daily at 9:30am, 11:30am, and 1:30pm, and the 2-hour ride costs $39 (£21) for adults and $25 (£13) for children age 2 to 12.

THE DOLPHIN EXPERIENCE

A pod of bottle-nosed dolphins is involved in a unique dolphin/human familiarization program at Dolphin Experience, located at **Underwater Explorers Society (UNEXSO),** next to Port Lucaya, opposite the entrance to the Westin & Sheraton at Our Lucaya (© **800/992-DIVE** or 242/373-1244; www.unexso.com). This "close encounter" program allows participants to observe these intelligent and friendly animals and hear an interesting talk by a member of the animal-care staff. At the world's largest dolphin facility, the conditions aren't cramped. In addition, dolphins can swim out to sea, passing through an underwater "sea gate" that prevents their natural predators from entering the lagoon; the dolphins later return of their own free will to the relative safety of their protected marine habitat. After a 25-minute ferryboat ride from Port Lucaya, you'll step onto a shallow wading platform and interact with the dolphins. At press time, the dolphin colony had 17 members. The experience costs $75 (£40) and is an educational, fun adventure for all ages. Children under 3 participate free, while it costs $38 (£20) for those aged 4 to 12. If you like to document your life's unusual experiences, you'll want to bring your camera. For certified divers, UNEXSO offers a "dolphin dive," wherein a school of dolphins swim out from their marine habitat in Sanctuary Bay for a closely supervised diver-to-dolphin encounter. The cost is $169 (£90). If business warrants, the dolphin dive is offered daily.

FISHING

In the waters off Grand Bahama, you can fish for barracuda, snapper, grouper, yellowtail, wahoo, and kingfish, along with other denizens of the deep.

Reef Tours, Ltd., Port Lucaya Dock (© **242/373-5880** or 242/373-5891; www.bahamasvg.com/reeftours), offers one of the least expensive ways to go deep-sea fishing around Grand Bahama Island. Adults pay $110 (£58) if they fish, $50 (£27) if they go along only to watch. Four to six people can charter the entire 13m (43-ft.) craft for $650 (£345) per half-day or $1,250 (£663) per whole day. The 9.6m (31-ft.) boat can be chartered for $425 (£225) for a half-day and $825 (£437) for a full day. Departures for the 4-hour half-day excursions are daily at 8:30am and 1pm, while the 8-hour full-day excursions leave daily at 8:30am. Bait, tackle, and ice are included in the cost.

GOLF

Since the closing of two of the island's older courses (The Ruby and The Emerald) after the hurricane damages of the early millennium,

Grand Bahama Island is not as richly accessorized with golf courses as it was before. But golf on the island recently experienced a resurgence, thanks to the improvement of the golf layouts described below. Each of them is open to the public year-round, and clubs can be rented from their respective pro shops.

Fortune Hills Golf & Country Club, Richmond Park, Lucaya (© 242/373-2222), was originally intended to be an 18-hole course, but the back 9 were never completed. You can replay the front 9 for 18 holes and a total of 6,916 yards from the blue tees. Par is 72. Greens fees cost $47 (£25) for 9 holes, $61 (£32) for 18. Carts are included in greens fees. Club rental costs $18 (£9.55) for 18 holes and $14 (£7.40) for 9 holes.

The best-kept and most-manicured course on Grand Bahama is the **Lucayan Golf Course,** Lucaya Beach at Our Lucaya (© 242/373-1333). Made over after Hurricane Jeanne of 2004, this beautiful course is a traditional golf layout with rows of pine trees separating the fairways. Greens are fast, with a couple of par 5s more than 500 yards long, totaling 6,824 yards from the blue tees and 6,488 from the whites. Par is 72. Greens fees are $120 (£64) for 18 holes, including a mandatory shared golf cart.

Its sibling golf course, with an entirely separate clubhouse and staff, is the slightly older **The Reef Course** ★★, Royal Palm Way, at Our Lucaya (© 242/373-1333). Designed by Robert Trent Jones, Jr. (who called it "a bit like a Scottish course but a lot warmer"), the course boasts 6,920 yards of links-style playing grounds. It features a wide-open layout without rows of trees to separate its fairways and lots of water traps—you'll find water on 13 of the 18 holes and various types of long grass swaying in the trade winds. Play requires patience and precise shot-making to avoid the numerous lakes.

At either of the above-mentioned golf courses, guests at either the Westin or Sheraton hotels, with which the courses are associated, pay between $90 and $140 (£48–£74), depending on the season, for 18 holes. Nonguests are charged between $110 and $160 (£58–£85) for 18 holes. Rates include use of an electric-powered golf cart.

HORSEBACK RIDING

Pinetree Stables, North Beachway Drive, Freeport (© 242/373-3600 or 305/433-4809; www.pinetree-stables.com), are the best and—with a boarded inventory of more than 50 horses—biggest riding stables in The Bahamas, superior to rivals on New Providence Island (Nassau). Pinetree offers trail rides to the beach Tuesday through Sunday year-round at 9 and 11:30am. The cost is $75 (£40) per person for a trail ride lasting 2 hours. No children under 8 are allowed. As a means of protecting the horses, the weight limit for riders is 200 pounds.

SEA KAYAKING

If you'd like to explore the waters off the island's north shore, call **Grand Bahama Nature Tours** (© 866/440-4542 or 242/373-2485; www.GrandBahamaNatureTours.com), who'll take you on kayak excursions through the mangroves, where you can see wildlife as you paddle along. The cost is $79 (£42) per person (children 11 and under pay half-price), with lunch included. Double kayaks are used on these jaunts, and children must be at least 3 years of age. For the same price, you can take a 30-minute trip by kayak to an offshore island, with 1½ hours of snorkeling included along with lunch. Call ahead for reservations for either of these tours. A van will pick you up at your hotel between 9am and 10am and deliver you back at the end of the tour, usually sometime between 3 and 4pm. A popular variation on this tour, which operates during the same hours and at the same prices, includes more time devoted to snorkeling above a series of shallow offshore reefs and slightly less time allocated to kayaking.

SNORKELING & SCUBA DIVING

Serious divers are attracted to such Grand Bahama sites as the Wall, the Caves (one of the most interesting of which is Ben's Cavern), Theo's Wreck, and Treasure Reef. **Theo's Wreck** ✸✸ is the most evocative site; it was a freighter that was deliberately sunk off Freeport to attract marine life. Today it teems with everything from horse-eyed jacks to moray eels. Other top locales include Spit City, Ben Blue Hole, Pygmy Caves, Gold Rock, Silver Point Reef, and the Rose Garden.

Underwater Explorers Society (UNEXSO) ✸✸✸ (© 800/992-DIVE or 242/373-1250; www.unexso.com), one of the premier dive outfitters in The Bahamas and the Caribbean, offers seven dive trips daily, including reef trips, shark dives, wreck dives, and night dives. Divers can even dive with dolphins in the open ocean here— a rare experience offered by very few facilities in the world (see "The Dolphin Experience," above).

A popular 3-hour learn-to-dive course, the "Mini-B Pool and Reef Adventure," is offered daily. Over UNEXSO's 30-year history, more than 50,000 people have successfully completed either this course or its similar predecessors. For $85 (£45), students learn the basics in UNEXSO's training pools and dive the beautiful shallow reef with their instructor.

A nearby competitor, **Reef Tours** (𝄐 **242/373-5880;** www. bahamasvacationguide.com/reeftours), offers well-recommended snorkeling tours. Lasting just under 2 hours each, they depart from Port Lucaya three times a day. Tours are priced at $35 (£19) each for adults and at $18 (£9.55) for children aged 6 to 12, with all equipment included. A variation on that program is a 3-hour "sail and snorkel tour." Departing daily at 9:30am and 1:30pm, it's priced at $45 (£24) for adults and at $25 (£13) for children aged 6 to 12.

WATERSPORTS IN GENERAL

Ocean Motion Water Sports Ltd., Sea Horse Lane, Lucaya Beach (𝄐 **242/374-2425;** www.oceanmotionbahamas.com), is one of the largest watersports companies on Grand Bahama. It offers a wide variety of activities daily from 9am to 5pm, weather permitting, including snorkeling, parasailing, Hobie Cats, banana boats, water-skiing, jet skis, windsurfing, and other activities. Parasailing, for example, costs $60 (£32) per person for 5 to 7 minutes in the air. Snorkeling trips cost $35 (£19; $18/£9.55 for kids under 12) for 1½ hours; water-skiing, $40 (£21) per 3.2km (2-mile) pull, $60 (£32) for a 30-minute lesson; Hobie Cats, $50 (£27) for the 4.2m (14-ft.), $75 (£40) for the 4.8m (16-ft.), $20 (£11) for a lesson; windsurfing, $30 (£16) per hour, $100 (£53) for a 2-hour lesson; kayaking, $20 (£11) for a single kayak, $25 (£13) for a double; water trampoline, $20 (£11) full day, $10 (£5.30) half-day; and banana boating, $15 (£7.95) per person for a 3.2km (2-mile) ride along a white-sandy beach. Call for reservations, especially for windsurfing.

Lucaya Watersports, Taíno Beach (𝄐 **242/373-6375**), also offers options for fun in the surf, including WaveRunners rented at $65 (£34) per 30 minutes and double kayaks costing $25 (£13) per hour for two passengers. The outfitter also offers double paddle boats, holding four people, for $25 (£13) per hour. The sunset cruises—a 2-hour sailboat ride offered every Wednesday between 5 and 7pm—are especially popular and cost $45 (£24) per person.

6 Seeing the Sights

Several informative tours of Grand Bahama Island are offered. One reliable company is **H. Forbes Charter Services Ltd.,** the Mall at West Sunrise Highway, Freeport (𝄐 **242/352-9311;** www.forbes charter.com). From headquarters in the International Bazaar, this company offers half- and full-day bus tours. The most popular option is the half-day Super Combination Tour, priced at $35 (£19) per adult and $25 (£13) per child age 5 to 12. It includes

---

Finds **A Sudsy Look at Grand Bahama**

You don't think of Freeport as brewery country, but the island is known for its Hammerhead Ale, a favorite of connoisseurs. The **Grand Bahama Brewing Co.**, Logwood Road, Freeport (*©* **242/351-5191**), a 10-minute drive northwest of Port Lucaya, near the airport, offers loosely scheduled 25-minute tours of its brewing facilities every Monday to Friday beginning at 10am, with the absolute last departure of the day at 4:40pm. The enterprise manufactures beer under two separate labels, Hammerhead and Lucayan, ranging from light lagers to stouts. Tours cost $5 (£2.65), but the fee is credited to any lager or ale purchases you might make.

---

drive-through tours of residential areas and the island's commercial center, stops at the island's deep-water harbor, shopping, and a visit to a wholesale liquor store. Departures are Monday through Saturday at 9am and 1pm; the tour lasts 3½ hours. Full-day tours, conducted whenever business warrants, last from 9am to 3:30pm. In addition to everything included in the half-day tours, they bring participants in a bus or van, with guided commentary, all the way to The Caves, near Grand Bahama Island's easternmost tip, for a price of $50 (£27) per adult, $35 (£19) per child.

See also "Beaches, Watersports & Other Outdoor Pursuits," above, for details on UNEXSO's Dolphin Experience, and "Shopping," below, for coverage of the International Bazaar and the Port Lucaya Marketplace.

Lucayan National Park   This 16-hectare (40-acre) park is filled with mangrove, pine, and palm trees. It also contains one of the loveliest, most secluded beaches on Grand Bahama, a long, wide, dune-covered stretch of sandy beach reached by following a wooden path winding through the trees. Bring your snorkeling gear so you can glimpse the colorful creatures living beneath the turquoise waters of a coral reef offshore. As you wander through the park, you'll cross Gold Rock Creek, fed by a spring from what is said to be the world's largest underground freshwater cavern system. There are 36,000 entrances to the caves—some only a few feet deep. Two of the caves can be seen because they were exposed when a portion of ground collapsed. The pools in the caves are composed of 2m (6½ ft.) of fresh water atop a heavier layer of salt water. Spiral wooden steps have been built down to the pools.

The freshwater springs once lured native Lucayans, those Arawak-connected tribes who lived on the island and depended on fishing for their livelihood. They would come inland to get fresh water for their habitats on the beach. Lucayan bones and artifacts, such as pottery, have been found in the caves, as well as on the beaches.

Settlers Way, eastern end of East Sunrise Hwy. ℂ **242/352-5438.** Admission $3 (£1.60); tickets available only at the Rand Nature Centre (see below). Daily 9am–5pm. Drive east along Midshipman Rd., passing Sharp Rock Point and Gold Rock.

Rand Nature Centre   This 40-hectare (99-acre) pineland sanctuary, located 3km (1¾ miles) east of the center of Freeport, is the regional headquarters of The Bahamas National Trust, a nonprofit conservation organization. Nature trails highlight native flora and "bush medicine," and provide opportunities for bird-watching. As you stroll, keep your eyes peeled for the lush blooms of tropical orchids or the brilliant flash of green and red feathers in the trees—wild birds abound at the park. You can join a bird-watching tour on the first Saturday of every month at 8am. Other features of the nature center include native animal displays, an education center, and a gift shop selling nature books and souvenirs.

E. Settlers Way. ℂ **242/352-5438.** Admission $5 (£2.65) adults, $3 (£1.60) children 5–12, free for children under 5. Mon–Fri 9am–5pm.

7 Shopping

Shopping hours in Freeport/Lucaya are generally Monday to Saturday 9am to 6pm. However, in the International Bazaar, hours vary widely, with shops usually closing a bit earlier. Most places are open Monday through Saturday. Some begin business daily at 9:30am; others don't open until 10am, and closing time ranges from 5:30 to 6pm.

PORT LUCAYA MARKETPLACE

Port Lucaya and its Marketplace supplanted the International Bazaar (see below) in the mid-1990s, when it became clear that the future of merchandising on Grand Bahama Island had moved. Today Port Lucaya Marketplace on Seahorse Road rocks and rolls with a spankingly well-maintained physical plant that's set within a shopping, dining, and marina complex on 2.4 hectares (6 acres) of low-lying, seafronting land. Regular bouts of free entertainment, such as steel-drum bands and strolling musicians, as well as recorded music that plays throughout the evening hours, add to a festival atmosphere.

The complex emulates the 19th-century clapboard-sided construction style of the Old Bahamas, all within a short walk of the most cutting-edge and desirable hotel accommodations on Grand Bahama Island, including the Westin & Sheraton at Our Lucaya. It's also within a minute's walk of the island's only casino, the Isle of Capri. The development rose on the site of a former Bahamian straw market. Today, in addition to dozens of restaurants and upscale shops, the Market incorporates rows of brightly painted clapboard-sided huts out of which local merchants sell handicrafts and souvenirs.

The waterfront location is a distinct advantage. Lots of the business that fuels this place derives from the expensive yachts and motorcraft that tie up at the marina here. Most of those watercraft are owned by residents of nearby Florida. You might get the sense that many of them just arrived from the U.S. mainland, disgorging their passengers out onto the docks that immediately flank the Marketplace.

Androsia   This is the Port Lucaya outlet of the famous house that produces handmade fabrics on Andros Island. Designs and colors capture the spirit of The Bahamas. The store sells quality, 100%-cotton resort wear, including simple skirts, tops, jackets, and shorts for women, and it also offers a colorful line of children's wear. Port Lucaya Marketplace. ✆ **242/373-8387.**

Animale   Trendy fashionistas, who know a lot about this sort of thing, would define this as a hot boutique with the kind of clingy sophisticated tropical fashion that makes any reasonably shaped woman look good. Come here for long cotton dresses that make the female form look more-than-usually provocative, and the kind of fashion accessories—oversize straw hats, chunky necklaces, animal-print scarves—that emphasize the feline, the *animale,* and perhaps, the seductress. In the Port Lucaya Marketplace. ✆ **242/374-2066.**

Bandolera   The staff can be rather haughty here, but despite its drawbacks, the store carries a collection of chic women's clothing that's many cuts above the T-shirts and tank tops that are the norm for many of its competitors. Port Lucaya Marketplace. ✆ **242/373-7691.**

Colombian Emeralds International   This branch of the world's foremost emerald jeweler offers a wide array of precious gemstone jewelry and one of the island's best watch collections. Careful shoppers will find significant savings over U.S. prices. The outlet offers certified appraisals and free 90-day insurance. Port Lucaya Marketplace. ✆ **242/373-8400.**

Corporate Casual Boutique   Positioned close to Giovanni's Restaurant, this women's clothing store is owned and operated by a sophisticated Bahamian press and public relations agent who's deeply familiar with dressing for success. You'll find clothing fit for a female executive climbing up the corporate ladder. Port Lucaya, Building 9. 𝒞 242/373-5626. There's another, even larger, branch of this enterprise in downtown Freeport, at #2 Millennium Mall on West Atlantic Dr. 𝒞 242/351-5620.

Flovin Gallery II   This branch of the art gallery located in the International Bazaar sells a collection of oil paintings (both Bahamian and international), along with lithographs and posters. In its limited field, it's the best in the business. It also features a number of gift items, such as handmade Bahamian dolls, decorated corals, and Christmas ornaments. Port Lucaya Marketplace. 𝒞 242/373-8388.

Les Parisiennes   This outlet offers a wide range of fine jewelry and watches. It also sells crystal, Versace wear, and perfumes, including the latest from Paris. Port Lucaya Marketplace. 𝒞 242/373-2974.

UNEXSO Dive Shop   This premier dive shop of The Bahamas sells everything related to the water—swimsuits, wetsuits, underwater cameras, video equipment, shades, hats, souvenirs, and state-of-the-art diver's equipment. Port Lucaya Marketplace. 𝒞 800/992-3483 or 242/373-1244. www.unexso.com.

THE INTERNATIONAL BAZAAR

The older and less glamorous of Grand Bahama Island's two main shopping venues, The International Bazaar has steadily declined since the collapse of the megaresort Crowne Plaza Hotel, immediately next door. Originally conceived as a warren of alleyways loaded with upscale, tax-free boutiques, and still plugging away valiantly at its location at East Mall Drive and East Sunrise Highway, it encompasses 4 hectares (10 acres) in the heart of Freeport. Frankly, today it's a pale shadow of what it was during its peak in the mid-1980s, when it boasted 130 purveyors of luxury goods, when the Marketplace at Port Lucaya was still a dream, and when busloads of cruise ship passengers would be unloaded in front of its gates at regular intervals. Today it's a bit tarnished and gives off a sense of dusty redolence in the streaming sunlight, with many shops permanently closed and with cracks in its masonry. Its aggressively touted role as an "international" venue seems a bit theme-driven and tired. Even worse, its rising competitor, the Port Lucaya Marketplace, is looking better every day.

Buses at the entrance of the complex aren't numbered, but those marked INTERNATIONAL BAZAAR will take you right to the gateway at the Torii Gate on West Sunrise Highway. The fare is $1 (55p). Visitors walk through this much-photographed gate, a Japanese symbol of welcome, into a miniature World's Fair setting (think of it as a kitschy and somewhat run-down version of Epcot). The bazaar blends architecture and cultures from some 25 countries, each re-created with cobblestones, narrow alleys, and a layout that evokes a theme-driven, somewhat dusty casbah in North Africa. In the approximately 34 shops that remain in business today, you might find something that is both unique and a bargain. You'll see African handicrafts, Chinese jade, British china, Swiss watches, Irish linens, and Colombian emeralds. Many of the enterprises represented here also maintain branches within the Port Lucaya Marketplace. Various sections evoke the architecture of the Ginza in Tokyo, with merchandise—electronic goods, art objects, and luxury products—from Asia. Other subdivisions evoke the Left Bank of Paris, various regions of India and Africa, Latin America, and Spain.

Some merchants claim their prices are 40% less than comparable costs in the United States, but don't count on that. If you're contemplating a big purchase, it's best to compare prices before you leave home. Most of the merchants can ship your purchases back home at relatively reasonable rates.

A **straw market** next door to the International Bazaar contains items with a special Bahamian touch—colorful baskets, hats, handbags, and place mats, and an endless array of T-shirts—some of which make worthwhile gifts or souvenirs from your trip. (Be aware that some items sold here are actually made in Asia, and expect goodly amounts of the tacky and tasteless as well.)

Here's a description of the best shops that remain in the bazaar.

ART
Flovin Gallery   This gallery sells original Bahamian and international art, frames, lithographs, posters, and Bahamian-made Christmas ornaments and decorated coral. It also offers handmade Bahamian dolls, coral jewelry, and other gift items. Another branch is at the Port Lucaya Marketplace (see above). In the Arcade section of the International Bazaar. ✆ 242/352-7564.

FASHION
Cleo's Boutique   This shop offers everything from eveningwear to lingerie. A warm and inviting destination, Cleo's prides itself on capturing the Caribbean woman in all of her moods. You can also find a wide array of costume jewelry beginning at $25 per piece. International Bazaar. ✆ 242/352-3340.

Paris in The Bahamas   This shop contains the biggest selection of luxury goods under one roof in the International Bazaar. The staff wears couture black dresses like you might expect in Paris, and everywhere there's a sense of French glamour and conspicuous consumption. You can find both Gucci and Versace leather goods for men and women; crystal from Lalique, Baccarat, Daum, and Kosta Boda; and a huge collection of cosmetics and perfumes. International Bazaar. © 242/352-5380.

Unusual Centre   Where else can you get an array of items made of walrus skin or peacock feathers? There's another branch at the Port Lucaya Marketplace (© 242/373-7333). International Bazaar. © 242/ 352-3994.

PERFUMES & FRAGRANCES
The Perfume Factory Fragrance of The Bahamas   This is the top fragrance producer in The Bahamas. The shop is housed in a re-creation of an 1800s mansion, in which visitors are invited to hear a 5-minute commentary and to see the mixing of fragrant oils. There's even a "mixology" department where you can create your own fragrance from a selection of oils. The shop's well-known products include Island Promises, Goombay, Paradise, and Pink Pearl (with conch pearls in the bottle). The shop also sells Guanahani, created to commemorate the 500th anniversary of Columbus's first landfall, and Sand, the leading Bahamian-made men's fragrance. At the rear of the International Bazaar. © 242/352-9391. www.perfumefactory.com.

8 Grand Bahama After Dark

Many resort hotels stage their own entertainment at night, and these shows are open to the general public.

ROLLING THE DICE

At press time, Grand Bahama maintained only one casino, the **Isle of Capri,** at Our Lucaya. Set within its own free-standing building on the grounds of the Westin & Sheraton at Our Lucaya, this is the big draw for anyone looking to gamble on Grand Bahama Island. Outfitted in a neutrally modern, not-particularly-ostentatious design, it contains a crescent-shaped bar, a restaurant, and games that include baccarat, Caribbean stud poker, blackjack, roulette, and aisles loaded with some 400 slot machines. It's open daily from 10am to 2am or later, and entrance is free. The Westin & Sheraton at Our Lucaya resorts, Royal Palm Way. © 242/373-1333.

Finds **Bahamian Theater**

Instead of one of those Las Vegas leggy showgirl revues, you can call the 450-seat **Regency Theater,** West Sunrise Highway (© **242/352-5533**), and ask what performance is scheduled. This is the home of two nonprofit companies, The Freeport Players' Guild and Grand Bahama Players. The season runs from September to June, and you are likely to see reprises of such Broadway and West End (London) blockbusters as *Mamma Mia!,* as well as contemporary works by Bahamian and Caribbean playwrights. Some really intriguing shows are likely to be staged every year by both groups, which are equally talented. Tickets cost from $10 to $20 (£5.30–£11).

THE CLUB & BAR SCENE

Located in the center of the **Port Lucaya Marketplace** waterfront restaurant and shopping complex, **Count Basie Square** contains a vine-covered bandstand where the best live music on the island is performed several nights a week, usually beginning around 7:30 or 8pm. And it's free! The square honors the "Count," who used to have a grand home on Grand Bahama. Steel bands, small Junkanoo groups, and even gospel singers from a local church are likely to be heard performing here, their voices or music wafting across the marina and the nearby boardwalk and wharves. You can sip a beer or a tropical rum concoction at one of the bars in the complex. (See "Where to Dine," earlier in this chapter, for details on a few of these, including **Fatman's Nephew** and **Shenanigan's Irish Pub.**)

Club Amnesia   This is one of the most popular discos and pickup joints on Grand Bahama Island, a local spot that seems a world away from the somewhat sanitized version of nightlife at the island's tourist hotels. It features a psychedelic interior outfitted with big mirrors, strobe lights, and Junkanoo colors. Recorded music grooves and grinds, and live bands are often imported either from the mainland of Florida or from nearby Caribbean islands. Crowds range in age from 18 to 35, and the cover charge, depending on who's playing that night, costs from $10 to $20 (£5.30–£11) per person (concerts cost up to $50/£27 per ticket). Open nights vary with the season, but it's a good bet that the place is operating Thursday to Saturday from 8:30pm till around 2am. East Mall Dr. © **242/351-2582.**

Margaritavilla Sand Bar   Arguably the hottest bar on island is this lively "jump-up" place opening onto an isolated stretch of Mather Town Beach, about a 15-minute drive southeast of Lucaya. It's really a one-room sand-floor shack, but a lot of fun. A weekly bonfire cookout is staged Tuesdays from 6:30 to 9:30pm, with fish or steak on the grill along with a DJ. The conch fritters and cracked conch and fries are some of the best on island, with main courses costing $15 (£7.95) and up if you'd like to stick around to eat. The place rocks on Wednesday night with younger Bahamians, although Sunday is for an older crowd that prefers singalongs. The bar swings open at 11am. As for closing times, the owner Jinx Knowles says it "might be 7 at night if it's quiet or 7 in the morning if it's jumpin.'" Millionaire's Row, Mather Town Beach. (✆ 242/373-4525.

Prop Club   Previously recommended in "Where to Dine," this sports bar and dance club flourishes as a singles bar that rocks at high intensity, fueled by high-octane cocktails. A lot of things seem to happen here, including occasional bouts of karaoke, live music, cultural showcasing of emerging Bahamian and Caribbean bands, and both Junkanoo and retro-disco revival nights. You can also expect a "get down with the DJ" night on Sundays and game nights on slow Mondays. The DJ arrives at 10pm every night. The Westin & Sheraton at Our Lucaya resorts, Royal Palm Way. (✆ 242/373-1333.

Index

See also Accommodations and Restaurant indexes below.

FROMMER'S® COMPLETE TRAVEL GUIDES

FROMMER'S® DAY BY DAY GUIDES

PAULINE FROMMER'S GUIDES! SEE MORE. SPEND LESS.

FROMMER'S® PORTABLE GUIDES

FROMMER'S® CRUISE GUIDES

Alaska Cruises & Ports of Call	Cruises & Ports of Call	European Cruises & Ports of Call

FROMMER'S® NATIONAL PARK GUIDES

Algonquin Provincial Park	National Parks of the American West	Yosemite and Sequoia & Kings
Banff & Jasper	Rocky Mountain	Canyon
Grand Canyon	Yellowstone & Grand Teton	Zion & Bryce Canyon

FROMMER'S® MEMORABLE WALKS

London	Paris	San Francisco
New York	Rome	

FROMMER'S® WITH KIDS GUIDES

Chicago	National Parks	Toronto
Hawaii	New York City	Walt Disney World® & Orlando
Las Vegas	San Francisco	Washington, D.C.
London		

SUZY GERSHMAN'S BORN TO SHOP GUIDES

France	London	Paris
Hong Kong, Shanghai & Beijing	New York	San Francisco
Italy		

FROMMER'S® IRREVERENT GUIDES

Amsterdam	London	Rome
Boston	Los Angeles	San Francisco
Chicago	Manhattan	Walt Disney World®
Las Vegas	Paris	Washington, D.C.

FROMMER'S® BEST-LOVED DRIVING TOURS

Austria	Germany	Northern Italy
Britain	Ireland	Scotland
California	Italy	Spain
France	New England	Tuscany & Umbria

THE UNOFFICIAL GUIDES®

Adventure Travel in Alaska	Hawaii	Paris
Beyond Disney	Ireland	San Francisco
California with Kids	Las Vegas	South Florida including Miami &
Central Italy	London	the Keys
Chicago	Maui	Walt Disney World®
Cruises	Mexico's Best Beach Resorts	Walt Disney World® for
Disneyland®	Mini Mickey	Grown-ups
England	New Orleans	Walt Disney World® with Kids
Florida	New York City	Washington, D.C.
Florida with Kids		

SPECIAL-INTEREST TITLES

Athens Past & Present	Frommer's Exploring America by RV
Best Places to Raise Your Family	Frommer's NYC Free & Dirt Cheap
Cities Ranked & Rated	Frommer's Road Atlas Europe
500 Places to Take Your Kids Before They Grow Up	Frommer's Road Atlas Ireland
Frommer's Best Day Trips from London	Great Escapes From NYC Without Wheels
Frommer's Best RV & Tent Campgrounds	Retirement Places Rated
in the U.S.A.	

FROMMER'S® PHRASEFINDER DICTIONARY GUIDES

French	Italian	Spanish